Factory Towns of South China

Factory Towns of South China
An Illustrated Guidebook

Edited by Stefan Al

香港大學出版社
HONG KONG UNIVERSITY PRESS

Hong Kong University Press
14/F Hing Wai Centre
7 Tin Wan Praya Road
Aberdeen
Hong Kong
www.hkupress.org

ISBN 978-988-8083-69-5

British Library Cataloguing-in-Publication Data
A catalogue record for this book is available from the British Library.

10 9 8 7 6 5 4 3 2 1

Printed and bound by Liang Yu Printing Factory Ltd., Hong Kong, China

Contents

Contents

Acknowledgements

Many have been instrumental in the making of this book, but I would like to express my gratitude to a few whose contribution has been exceptional. First, I thank Ananya Roy and Greig Crysler for providing me with the theoretical tools to be able to imagine this book. Publisher Michael Duckworth and Jennifer Flint have been courageous in taking on a challenging and unconventional project. I am also grateful to David Lung, Paul Leung and Mr. Ng for their unwavering and generous support. Of the contributing editors I would like to thank especially Paul Chu Hoi Shan who suggested the idea to study factory towns, and Casey Wang, Claudia Juhre and Alexander Giarlis for their role in shaping the case study research. Jia-Ching Chen helped identifying essay topics and contributors. A special thanks goes to the MUD Class of 2010, to Anthony Lam Cheuk Wang who has significantly influenced the graphical layout of this book, and to Po Hei Chu, Chris Cawkwell, Nevin Nanyan Yu, and Daniel Fung who provided tremendous assistance in finalizing the work. Finally, I would like to thank the factory owners who agreed to let our researchers access the factory compounds, plus the factory workers who were willing to share their life stories.

Acknowledgements

This publication was made possible thanks to the generous donation of Mr. Ng Wing Chi of the The Zai Yuan Cultural Foundation.

我們充心感謝在園文化基金吳榮治先生的慷慨捐助，使這本圖冊可順利出版。

An industrialist for the best part of my life, I have witnessed the heyday of the manufacturing industry in Hong Kong. I often look back with mixed feelings to the days when I moved around factories, surrounded as I was by machinery roaring out loud as if to protest their being made to work almost non stop twenty four hours a day. Industry no longer takes a strong hold in Hong Kong. But no one can deny that it has made immeasurable contribution to the local economy.

This invaluable publication, *Factory Towns of South China: An Illustrative Guidebook*, may not echo everything we have seen in Hong Kong, but we may nonetheless find some traces of resemblances. I support the publishing of this book to show my personal appreciation of the significant role played by the manufacturing sector in the history of Hong Kong's economy. My fond memories will not soon go away.

Ng Wing Chi

作為一個在工業界奮鬥大半生的廠商，親身經歷了香港工業曾經興盛的年代。回想當年在工廠林立和機器轟鳴中穿梭的日子，心中不勝感慨。如今，香港工業雖已在本地逐漸淡出，但它對香港崛起所作出的貢獻卻功不可沒。

　　這部《華南工廠城：圖示旅遊書》介紹的雖然不盡是當年香港工業的情況，但從這些似曾相識的描述與畫面中，過往曾經目睹和經歷過的點點滴滴似乎依稀可見。謹以對此書的支持，一表心意，權作對那段歷史無法舍卻的緬懷與紀念。

吳榮治

With the outbreak of the Korean War in the 1950s, countries all over the world banned all Chinese imports. The resultant ripple effect hit Hong Kong hard as at the time it relied mainly on the entrepot trade. People soon found a new hope in turning their major economic activity to industry and manufacturing. No one could ever imagine that this small twist in history would start the transformation of Hong Kong from a fishing port to an international city.

In the 1960s, the manufacturing industry became more established. Factory buildings mushroomed. People worked long hours in factories and Hong Kong products were exported to countries all over the world. "Made in Hong Kong" was a label that marked high-quality products and this placed Hong Kong on the world map.

With the opening up of the People's Republic of China in the 1970s, Hong Kong manufacturers began to move their factories northwards, across the border to the Pearl River Delta. Making good use of their invaluable experience gained over a number of decades, these manufacturers successfully moulded the Pearl River Delta into a major manufacturing hub of China. More recently, Hong Kong manufacturers have begun to shift their business further north to the Yangtze River Delta and even to Northern China and the inland area. We have no doubt that these spirited entrepreneurs will continue to use their talent and experience to create yet another success story.

Paul S. W. Leung
Chief Executive Officer
The Chinese Manufacturers' Association of Hong Kong

二十世紀五十年代，朝鮮戰爭硝烟突起，香港曾經賴以生存的轉口貿易在國際社會對華禁運的浪潮中頃刻坍塌，生計一時堪憂的香港人在尚未興起的加工製造業中找到了希望，他們走進工廠，開始用自己的雙手打造未來。沒有人想到，歷史的一個小轉彎，卻意外的開始了這個小漁港逐步邁向國際大都會的歷程。

Acknowledgements

　　六十年代，香港工業在探索中漸漸成長、日益成熟。白手起家的廠商們開始自立門戶，一間間工廠大廈拔地而起，人們在轟隆的機器聲中，將親手打造的工業品送往世界各地。「香港製造」的產品跨越千山萬水，在歐美市場上大放異彩，也讓這個寂寂無名的城市從此聲名鵲起。

　　時至今日，香港工業已隨著內地改革開放的浪潮大舉北遷。幾十年間，香港廠商的足跡遍布珠江三角洲，他們用長期歷練而來的敏銳觸覺和豐富經驗，引領當地成為全中國輕工業最為發達的地區。如今，他們已將目光移向長江三角洲，以及更遠的北方和內陸地區。在那裡，他們一如既往的發揮著飽含智慧和激情的香港工業家精神，為當地的工業建設帶出新的動力和靈感。奮鬥永無止境的香港廠商將在廣闊的中華大地上續寫夢想、創造新的傳奇！

香港中華廠商聯合會
行政總裁梁世華

Credits

Editor:

Stefan Al

Contributing Editors:

Paul Chu Hoi Shan, Alexander Giarlis, Claudia Juhre, Casey Wang

Cover Design:

Anthony Lam Cheuk Wang

Layout Design:

Anthony Lam Cheuk Wang, Po Hei Chu, Ka Kie Kwok, Jingshu Chen, Fatima Lee

English Case Studies Editing:

Chris Cawkwell, Daniel King Him Fung

Chinese Translation of Essays:

Eunice Chen Mengyi

Graphic Editing:

Anthony Lam Cheuk Wang, Daniel King Him Fung, Po Hei Chu, Alvin Cheung Heng Kan, Nevin Nanyan Yu, Chanchan Chen

Infographics:

Urbanization: Fatima Lee, Nevin Nanyan Yu, Nusrat Wahid, Chris Cawkwell

Demographics: Po Hei Chu, Xuyuan Chai, Lauren, Edwin Chan, Yin Ki Ho

Economics: Ruimin Chen, Jingshu Chen, Suning Wang, Nita Gandwinatan

Infrastructure: Alvin Cheung Heng Kan, Jierong Chen, Anthony Lam Cheuk Wang

Cities Overview and History:

Hong Kong: Nita Gandwinatan

Shenzhen: Fatima Lee, Nevin Nanyan Yu, Nusrat Wahid

Dongguan: Po Hei Chu, Xuyuan Chai, Lauren, Edwin Chan, Yin Ki Ho

Guangzhou: Ruimin Chen, Jingshu Chen, Suning Wang

Foshan: Alvin Cheung Heng Kan, Jierong Chen, Anthony Lam Cheuk Wang

Zhongshan: Ka Kie Kwok, Chris Cawkwell, Xiaoteng Xiao

Factory Town Case Studies:

Kwun Tong Industrial Town: Nita Gandwinatan

Fuyong Town: Nevin Nanyan Yu

Shekou Industrial Zone: Fatima Lee

Nancheng District: Po Hei Chu

Huangjiang Town: Lauren Chai

Donghuanjie Town: Ruimin Chen

Liwan District: Suning Wang

Shiwan Town Artistic Ceramic Factory: Alvin Cheung Heng Kan

Shiwan Town Ceramic Tilling Factory: Anthony Lam Cheuk Wang

City Center: Chris Cawkwell

Factory Futures:

Foshan Industrial Design Town: Anthony Lam Cheuk Wang

Printscape: Jingshu Chen

Villaging Industry: Suning Wang

World Factory Adventure: Nevin Nanyan Yu

Regional Map:

Nevin Nanyan Yu

Factory Towns of South China
An Illustrated Guidebook

Stefan Al

Department of Urban Planning and Design
The University of Hong Kong

In 2008, when a British man discovered photos of what appeared to be a young factory girl posing at an assembly line on his brand new iPhone, the Shenzhen factory worker became an overnight Internet superstar. The photos were uploaded onto an online forum and went viral. People all over the world started to speculate about the identity of "iPhone Girl."[1] In reality, she is one of the many rural migrants who have flocked to major cities in China in search of a job. Like many "factory girls" and "factory boys," she worked for a large manufacturing corporation, namely, the Taiwanese electronics giant—Foxconn—the world's largest manufacturer of electronic components.

Foxconn City is a walled complex that measures about three square kilometers. It is located in Shenzhen and is home to 420,000 factory workers.[2] The compound itself is practically a self-contained city with its own fire brigade, hospital, bank, television broadcasting station and even Foxconn-stamped manhole covers. The photo of iPhone Girl only shows a glimpse of what occurs within the walled compound. However, it has opened a window to allow consumers to see past the fine print "Assembled in China." Through modern technology and efficient means of transportation, many major international corporations are able to implement offshore manufacturing in countries where labor is cheap. These laborers work long hours and make only a few dollars a day. It is an ironic and poignant fact that iPhone Girl will probably never be able to afford an iPhone.

When China began its economic reform in 1978, factory owners saw it as an opportunity to utilize the country's growing labor supply, whose low cost and docility have been maintained by deepening inequalities and limitations on workers' rights. They brought jobs into China, which in turn attracted the poor rural residents to migrate to cities like Shenzhen in hopes for a better life. However, the official number of migrant workers is controlled through China's household registration system, or *hukou*. This system was codified in the 1950s to constrain the movement of villagers to urban areas by designating all Chinese citizens as either "rural" or "urban" residents and by requiring official permission for permanent migration. Despite government control, major cities like Shenzhen experienced a population spike. What used to be a fishing village with a population of 280,000, Shenzhen rapidly became a megacity when it was appointed to be a Special Economic Zone in 1980. Within thirty years, the city's population increased fiftyfold to an estimated 14 million residents. Without a doubt, southern China has become the "factory of the world" with the largest industrial region on earth.

In spite of decades of rapid growth in the south of China, this new global center of production is relatively invisible to the West. The mass-produced consumer products distributed all over the world and to a myriad of malls come primarily from one region in the south of China, the Pearl River Delta (PRD). The delta spreads around the Pearl River estuary in Guangdong Province, where the river flows into the South China Sea. The PRD is a 26,000-square-kilometer megacity region with a population of 120 million, and houses many of the world's largest manufacturing companies. It is also home to a floating population of more than 30 million migrant workers who move in and out of the towns based on the ebb and flow of their hometown festivals and work opportunities.

"Shenzhen speed," a term referring to the velocity of urbanization in Shenzhen, has now become common vernacular. The city and other surrounding urban areas have transformed so rapidly that they are no longer recognizable. The region has traded its picturesque agrarian qualities for the grim industrial metropolis— commonly recognized by the urban sprawl, central traffic congestion and environmental degradation. Interests of private developers including factory owners have mainly led the haphazard growth. However, the emergence of these gritty industrial landscapes scattered along the Pearl River Delta must be seen within the context of volatile shifts of retail-led value chains in a global political economy. Although these landscapes lie conveniently out of sight from the centers of consumer society, they make up the other side of this Janus-faced economic geography.

This book documents these South China factory towns, exposing the gritty establishments, their crowded dormitories and the monotonous labor carried out by factory workers. Although much research has examined the political economy and growth of the PRD, little effort has gone toward understanding its factory towns as places with their own urbanisms. The dynamics behind this urban typology can be both architecturally astounding as well as ethically disturbing. These factory towns attract individuals to migrate from their villages in search of a better life. Some of these factory towns function as self-contained centralized cities, with as many as 400,000 workers living within the compound. Other factories lie scattered in larger villages to mask their existence from the authorities, in order to evade governmental crackdown on the production of fake consumer goods and illegal casino machines. Little is left of the utopian impulses of the Western company town experiments of the nineteenth century, or the social factors in communist China's work unit, the *danwei*.

From an architectural point of view, some of these older government-established factory complexes are astonishing cultural heritage sites. However, over time, the facilities slowly deteriorate in physical terms as well as in long-term sustainability as factory owners face new environmental and labor regulations. In contrast to the horrid living conditions offered by older factories, some major corporations are building factory towns that resemble luxury resorts, with physical attributes such as marbled floors, green lawns and dormitory bungalows. This is done to attract the increasingly demanding labor cache. Despite the five-star façade offered by these newer factories, the factory towns are currently caught in a moment of turmoil. In 2010, a number of factories located in the south of China made headlines

in newspapers across the globe with distressing images of factory worker suicides and strikes. Of all the factory towns in South China, Foxconn City suffered the largest impact, with a staggering number of fourteen reported suicide deaths within an eleven-month period, including a double suicide. The suicides were rumored to be driven by the long working hours, alienation, low wages and strict company deadlines. In order to prevent workers from leaping off heights to death, the company ended up attaching large safety nets to the factory buildings, to act as suicide prevention nets.

While Foxconn struggled with increasing suicide rates, others like the Honda Auto Parts factory in Foshan suffered from strikes, symptomatic of a moment in which millions of laborers are beginning to be more assertive in their demands for their working environment, rights and higher wages. The rise of minimum wages was by far the most alarming news to both producers and consumers as they began to worry about an increase in the cost of goods. Additionally, the Chinese government pressured these companies to implement clean, environmentally friendly and high-value-added manufacturing practices. Further, the influx of foreigners and migrants to the south of China has also contributed to inflation of land prices. Adding fuel to the fire, the global financial crisis dealt a major blow to already struggling companies. As a result, particularly smaller low-value-added companies were forced to pack up, and some factory towns began to slowly empty out. Ironically, these are the same factories that were largely responsible for the Chinese economic miracle. "China does not want us anymore." This quote from a representative of the Chinese Manufacturers' Association reflects the perception of severity

stemming from China's new laws and legislation with regard to commercial production. The foreign investors who once saw South China as a business opportunity are now searching the globe for more profitable conditions, in China's western and central cities and in countries like Vietnam and Indonesia.

Now as some factories lie abandoned, a critical evaluation of the factory town is overdue. A clue to a possible future direction of the factory town can be found in the existing factory town types. The name "factory town" stands for a collection of industrial buildings that can be completely different in terms of organization and structure. Some function as isolated cities dominated by a single company, much like a company town, while others are like industrial districts in which different companies share facilities and services. At some places, workers live within the factory compounds in dormitories; at others, they live off-site in dense urban villages or bunk bed-filled apartments. Some building complexes are architecturally stunning industrial heritage sites worthy of reuse, while others have been built to be discarded. This taxonomy hints at potential futures for the factory towns.

It suggests that the model of the isolated factory town is defunct, since it alienates workers from the city, and it expires more quickly because it is more difficult to redevelop for a different purpose. This model made sense when corporations entered the still undeveloped Pearl River Delta and had to build communities from scratch, including dormitories, kindergartens, movie theaters, and hospitals within the factory compounds. Now that the surroundings are fully urbanized, factories can return these services to the city, and link to urban areas with public transportation. Then, in view of the rapidly shifting conditions of production and consumption in the global economy, the afterlife of factory complexes should be considered. Factories could be designed as temporary structures that can be demounted, or as long-lasting buildings or infrastructure with a post-industrial future in the city. One factory owner even imagined his factory to sit on a boat, so that it could sail from country to country depending on minimum wage fluctuations.

Whatever the future holds, it is important to understand the present condition. This book attempts to provide a glimpse of life in the factory town by adding images to stories. It uses the genre of the illustrated guidebook as a way to make visible the living conditions of the worker, in addition to popularizing otherwise less accessible research to an audience beyond the urban scholar, which is bilingually presented to both English and Chinese readers. The illustrated guidebook is a genre that appears particularly relevant to the research of urban environments, as it is lavishly decorated with maps, diagrams, photos and drawings that might as well appear in an urban design journal. In addition, the illustrated guidebook allows for a comprehensive and balanced view through supplementing visual information with stories, anecdotes and quantitative data. Urban researchers, often confined to more traditional forms of writing, have yet to exploit the genre.

Besides being visually rich and accessible to a broader audience, the genre is inherently interdisciplinary. The section on background facts in the book— Urbanization, Demographics, Economics, and Infrastructure— covers a wide range of perspectives on the phenomenon, from the disciplines of urban planning, geography, architecture, sociology, and anthropology. In addition to

visual representations of data, various scholars and experts have contributed essays to provide a deeper understanding on the topic. For instance, migration statistics are supplemented with articles that explain how such a migrant population is structurally produced by the household registration system, or what it means for migrant workers to belong to multiple places. Such a multiperspectival approach enables a more intricate and comprehensive understanding of the topic.

The following section of the book features the factory town case studies conducted by graduate students in the Urban Design Program of the University of Hong Kong. Students, having studied the factories and daily lives of the workers, mapped out and zoomed into various dimensions of the factory town which are now presented under the headings: Regional Map, Factory Buildings, Production Line, Shopping Guide, Wining and Dining, Accommodation, Employee of the Day, and Around the Clock. Some of them struggled to get access beyond the barbed wire that encircled compound walls of the factory complexes, and at times were even threatened by security guards and watch dogs. But others were welcomed warmly into factories and presented with ample product samples. With them, workers shared stories ranging from the pressures of hard and repetitive physical labor, to aspirations for upward social mobility for their children and themselves. Every so often they expressed feelings of isolation and boredom, or happiness found in pastime pleasures and assembly line romance.

In order to present a multifarious narrative, the case studies are sampled in such a way as to show a wide range of factory towns distributed throughout the South

China region, manufacturing products as diverse as ships, cars, video game machines, LED displays, ceramic tiles and sculptures, greeting cards, soy sauce, and even action figures.

The sequence of the case studies mirrors the process of development in China. Traveling counterclockwise around the Pearl River Delta, from Hong Kong, to Shenzhen, Dongguan, Guangzhou, Foshan and Zhongshan, one can witness different phases of capital accumulation, which partly explains the industrial variation amongst different cities in the Pearl River Delta. Hong Kong has long retired its industrial manufacturing, which it housed in vertical factories, and had exported it to Shenzhen in the 1980s. Shenzhen is now shifting up to high-value-added manufacturing and information technology, and so is Dongguan— previously known for its labor-intensive manufacturing such as toys, textiles and footwear—moving toward producing IT products such as computers parts. Guangzhou, capital of the Guangdong Province, has most of the older state-owned factories, and ambitiously seeks to expand in order to reclaim its historical importance. Meanwhile, the low-value-added manufacturing industries are relocating to the relatively underdeveloped Foshan and Zhongshan—known for producing garments, food products and ceramics—and to China's inner cities, a move which may gradually reduce the unequal regional development within China.

This is not a typical guidebook. It is not written with tourists in mind as the readership, but from the perspective of a factory worker. It does not cover tourist sights, but features the facilities of factories, representing the current situation in which factories compete against each other to attract labor. It does not just document the status quo, but seeks to uncover future

Introduction 前言

possibilities. Serving as a potential guide are the provocative design solutions, incorporated as "real estate advertisements." This project thus seeks to subvert the genre, embedding it with a different political purpose. In this way, it attempts to be a *détournement* from the typical illustrated guidebook.

This book's images fit in a politics of visibility. The book was produced from shopaholic Hong Kong. A white haze of polluted particles often covers the "city of malls," without showing the least physical trace of the south Chinese factories. The shroud temporarily limits visibility to the adjoining mainland factory region, concealing the origin of the commodities in the local shopping windows. Disguised in flashy graphics and the genre of the guidebook, this book attempts to be just such a collection of traces and particles, yet one that acts as a

"gentle" reminder of the existence of the south Chinese factory towns, the transitory home of millions of iPhone Girls. If the photos left on the phone had unintentionally given a face to an anonymous and invisible factory girl, then this book is a deliberate attempt to bring to the foreground real lives and places within the compounds of South China factory towns.

Notes

1. For a more in-depth discussion on "iPhone girl" see Ananya Roy, "Postcolonial Urbanism: Speed, Hysteria, Mass Dreams." In *Worlding Cities: Asian Experiments and the Art of Being Global*, edited by Ananya Roy and Aihwa Ong, 307–332. Oxford: Wiley-Blackwell, 2011.
2. Austin Ramzy, "Chinese Factory under Scrutiny as Suicides Mount." *Times*, May 26, 2010.

華南工廠城：圖示指南手冊

中國在經濟改革開放後，廉價的勞動力受到外國投資者的注意，工業迅速發展起來。在中國南方，很多外資公司都展開了大規模的工業生產，建立了不少擁有完善配套設施的「工業城」。工人在工業城中工作、居住及生活，雖然待遇不斷改善，工業城的環境質素亦不斷提高，但封閉的環境及單調的生活構成了種種問題，其中以富士康廠房的自殺事件最為轟動。

本書不是一本普通的「工業城指南」。筆者從工人、建築規劃及社會倫理的角度出發，就中國南方工業城的現況作出討論。透過不同的個案研究，記錄了工業城的規劃及類型、工人在工業城裏的生活和工作情況，以及他們面對的問題，繼而探討在日新月異的經濟及社會情況下，工業城未來的發展路向。

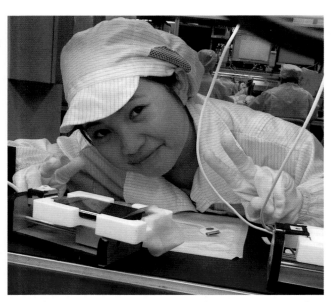

Images left by a factory worker on an iPhone caused worldwide interest in Foxconn City's smiling "iPhone Girl."

Recent view of a 1950s-era danwei residential compound in Beijing

The Danwei
Socialist Factory Town in Miniature?

David Bray
Department of Sociology and Social Policy
The University of Sydney

China's cities are being rebuilt on a phenomenal scale with amazing speed, and are driven headlong into the twenty-first century by an apparently insatiable demand for factories, condominiums, office towers and shopping malls. But if you look carefully down some of the backstreets of the old industrial districts, you can still find architectural remnants of an earlier era—small clusters of three- or four-story brick apartment blocks—austere, unadorned and, these days, rather run-down. Believe it or not, these drab blocks, built in the 1950s and 1960s, were once seen as the pinnacle of modern living, the pride of those who lived in them and the envy of those who

did not; for they housed the new "masters of society," the workers who were building a new socialist China. Adjacent to these residential complexes, and usually enclosed within the same compound, once stood the factories and workshops of the socialist planned economy. These combined factory/residential complexes—the work units, or *danwei*, of Maoist China—provided employment, housing, education, healthcare, welfare services and recreation for workers and their families; they were the building blocks not just for an ambitiously industrializing economy, but indeed for constructing a utopian new form of collectivized urban life. While this brand of utopian planning no

doubt failed in the end, its key result was to create a standardized and universalized form of urbanism in China founded on the *danwei* as its basic cell. In this way, the Chinese city of the Maoist era was structured more as a collection of mini factory towns (*danwei*) than as an integrated urban system.

It is no great exaggeration to contend that the *danwei* was *the* foundation of urban China for about forty years from the mid-1950s to the mid-1990s. It was the source of employment and material support for the majority of urban residents; it organized, regulated, policed, trained, educated and protected them; it provided them with identity and "face"; and it formed integrated communities through which urban residents derived their sense of place and social belonging. This "sense of place" seems to have been particularly reinforced by the fact that each *danwei* was enclosed by a high wall forming a discreet compound that separated the *danwei* and its residents from the surrounding streets and city. Walls have been key features of Chinese cities for centuries; even today we can find remnants of ancient city walls, temple walls and the walls which enclose traditional courtyard-style homes. But why, after the founding of modern socialist China in 1949, did the new government continue to build walls? Some historians have interpreted this apparent historical continuity of wall building in cultural terms, suggesting that it demonstrates that Chinese culture is closed-off, inward-looking and obsessed with control and containment. According to this analysis, the various types of walls that exist in China, from the Great Wall to the traditional walled family compound and the modern

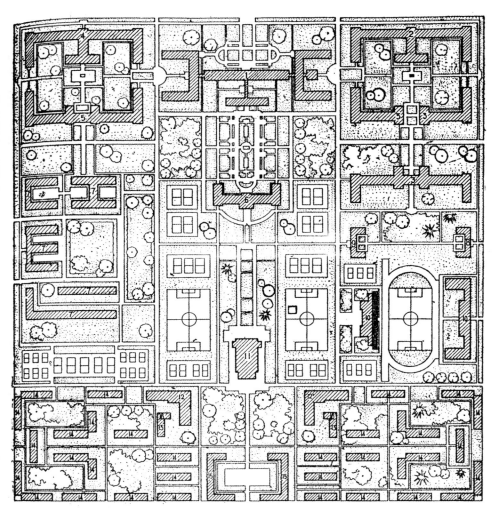

Plan for Xi'an University of Communications. Note the strong axiality of the design–a central vertical axis and two subsidiary side axes. The main entrance to the danwei is at top-center, directly in front of the main administrative building (zhulou).

Legend: 1. main administrative building (zhulou); 2, 3, 4 and 5. teaching and research buildings for various departments; 6. library; 7. work experience factory; 8. medical clinic; 9. Trade Union club; 10. covered drill ground; 11. the Great Hall; 12. student dining hall; 13. bath house; 14. student and unmarried staff dormitories (married staff reside in apartments in an adjacent residential compound); 15. welfare services.

Source: Du Erqi (杜爾圻). 1956. " 高等學校建築群的布局和單體設計 " ("The Arrangement of Building Clusters and Individual Building Designs for Colleges of Higher Education.")《建築學報》5: 1–27.

Life inside the danwei was centred on collective-oriented activities

wall enclosing the *danwei*, should all be understood as repetitions of a universal Chinese cultural trait. In my view, this argument is too simplistic because it ignores the very different dynamics occurring within the walls. If we go inside, we see, for example, that the socialist *danwei* is designed and organized entirely differently from the traditional courtyard home. Of course, there clearly is a historical continuity in the utilization of walls, but this is simply because walls continue to be seen as boundaries for demarcating social space in China: the walls of the traditional courtyard home marked the realm of the traditional family, while the walls of the *danwei* mark the domain of the socialist workplace which had become the new basic unit of urban society.

While each *danwei* became virtually a self-contained community, there was also a remarkable degree of uniformity in the appearance and spatial layout of the archetypal

danwei. This was because the Communist authorities decided very early to bring urban planning, architecture, civil engineering and the construction industry under central bureaucratic control. As a result, design and construction methods were standardized on a national scale, and all new residential and industrial structures had to conform to a narrow set of design parameters. The austere architectural style that emerged reflects both a modernist aesthetic and the economic austerity of the era; but more significantly, the spatial layout of the *danwei* was the result of carefully considered planning, designed ultimately to facilitate a transformation in the nature of urban life. Specifically, the planners sought to promote socialist collectivized living in order to transform the urban population into politically enlightened proletarians loyal to the new socialist state. The spatial form which emerged, then,

was informed by two interrelated design principles: the arrangement of key buildings along a central axis symbolized the primacy of the socialist state as well as the centrality of labor within the *danwei*, while the arrangement of living space around common facilities was intended to create an environment conducive to the development of socialist collectivity and proletarian consciousness. *Danwei* members spent most of their time within the *danwei* compound; hence their daily lives were shaped not only by the routines and rhythms of labor but also by the physical environment within which they circulated.

Entering through the main gate of a typical *danwei*, you arrive into a large open forecourt beyond which stands the architectural focal point of the complex: the *zhulou*, or "principal building." The *zhulou* usually housed the main administrative offices for the *danwei*, including offices for the Party branch committee and other senior *danwei* officials. Its prominent positioning symbolized the centrality of the Party and its leadership role in the everyday life of the *danwei*. In traditional China, power lay concealed deep behind layers of walls, far removed and remote from the ordinary subject. By contrast, the architectural language of the *danwei* spoke to a more open, populist and at times, egalitarian face of state power. In short, while the spatial symbolism of the *danwei* represented the centrality of Party and State to the life of the *danwei*, it also embodied the ideals of Mao's famous "mass line"—namely, that leaders must live and work amongst the masses.

Walking past the *zhulou*, you will find the other important buildings of the *danwei* compound arranged sequentially along the central axis. Where the function of the *zhulou* was usually related directly to the Party and central government, other buildings were generally associated with the business of the particular *danwei*. These buildings housed the major workshops or plants for a factory, the offices for an administrative department, or the lecture theaters and classrooms for an educational institution. As with the *zhulou*, the central positioning of these buildings imparted an important symbolic meaning: it denoted the centrality of labor in the life of the *danwei* and the socialist nation. The *raison d'être* of the *danwei* was the organization of labor; therefore, within the *danwei* compound, daily life revolved around the demands of production—whether it be production of material goods, knowledge or information. It is not strange to find then, that the *danwei* was organized spatially to reflect the privileged position that socialism accorded productive labor. Socialism was predicated upon *both* an improvement in the material conditions of life *and*

the production of a proletarian consciousness emerging out of participation in collective labor. *Danwei* designers clearly sought to produce a form of space in which both the productive and the spiritual effects of labor could be nurtured.

Collective life within the *danwei* was arranged at a number of different levels. At the most basic level of collectivity, every three to five families shared toilets and kitchens within each basic housing unit (*danyuan*). At the next level, each two to three buildings shared facilities like laundries, bicycle sheds and open space for recreation. Finally at the *danwei* level, all residents shared facilities like canteens, medical clinics, bathhouses, meeting halls, sports grounds, kindergartens, primary schools, and so on. Clearly, everyday collective life within the *danwei* cannot be considered a monolithic whole; rather, the nature of collective interaction changed between the various activities that constituted the daily life of a *danwei* member. While the *danwei* constituted the basic unit of collective identification, *danwei* members undertook many of their daily activities amongst smaller collective groupings.

As with most utopian schemes, the *danwei* system failed on a number of fronts: most notably it proved inefficient as an economic model, and instead of leading towards a more egalitarian social structure, became synonymous with structural inequality (both within and between *danwei*) and the corrupt abuse of power. Urban economic reform and restructuring, beginning in the early 1980s, gradually undermined many of the precepts and practices of the Maoist *danwei* system. Yet it was not until the late 1990s that the Chinese government, under Premier Zhu Rongji, took the ultimate step of severing the link between

workplace and living space: as part of a major restructuring of the state sector, from 1998 onwards state-owned enterprises were forbidden to provide housing for employees. In this context, it seems a great paradox that one of the key features of private sector industrial operation in the factory towns of southern China today is to provide living space and rudimentary services (dormitory accommodation, dining halls etc.) for employees. However, while there may be some superficial similarities between the Maoist *danwei* and the contemporary factory complex, the operational logic that informs them is entirely different: where the former sought to create an egalitarian socialist society, the latter merely pursues the neoliberal objective to minimize the costs of labor reproduction.

For a more detailed discussion of these issues, see D. Bray, *Social Space and Governance in Urban China: The Danwei System from Origins to Reform* (Stanford, CA: Stanford University Press, 2005).

單位：社會主義工廠──微型城鎮？

單位制度，是中國過去城市建設的指標。工人們居住在三、四層的紅磚公寓，為了建設中國社會主義而努力，在住宅區毗鄰，通常設置工廠和工作間等社會主義經濟的規劃。單位制度在毛澤東主導下，結合了工作及居住，為工人及其家人提供就業、住房、教育、醫療、福利服務和娛樂等，並以烏托邦的城市生活為目標。雖然沒有達到烏托邦式的理想，但單位制度為中國的城市提供了標準化及同一規格的發展模式，成為中國城市發展規劃的基本單位。當然，基於低效率和不平等的社會結構，單位制的失敗是無可避免的。近年來，中國南方的工業發展迅速，很多工廠亦會為工人提供居住地方，但主要是為了節省開支，並非為建立平等的社會主義。

Genesis and Evolution of Chinese Factory Towns in the Pearl River Delta
From Hong Kong toward Shenzhen

Laurence Liauw
Faculty of Architecture
The University of Hong Kong

Since the 1970s, the Pearl River Delta (PRD) has been a "factory to the world," producing a multitude of goods for global export, inverting the earlier practice since 1949, when China mainly manufactured for itself. The postwar Chinese factory towns were located in northern China and around Shanghai, while South China remained largely agrarian. Hong Kong, then still a British colony, was industrializing rapidly from the 1950s to the 1970s in response to the global demand for cheap consumer goods such as textiles, toys and electronics, supported by its open financial markets and advanced shipping industry. It was the 1960s' "golden age" of industry and shipping that founded Hong Kong's wealth and regional trading center status as a "window into China." With its trading expertise, rule of law, and abundant foreign capital, Hong Kong was the original global Chinese factory town prototype before any other Chinese city in the modern period after 1949. A typical urban transformation can be seen in Hong Kong's Kwai Chung district, which has evolved within thirty years from a fishing village to a factory district, and which has then taken on residential, container terminal, and leisure functions. This original economic urban model begun in Hong Kong has recast itself across the border, and continues to influence China's cities. Since China's Open Door Reform policies in the 1970s, most Hong Kong factories have relocated to the Mainland, and mostly to the

PRD. The "Made in Hong Kong" global brand shifted to the "Made in China" brand of today. Owing to such dynamics at work, one can trace back to the origins of a Chinese factory town and see how its evolution was influenced by changing politics, economics and society in China.

The genesis of a typical factory town in the PRD follows a generic pattern and cycle of development [see text inlays below]. In the beginning, many residents go from being farmers to becoming construction workers, with the working population consisting of some locals but mostly migrants.

[Factory towns are built by and for migrants, thereby making migration the driving force of industrialization in rural areas.] Small-sized speculative standard factories literally rise from the farmlands as brick and tin sheds replace paddy fields. [Factories are built speculatively even before industry arrives. Investment agents then seek out buyers or tenants.] Building mud tracks and factories provides jobs for the influx of construction workers who have come in anticipation of an emerging factory town. The first factory towns in the 1970s were formed from urban villages, starting with Shenzhen's

Hong Kong factory town in the 1960s

Kwai Chung district in Hong Kong

Shangbu, China's first experimental capitalist model village, which has evolved into today's Huaqiangbei downtown district.

China's "world factory" has been exporting to the world since 1979, with the PRD as the "dragon's head" boasting an average GDP growth rate of over 20 percent per annum. Hong Kong initially provided expertise and capital investment in establishing factories and international trading contacts, but since the 1990s, global industries have set up factories all over China. Hong Kong still accounts for about 60 percent of foreign direct investment within the PRD, and Hong Kong owners employ 11 million workers in the region Industrialization and rapid growth of the Chinese economy since 1979, from a GDP of RMB 362.4 billion (at the 1979 US$ exchange rate of 1.49) in 1978 to US$4.99 trillion (at current exchange rates) in 2009, has brought with it urbanization at unprecedented scales not seen before in history. Four hundred million people have migrated to cities from rural areas, increasing China's urbanization rate from 20 percent in 1979 to 45 percent in 2009. In the coming twenty years up until 2030, China expects another 400 million urbanizing

towards a central government targeted urbanization rate of 60 percent. This trajectory follows the predictable path of national development from modernization (1949–79) to industrialization (1979–90) and urbanization (1990s to the present and beyond).

As China rapidly transforms from a rural to an industrial to an urban economy, factory towns become an intermediate stage in China's move toward the status of a developed country. [*After factories are established, entrepreneurs arrive setting up small shops, specializing most notably in cell phones, food and clothing. Factory girls dominate the landscape, making the average resident age of many PRD factory towns in the early twenties.*] The difference between the Chinese industrialization model and that of factory towns in Europe (Manchester and the Ruhr region) and the United States (Lowell, Massachusetts and Pittsburgh) in the nineteenth century is that expertise, technology and capital were imported in the former to take advantage of local labor. China's industries currently account for 47 percent of its GDP, while agriculture accounts for only less than 10 percent. At this stage of China's development, the side effects

of industrial expansion emerge as pollution, poor public health and environmental costs to the country. Cities' regional growth propels infrastructure expansion at a territorial level, leading to general urban sprawl. [*Factories specialize in subcomponents that are assembled elsewhere at larger factories. When foreign investment arrives with the establishment of large assembly plants, the local government wakes to action.*]

The proliferation of Chinese factory towns of under 1 million in population has outstripped the growth of megacities, and will continue to constitute the main driving force of urbanization (over 40 percent, according to McKinsey Global Institute) in the next twenty years. This "bottom-up" growth and "self-organization" model of factory towns in the PRD has triggered copycat development in other regions. [*Ex-farmers have become property developers of modern housing blocks for cash-rich villagers, and hotels begin to proliferate for business and leisure purposes. At each "town center," the ubiquitous McDonald's-and-Kentucky-Fried-Chicken consumerscape marks the arrival of a generic town. Signboards advertising vocational training schools are seen everywhere.*] This small factory town model (with a population under 1 million and not qualifying for city status) is seen as flexible, efficient and effective, mostly evading control by the central government and retaining more earned income. Local governments in such towns typically sell land via joint ventures to developers of industrial and residential developments, earning over 50 percent of their income this way. [*Local politicians stay in power typically for five-year terms of office, the quick turnover depriving many towns of sufficient time and willpower to build public institutions such as schools, hospitals.*]

Professional services such as banks and lawyers are often missing due to the speed and 'political' nature of development.] Small towns are formed as agglomerations of "street-districts" with support from district governments in building public utilities. New regional infrastructure eventually connects the fragmented urban fabric of "street-districts" into a township.

China's national Five-Year Plans (currently the 12th since 1949) regularly updates development policies of the central government for economic transformation, social and urban reform. Domestic consumption-led development and sustainable low carbon policies are the new focus. The National Development and Reform Commission's *2008 Outline Plan for the Reform and Development of the PRD (2008–2020)* advocated for advanced manufacturing and modern service industries. Recent reform in workers' labor laws and antipollution environmental policies of the central government has reconfigured the economy and the industrial landscape, affecting many

of the PRD factory towns rocked by labor riots and environmental scandals. [*Police presence is now necessary to check the occasional workers' riot exacerbated by new labor laws. Constant migration into such factory towns could be swayed by competition between nearby industries, and workers would eventually migrate away as the factory town's industries and raison d'être expire.*] Maturing factory towns could either lead to shrinkage and expiry (as in the cases of Manchester and Detroit), or would be upgraded to form even larger self-sustainable industrialized agglomerations. The PRD megaregion of 48 million people (expected to expand to over 100 million by 2030) competes with other coastal megaregions of hundreds of factory towns emerging around the Yangtze Delta (Shanghai) and the Bohai region (Beijing-Tianjin). There are now more than 150 million migrant workers mobile in China. Major macroeconomic shocks to the system—the incidents of 1989 (Tiananmen Square incident),

1997 (the Asian financial crisis), 2003 (SARS), and 2008 (the global financial crisis)—have destabilized but not derailed the industrialization and urbanization momentum. Despite intermittent shocks, China's factory towns and centrally planned urbanization continue undeterred in their "Long March" toward progress and modernization. [*The 2008 financial crisis saw a hollowing out of over 600,000 workers from the PRD at one stage. Smaller towns formed with more than 75 percent of migrant worker residents would be transformed into ghost towns overnight, with the ebb and tide of industrial cycles and migration. But factory towns continued to be born, to grow, expire and evolve (just as Hong Kong did) with the continued resilience of the Chinese economy.*]

Shenzhen, the first Special Economic Zone set up by Deng Xiaoping, serves as a prototype (after Hong Kong) for the genesis, evolution and metamorphosis of contemporary Chinese factory towns, changing from agriculture to industry to becoming a postgeneric city. Emerging from a condition

PRD factory in paddy fields

Urban sprawl around factories in PRD

China Daily, 8 January 2009. Retrieved from: http://www.chinadaily.com.cn/bizchina/2009–01/08/content_7379756.htm.

World Bank data and statistics on China. Retrieved from http://web.worldbank.org.

"Hidden Pearl River Delta." *Urban China Magazine*, 13. China Periodical Press Center, Shanghai: 2006.

Terry, Edith. *Beyond the Pearl River Delta*. Hong Kong: Civic Exchange, 2008.

Mumford, Lewis. *The City in History*. New York: Harcourt, Brace and Co., 1961.

of insignificance and having almost nothing that resembles a city in 1979, Shenzhen first built standard industrial types, then global businesses and expanding urban fabric. It is an important case study for how local factory types evolved into global factory types, morphing into international business centers. Shenzhen is highly mobile and adaptive, with its migrant residents having adapted and upgraded their skills. Districts like Shangbu became today's Huaqiangbei electronics center; the Overseas Chinese Town district evolved from manufacturing to tourism and creative industries; Guangming District is developing sustainable high-tech industries; and Bao'an plans to transform itself from a polluting industries district to an ecological CBD "water city" with a population of 1.5 million. Such is the evidence, ambition and willpower of this prototype factory city, modeled after Hong Kong but in some ways already superseding it, that it has seen its population grow from 30,000 in 1979 to over 15 million today (including migrant workers), with its GDP also rapidly rising. With Shenzhen's track record

in the PRD, its liberal dynamism and promise. While Shenzhen enjoys an impressive track record in the PRD, with its liberal dynamism style of development and promise of the future, the challenge remains for other Chinese factory towns aspiring to postgeneric evolution: How to be similarly successful as Shenzhen, and also how to differentiate themselves in order to compete?

References

Outline Plan for the Reform and Development of the Pearl River Delta 2008–2020. National Development and Reform Commission, December 2008.

Liauw, Laurence. "Kwai Chung Hong Kong and Songgang Shenzhen Post-Industrial Studies." Chinese University of Hong Kong, School of Architecture, March Urbanization Studio 2007–8.

Liauw, Laurence. *AD New Urban China*. London: Wiley, 2008.

Hessler, Peter. "The Road Ahead." *National Geographic*, May 2008.

"Preparing for China's Urban One Billion." McKinsey Global Institute, March 2008.

珠江三角洲內中國工廠城的起源與衍化：從香港到深圳

第二次世界大戰後，香港經歷了快速的工業化，從一個小漁村發展為世界聞名的工業城鎮。中國改革開放後，香港的發展模式為中國日後工業城鎮的發展提供了原型參考。中國工業城鎮的發展與國家的發展相關，於不同階段分別受到現代化、工業化及城市化的影響，形成一個廣泛而可供參考的發展模式。最初，城鎮透過現代化及工業化，由農業轉型為小型的工業發展。工業城鎮是城市化發展中的過渡階段，以有機地聚集、有效率的小型工廠，為地方發展的基礎。這些小型工廠的集中地，經過地方政府的配套後，成為城市發展的基礎構成單位。

深圳是中國最早開發的工業城鎮之一，印證了上述的發展模式，是繼香港成為中國工業城鎮發展的另一個原型，亦為相關研究提供了重要的案例。自 1979 年起，深圳首先發展成標準的工業城鎮，再轉型開展全球商業，擴張城市面積，顯示了地方的工廠如何衍化成為全球性的工廠。

The Side Effects of Unregulated Growth
Can the Pearl River Delta Reverse Thirty Years of Environmental Degradation?

Claudia Juhre
Department of Urban Planning and Design
The University of Hong Kong

After thirty years of astounding and highly celebrated economic growth at breakneck speed, the Pearl River Delta is lately famed for a less remarkable achievement. The PRD has become one of China's most polluted and ecologically disturbed urban constructs.

Environmental degradation is troubling the mega region. Aging and highly-polluting industries supported by poorly developed infrastructures, exponential population growth, and extensive rural and urban sprawl are dominating the PRD's factory landscape. Natural assets, namely, water, air, soil and biodiversity, have been reported by the World Bank and the United Nations to be seriously and irreversibly damaged. Consequently, people's health and livelihoods are declared as threatened in many areas of the PRD. Acid rain, smoggy skies, ink-black rivers and electronic waste villages have lately caused cynical international travel suggestions, such as the most "attractive" pollution day trips from Hong Kong.[1] Not only internationally but also internally, this manifest "homemade" environmental decline, no longer capable of being ignored, has been recognized to be threatening the future development of the PRD.

"The Pearl River Delta has paid a great price in terms of environment and resources for the economic miracles it has created," said Pan Yue, vice minister of environmental protection at the Green China Forum in Shenzhen,

Guangdong in 2008. "Pollution is a threat to the delta's development." Vice Minister Shi Jiangtao was also quoted saying in Shenzhen.[2]

Many of today's problems can be traced back to the PRD's urbanization process starting with the political reforms in 1978. The main goal of the central government was to kick-start economic growth by moving away from central planning to a more market-orientated system. This further implicated a laissez-faire approach on local governing by loosening control over land use and ownership statutes. Regional legal planning frameworks guaranteeing a long-term sustainable development were non-existent. Thus local governments were competing in an ill-coordinated manner to attract foreign and domestic investment by offering cheap and available labour, low-cost natural resources, and low land prices. As an additional asset, with the absence of macro-scale environmental planning legislation, environmental protectionism or pollution control was completely neglected. This stirred a random chaotic rural industrialization specialized in manufacturing low-end, labour-intensive and high energy-consuming products with a low profit margin. The environmental costs are multiple. Factory constructions themselves are built to poor standards, many without emission filters, water filtering systems or appropriate waste facilities, causing direct output into natural waters, air and soil and threatening surrounding

rural livelihoods. Due to sprawling factory arrangements, retrofitting of municipal cleaning facilities is extremely difficult. Polluting infrastructure which convey heavy truck, car and ship traffic have additionally destroyed existing habitats and nature reserves. The PRD's estimated 200,000 factories have attracted approximately 30 million migrant workers, many of whom are of unregistered or illegal status. This transient population poses further burdens to local governments: unsustainable temporary settlements, lacking a clear taxation system for the provision of healthcare, education and waste facilities for this population in flux, causing unstable social conditions. Many factory towns which enabled the rise of the PRD as one of China's outstanding success stories are of poor urban quality, with a lack of community services and sense of belonging. On the other hand, they have fed excessive individual consumption patterns among the "new" Chinese middle class who are experiencing rising wealth; ownership of multiple automobiles, oversized individual households and wasteful lifestyles contribute a substantial component of this pollution chain.

Although some government officials argue that China's economic growth is not a main contributor to the PRD's environmental deterioration, law and policymakers in China generally agree that enforcement of environmental laws has been ineffective.[3] A national environmental law framework has been introduced in China since the late 1970s as part of the political reforms. During the 1980s, environmental conservation and protection was written into the constitution, and an independent unit to monitor pollution control programs—the State Environmental Protection Agency (SEPA)—was founded. Meanwhile, at the highest level, the Environmental Protection and National Conservation Committee directly under the National People's Congress and which comprised several ministries and governmental agencies, is responsible for the drafting and execution of national environmental protection laws. There has been no lack of ambitious environmental policies, laws and programs, but China's highly fragmented and decentralized political and geographical landscape often hinders these laws from achieving their intended efficacy. Generally, provincial and municipal governments can act with a high degree of independence, installing their own local laws as long as they are roughly in line with national laws, and are subject to little monitoring from above. In order to stay competitive, and paying heed to the central government's aim of achieving maximum growth, environmental matters have been ignored in the PRD and industries are hardly discouraged from reducing pollution or energy insufficiency. Tough media controls, the absence of action groups and inadequate education have caused a lack of awareness of health implications and future resource availability within the society as a whole.[4] Only a few internationally monitored events like the recent Asian Games or incentives through globally initiated research programs have shown mentionable results toward ecological or environmental improvements in the region.

Since 2007, the PRD is becoming less attractive than other industrial hubs such as the Yangtze River Delta, Vietnam and India for investment and settlement; the competition has grown significantly.

As an answer to the 11th Five-Year Plan calling for long overdue emission and water pollution control measures, *The Outline Plan for the Reform and Development of the Pearl River Delta (2008–2020)* released by China's National Development and Reform Commission holds great promise for the PRD's future.[5] It is targeted to bring in more sophisticated, high-end industries such as IT, biomedicine and tourism, similar to a Hong Kong or Singapore model, to transform the PRD into a clean, modern production and service sector base.[6] This ambitious program sounds like a good solution, but there is one major omission in the government's vision. At the current state of the PRD's environmental degradation, clean, sophisticated high-end industries are not attracted to move into the PRD yet. Educated labor, research and cultural facilities are lacking. The outline plan also does not offer a solution for a sensible path of transformation for the PRD. Many voices have suggested an ad hoc elimination process for unpopular and inefficient industries. This would not be the first time big changes have taken place in China overnight. Still, those industries with a history of thirty years' industrial bloom will leave behind an immense heritage of environmental destruction, which needs to be tackled first in order to regenerate the PRD as China's first advanced clean industries hub.

Despite certain environmentalists dismissing the program as an impossibility, the Guangdong government has described the upcoming developments as a positive challenge in a long-term solution.

Notes

1. See http://www.cnngo.com/hong-kong/play/pollution-tourism-see-amazing-polluted-sights-around-hong-kong-865637.
2. *South China Morning Post,* Hong Kong, September 13, 2008.
3. Caitlin Morray, "An Ill Wind: Air Pollution in the Pearl River Delta," *Pacific Rim Law & Policy Journal* 19 (2010), J. 217.
4. Ibid.
5. National Development and Reform Commission Policy Release.-The Outline of the Plan for the Reform and Development of the Pearl River Delta (2008–2010). January 2008. Retrieved at http://en.ndrc.gov.cn/.
6. Yue-man Yeung, "The Further Integration of the Pearl River Delta: A New Beginning of Reform," *Environment and Urbanization Asia*, 2010, 1: 13–26.

無規範擴張下的副作用：珠江三角洲可否改變三十年間環境退化

經過三十多年來的高速經濟發展，珠江三角洲已成為中國其一個污染最為嚴重的地區。基礎建設的不足，加上高污染工業的老化、快速的人口增長、過度的城市擴張等，都是污染的源頭。由於環境受到破壞，人們的健康及生計亦受到威脅。自從 1978 年中國改革開放以來，珠江三角洲的城市化過程過於着重經濟發展。為了發展經濟，地方政府向外來投資提供很多優惠，卻完全忽略了環境保護的重要性，沒有對環境污染作出有效監控。工廠的生產過程追求最大利益，但對於環境保護的配套不足。雖然國家對於環境污染有法可依，但地方政府為了增加競爭力，選擇性地執法。加上媒體的控制、缺乏壓力團體的監察及教育，社會亦忽視了環境保護的重要性。近來，面對其他地區的競爭，珠江三角洲推出一系列環境保護的措施，但能否真正解決環境污染的問題仍然言之尚早。

Air

Seventy percent of China's energy is generated by burning mainly unfiltered coal, which famously lies in the PRD's low-lying sub-basin under hazy skies. Many low-margin processing industries consume huge amounts of energy without emission filtering facilities. In 2008, a total of 75 hazy days were recorded in Guangdong, a record high since 1949.[1] Smog, produced mainly through car and cargo ship emissions, ranked as the number one regional air pollutant. In 2003, Hong Kong and Guangdong set a target in the *Pearl River Delta Regional Air Quality Management Plan* to reduce the four main pollutants up to 50 percent by 2010.[2] During the global crisis in 2008 and the Asian Games in 2010, factory closures relieved the situation short-term, but long-term improvements have been slow according to reports by the Chinese government and by scientists internationally. Quality standards are set far below as recommended by the World Health Organization, and most PRD cities have failed to meet the requirements of the Air Quality Information Transparency Index.[3] Lung cancer is regarded as the number one deadly illness in China. In Guangzhou's hospitals, numbers of diagnoses have risen seven times since the 1970s. Indoor or subterranean air pollution on badly ventilated factory floors, at mines or landfills create a huge health risk for low-wage workers. Cargo ships have been recognized as a lethal smog source, which have not been remotely targeted by legislation either in Hong Kong or Mainland China.[4]

Water

The Pearl River is China's third longest river after the Yangtze and Yellow Rivers, with a catchment area of 453,000 square kilometers. With the PRD's factory boom on the eastern delta, the polluting agricultural run-off in the west and rapid population growth in the entire region, water quality has been deteriorating. The Pearl River and its tributaries are serving 47 million inhabitants with drinking water in the PRD alone. In 2007, the Ministry of Water Resources designated more than 60 percent of its waterways as "polluted." Even if boiled, water is unsuitable for household consumption. A 2009 study by Greenpeace reported that industrial outputs are treated insufficiently, and that household sewage mostly entered the waters untreated in the PRD. In 2008, 53.4 percent of the province's rainfall in the first six months was

Guangzhou haze. Source: www.alistairruff.com.

Hong Kong haze. Source: www.alistairruff.com.

categorized as acid rain.[5] Health problems are significant, caused by heavy metal and organic traces in water and food, with their worst manifestation in so-called "cancer villages." Thirty-seven of these officially recorded settlements with extraordinarily high cancer rates are in Guangdong, located close to mining sites, steel plants or electronic waste recycling hubs.[6] The most recent scandal uncovered in February 2010 by the Chinese Academy of Science revealed that 10 percent of China's 250,000 million hectares of farmland was contaminated. As a consequence, 12 million tons of rice grain was unusable due to the risk of metal poisoning risk. A total loss of RMB 20 billion was projected.[7]

Biodiversity

The delta's most sacred resource are the flood plains in the estuaries, with highly valuable wetlands, mangroves and coral reefs hosting rich wild life such as birds, fish and insects. Those natural coastal communities have been destroyed by land reclamation and heavily damaged by heavy water pollution. Sixty percent of all wetland, floodplains and mangroves have been destroyed.[8] Marine wildlife is threatened; from among 381 fish species, 91 are endangered. The white dolphin unique to the area is also endangered. In 2006, the UNEP United Nations Environment Program declared the Pearl River Estuary as "dead," with 95 percent of the estuary being excessively contaminated. The topography of the PRD's mountainous landscape has been extremely altered for coal, steel and stone mining and for the mass construction of luxurious residential developments. Most forests that remain are

mono-culture for production purposes, and do not contribute to biodiversity. Heavily managed farmland with extensive use of pesticides leaves little hope for wildlife. Increased number of floods and a prediction of a 30-centimeter sea level rise at the mouth of the Pearl River are announcing the first signs of the global climate change.[9]

Waste

The growing volumes of domestic and hazardous wastes present considerable risks. The cost of discharging waste in the PRD is low. Most wastes go into solid landfills without prior treatment. Only few specialized treatment plants for industrial waste have been installed, and recycling as a concept is only beginning. The landfills are not well secured, and many substances leak into the groundwater. The local community has objected to the planning of waste-burning stations. Illegal recycling of electronic waste smuggled from around the globe into the PRD as ship cargo is a major threat. This has led some villages to transform into electronic

waste villages ("e-waste villages"). Poor villagers are taking the old electronic appliances apart with the crudest, most polluting and health-risking methods such as acid baths, burning or melting. These procedures are causing higher physical clean-up costs than the actual value of the raw materials regained. E-waste villages are known for a high incidence of illness among their populations. Textile, paper and printing industries also leave behind the most harmful waste products.

廣東省一帶，尤其以珠江三角洲為中心的區域，正面臨嚴重環境污染的挑戰。本文分別闡述空氣、水、生物多樣性及垃圾污染的具體情況，展示了珠三角正面對的環境難題。儘管政府已經作出努力，但陰霾天的數目創歷史新高，「癌症村」令人不寒而慄，生物多樣性的減少和電子垃圾污染的增加亦讓人瞠目。廣東省所面臨的困境，表明了環境污染的嚴重與危害性，面對這些迫在眉睫又無法迴避的問題，人們不僅需要勇氣，更需要智慧和對策。

E-waste recycling in Guiyu. Source: www.alistairruff.com.

Notes

1. See http://www.chinadaily.com.cn/bizchina/2009–11/12/content_8954323.htm.

2. Hong Kong Special Administrative Region Government (HKSARG) and Guangdong Provincial Government (GPG), *Pearl River Delta Regional Air Quality Management Plan (the Management Plan)*. December 2003. See http://www.epd.gov.hk/epd/english/environmentinhk/air/prob_solutions/files/plan_english.pdf.

3. Institute of Public and Environmental Affairs and Renmin University Center of Law, "Air Quality Information Transparency Index (AQTI)," January 18, 2011. Available for download at: http://www.ipe.org.cn/Upload/IPE 公告 /AQTI-final-20110118.pdf.

4. Greenpeace Southeast Asia, *Poisoning the Pearl: An Investigation into Industrial Water Pollution in the Pearl River Delta*. October 28, 2009. Available for download at: http://www.greenpeace.org/raw/content/eastasia/press/reports/pearl-river-delta-2009.pdf.

5. Ibid.

6. Lee Liu, "Made in China: Cancer Villages," *Environment Magazine*, March/April 2010. Retrieved from: http://www.environmentmagazine.org/Archives/Back%20Issues/March-April%202010/made-in-china-full.html.

7. See http://newsfeed.time.com/2011/02/23/12-million-tons-of-chinese-rice-contaminated/ and http://topics.scmp.com/news/china-news-watch/article/Millions-of-hectares-%20of-farmland-and-12m-tonnes-of-grain-contaminated and http://english.peopledaily.com.cn/90001/90776/90882/7067431.html.

8. Maplecroft, *Pearl River Delta: Environment and Climate Change*. 2006. Available at http://www.maplecroft.com/mc_portfolio/pdf/PR_PRD.pdf.

9. Ibid.

Global Megalopolis 全球巨型城市

A megalopolis is a clustered network of cities with a population of about 10 million or more.

巨型城市泛指聯繫三個或以上的城市，而城市人口達 1,000 萬或以上。

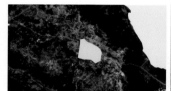

Mexico City, Mexico - 40m
墨西哥城，墨西哥 - 4000 萬

Chi/Pits, USA - 54m
匹茨堡，美國 - 5400 萬

Cairo, Egypt - 16m
開羅，埃及 - 1600 萬

Sao Paulo, Brazil - 43m
聖保羅，巴西 - 4300 萬

Buenos Aires, Argentina - 20m
布宜諾斯艾利斯，阿根廷 - 2000 萬

Lagos, Nigeria - 22m
拉戈斯，尼日利亞 - 2200 萬

In 1800, only 3% of the world's population lived in cities. The figure had risen to 47% by the end of the twentieth century. In 1950, New York City was the only urban area with a population of over 10 million, and there were only 83 cities in the world with a population over 1 million. Today there are 25 urban areas with a population over 10 million and 468 cities with a population over 1 million.

1800 年，只有 3% 的世界人口居住在城市，到 20 世紀末，城市人口已增至 47%。1950 年，紐約市是唯一一個人口超過 1,000 萬人的城市，而當時世界上只有 83 個城市的人口超過 100 萬。現時人口超過 1,000 萬的有 25 個城市地區，而人口超過 100 萬，則有 468 個城市。

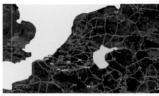

Rhine Ruhr, Germany - 11.5m
萊茵魯爾，德國 - 1150 萬

Istanbul, Turkey - 20m
伊斯坦布爾，土耳其 - 2000 萬

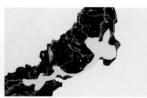

Tokyo, Japan - 80m
東京，日本 - 8000 萬

Central Spine, UK - 40m
中部地區，英國 - 4000 萬

Beijing, China - 23m
北京，中國 - 2300 萬

YRD, China - 88m
長江三角洲，中國 - 8800 萬

NE Seaboard, USA - 55m
東北海岸，美國 - 5500 萬

PRD, China - 120m
珠江三角洲，中國 - 1.2 億

Seoul, South Korea - 45m
首爾，韓國 - 4500 萬

Delhi, India - 28m
新德里，印度 - 2800 萬

Bangkok, Thailand - 25m
曼谷，泰國 - 2500 萬

West Coast, Taiwan - 18m
西岸，台灣 - 1800 萬

Mumbai, India - 55m
孟買，印度 - 5500 萬

Jakarta, Indonesia - 36.5m
雅加達，印度尼西亞 - 3650 萬

Manila, the Philippines - 33m
馬尼拉，菲律賓 - 3300 萬

19

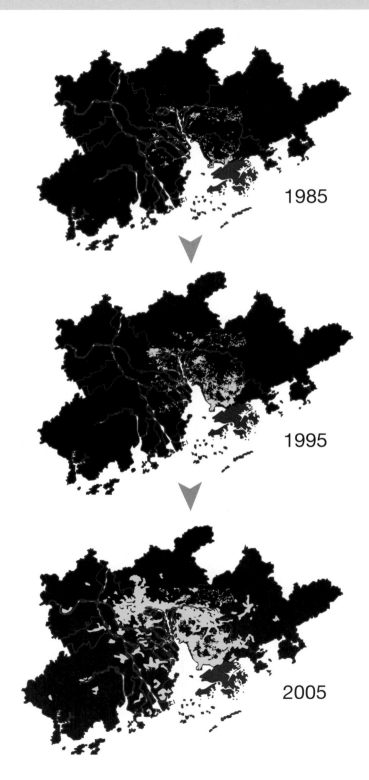

1985

1995

2005

Urbanization of the Pearl River Delta
珠三角城市化

Urban Growth in a Thirty-Year Span
三十年間的城市擴張

The Pearl River Delta has experienced a rapid growth in population mostly consisted of a "floating population" in a span of thirty years. In 1985, there were only two major cities in development: Guangzhou and Shenzhen. Moving on to 1995, most of the cities in the PRD were well-established with their own city centers. As of 2005, these became megacities that merged with each other to create a megapolis in the PRD.

在這短短 30 年的時間裏，珠江三角洲經歷了人口的快速增長。1985 年時，只有廣州和深圳兩個根深柢固的城市。到了 1995 年，所有珠三角的城市都有發展成熟的城市中心區。從 2005 年起，珠江三角洲裏出現了一個新現象，就是城市合併化。

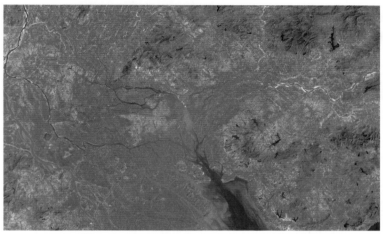

1979

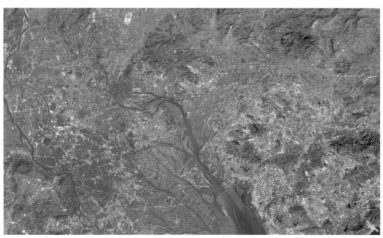

2003

Red indicates vegetation and grey reveals buildings and paved surfaces in these false-color images.
Source: NASA Landsat.

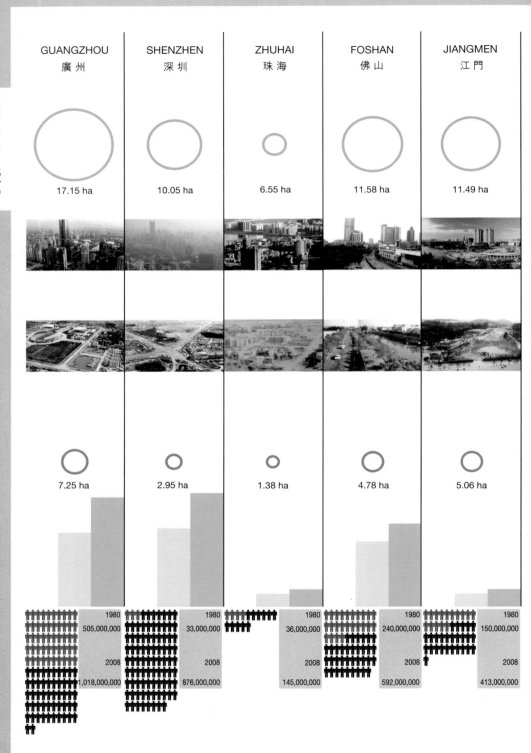

GUANGZHOU 廣州	SHENZHEN 深圳	ZHUHAI 珠海	FOSHAN 佛山	JIANGMEN 江門
17.15 ha	10.05 ha	6.55 ha	11.58 ha	11.49 ha
7.25 ha	2.95 ha	1.38 ha	4.78 ha	5.06 ha

1980 505,000,000	1980 33,000,000	1980 36,000,000	1980 240,000,000	1980 150,000,000
2008 1,018,000,000	2008 876,000,000	2008 145,000,000	2008 592,000,000	2008 413,000,000

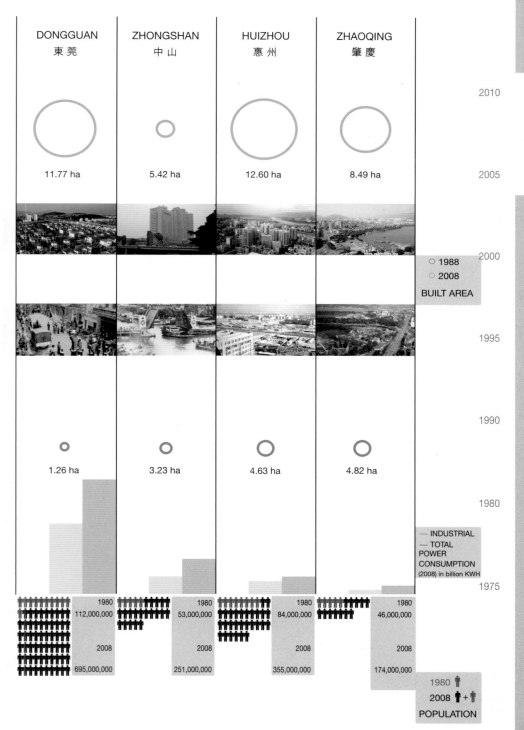

DONGGUAN 東莞	ZHONGSHAN 中山	HUIZHOU 惠州	ZHAOQING 肇慶

2010

11.77 ha | 5.42 ha | 12.60 ha | 8.49 ha

2005

2000

○ 1988
○ 2008
BUILT AREA

1995

1990

1.26 ha | 3.23 ha | 4.63 ha | 4.82 ha

1980

— INDUSTRIAL
— TOTAL
POWER
CONSUMPTION
(2008) in billion KWH

1975

DONGGUAN	ZHONGSHAN	HUIZHOU	ZHAOQING
1980 112,000,000	1980 53,000,000	1980 84,000,000	1980 46,000,000
2008 695,000,000	2008 251,000,000	2008 355,000,000	2008 174,000,000

1980 👤
2008 👤 + 👤
POPULATION

23

Migration without Integration
Workers between Countryside and City

Eli Friedman
Department of International and Comparative Labor
Cornell University

Poster from Liang's room in Guangzhou

According to a recent survey by an official trade union organization, 99 percent of migrant workers in the industrial hub of Shenzhen would rather stay in the city than return to their hometowns.[1] Analysts often note that this indicates a huge cultural change from the earlier generation of migrant workers, who tended to come to the city for short periods of time to earn money but always intended to return home. While there is no denying that many migrant workers aspire to lead modern, urban lives, they still maintain a conflicted relationship with the city. The experiences of Liang Hui,[2] a twenty-one-year-old worker in Guangzhou, demonstrate the tensions many migrants feel as they shuttle between city and countryside, never fully at home in either place.

I first visited the Hitachi elevator factory where Liang was employed while on a delegation of visiting trade unionists from the United States. With leaders from the Guangzhou Federation of Trade Union, we zipped in from the central city on an air-conditioned bus, passing by piles of trash, streams choked with gray effluent, and overcrowded tenements inhabited by villagers and migrant workers, and were ushered directly into the gated grounds of the factory.

The union at Hitachi had been showered with official recognition over the previous years, including such honors as a "Model Workers' Home" and an "Advanced Trade Union Unit." The shop floor was impeccable, with neatly uniformed workers operating highly advanced machinery. In meetings with the union leaders, we heard about their democratic practices, worker involvement, and the overall good conditions that employees at Hitachi enjoyed. This joint venture between Japanese Hitachi and a local state-owned enterprise appeared to embody the ideal of a high-tech, efficient, harmonious workplace in line with imagined "international standards."

Skeptical of their seamless presentation, several days later I ventured to the residential area abutting the Hitachi factory to try to talk to some of the workers directly. It was while wandering the streets in this area that I spotted a young man in the blue jumpsuit that all Hitachi workers wear. This was the first time I met Liang Hui. As I approached and greeted him in Chinese, his eyes light up in surprise. Enthralled with my ability to speak the language, we ended up chatting on the street for nearly an hour. He wanted to know all about America. It was not long before we developed a friendship, and I began visiting Liang every so often to chat or get dinner.

It turned out that things at Hitachi were not nearly so rosy as the union leadership had described. With starting wages of RMB 1,400, it was better than many neighboring factories, but seemed a paltry sum when the workers thought about trying to start a family or buy an apartment in the city. Liang needed the money because, as he frequently said, his family's "conditions were not very good," and his sister had an illness that required expensive medicine. Although Liang was a "regular worker," many of his friends were "interns," sent to the factory by their technical schools as cheap labor. These interns, making up perhaps half the workforce in some workshops, had none of the legal protections or benefits that regular workers enjoyed.

Despite the low wages, things for Liang were nothing like the horrendous conditions often associated with Chinese sweatshops. The shop floor where he worked was clean and well lit, and he had at least one day off a week. He lived alone in a relatively large, clean room with his own bathroom. He had a computer that

he spent a considerable amount of time on chatting with friends, watching movies, and playing games.

But despite the fact that he was not suffering severe material deprivation, things in Guangzhou had not worked out for him exactly as he imagined they would. He told me that, "Before [I left home] I thought Guangzhou was a very beautiful city, but when I came here I found out it isn't beautiful."[3] From watching TV he had an idea that Guangzhou was going to be a flashy, exciting city and that it would be more "fun" (*haowan*) than his hometown of Zhanjiang in rural western Guangdong. After arriving in the grim industrial suburb of Dashi, he realized that the Guangzhou from TV did not exist for him or people like him. Even though Liang's hometown is in the same province as Guangzhou, when he arrived he found that the most difficult issue was language. The dialect in Zhanjiang is quite different from that of Guangzhou, and so he was forced to use his heavily accented Mandarin to communicate. He said this made locals look down on him, so he worked hard at mastering Cantonese, watching TV programs every night after work. Eventually he picked it up, but he retains a heavy accent in both Mandarin and Cantonese.

But if Liang is not completely at home in Guangzhou, he now also looks like an outsider when he goes back to his hometown. On a weekend trip to his hometown that I took with him over Tomb Sweeping Day, I couldn't help but notice how different he was from those who had stayed behind. The first shock was that his parents, only in their forties, could not speak a word of Mandarin or Cantonese— only their local dialect. Suddenly Liang's trilingualism, awkward as it was, appeared as a mark of incredible worldliness, an indelible social marker of time spent in the metropolis. Small physical differences suddenly became increasingly obvious: people from the village were darker, had rough hands, deeper wrinkles at an earlier age. By contrast, Liang was quite pale with a willowy build, and he sported a carefully coiffed spiky hairstyle. His delicate, well-manicured hands made it nearly impossible to imagine him working in the fields.

Of course, many of Liang's friends from childhood were just like him and had also gone to the city for work, leaving mostly the older generation behind. Some of them had assembled back in the village during the national holiday. Among the young people I met, none of them had stayed behind to work the fields, and you could tell it from their appearance. Everyone gathered in the evening to reminisce about younger days and to swap stories about life in the city.

Perhaps it was my very foreignness which made Liang more comfortable talking to me about certain things than he might be with the people he grew up with. This openness was most evident in the frequency with which he would comment on the attractiveness of other men. Pointing out handsome men that we saw or discussing famous male actors—posters of whom covered his room back in Guangzhou—became a common refrain for him, something he likely wouldn't be able to do easily with a hometown friend.

If being in same-sex relationships in Chinese cities is still taboo, it would have been impossible for him to imagine it in his village. While Guangzhou maintains an underground queer community, the village likely offers no such opportunities.

And yet, as we squatted on the side of a squalid ditch waiting for the bumpy twelve-hour bus ride back to Guangzhou, Liang told me that his dream was to be able to earn enough money to buy a three-story house in his hometown. Despite the degree to which he was clearly not "local" anymore, his discovery that Guangzhou is "not that beautiful" had deeply affected him. One cannot help but wonder whether he is simply "eating from the bowl but eyeing the pot," and that a return to the countryside might present a whole new set of cultural and social challenges for him.

The question of whether young migrant workers like Liang return home or stay in the city is going to be crucial in determining the social, economic, and political future of China. For the past thirty years of marketization, cities have not had to bear the cost of social reproduction, as migrants have tended to return to the countryside to have children. Currently, the countryside exists as a sort of "safety valve," where workers can secure a basic subsistence if they are laid off or can't otherwise find work. But increasingly, the material and cultural needs of youth cannot be met on the farm. As this setup changes, cities must figure out how to integrate millions more residents, including a massive increase in the scope of social service provision. If even those few migrants like Liang who *want* to return home face enormous economic and cultural challenges in realizing this aspiration, it seems that things can only move in one direction. These youth from the countryside will have to fight tooth and nail for a secure, dignified, and fulfilling life in the city; their ability to do so holds incredible implications not just for urban development in China, but also for the future of the nation as a whole.

Notes

1. "Diaocha cheng Shenzhen xin shengdai mingong 99% bu yuan huixiang, jun yuexin 1838" [Investigation reveals 99% of new generation of migrant in Shenzhen don't want to return to the village, average monthly salary is 1838], *Shenzhen Wanbao*, July 15, 2010.
2. Pseudonym.
3. Conversation with the author. April 2009.

非融合的移民：都市與鄉村間的工人

本文通過深入訪談，展示第二代外地務工人員生活的多方面，揭示他們所面對的衝擊與壓力，藉此喚起城市，甚至整個國家更關注如何讓工人融入城市生活。這是在城市、國家層面上需要重視的議題，因為工人已成為城市不可或缺的成員，而且對國家的過去、現在與未來，有着重要的貢獻。

Workers at a Honda supply plant in Foshan gather near the factory gate during a strike in South China's Guangdong Province in May, 2010. Honda Motor Co. reported that production at its four car plants in the Mainland were temporarily halted due to strike. Source: South China Morning Post.

Strike

Minnie Chan
The South China Morning Post

The recent wave of strikes at factories in southern mainland China was triggered by one bold worker who decided to stick his neck out.

Early on the morning of May 17, Tan Guocheng, a twenty-four-year-old worker in the gearbox department at the Honda Auto Parts factory in Foshan, Guangdong, pressed an emergency button that shut down the production line. It was a symbolic strike signal that not only awakened his 1,900 underpaid coworkers but also millions of workers in the Pearl River Delta.

"We had waited for a leader to give us such a signal for a long time," a worker at the factory said.

"The workers talked about going on strike for better pay several years ago when we found that our ¥900 (HK$1,029) a month basic salary had almost been eaten up by inflation, while our company still made a profit of US$1.4 billion … Many of us considered going on strike for better pay, but no one had enough courage to take action."

Tan, a Hunan native who once had the dream of joining the Mainland's burgeoning middle class, said he had planned the strike after submitting his resignation. "I just wanted to fight for some benefits for my coworkers before I left," he said.

Several coworkers from his hometown supported him when he

promised to lead the strike, with Xiao Lang, who also decided to resign, becoming another strike leader.

Drawing inspiration from the nonviolence and noncooperation practiced by Mahatma Gandhi in India in the 1920s and 1930s, they set down two strict rules for the strike: no damaging of machines or facilities at Honda; and no fighting with people holding different opinions, including the Japanese management.

"We said we should stick to the two rules because we are telling the public that we are all well-educated people and our fight is rational and reasonable," Tan said.

On the first day of the strike, just a few hundred workers walked off the job. Three days later, Tan and Xiao led more than forty workers' representatives in negotiations with Honda's management, demanding a minimum pay rise of ¥800.

Management promised to give them an answer two days later, on May 22, but put Tan and Xiao on a train to Hunan that morning. The workers were then offered pay rises of ¥55 a month and told that Tan and Xiao had been sacked.

But if management believed such a tough response would cow the factory's workers into submission, it was mistaken. It actually brought all 1,900—mostly aged between nineteen and twenty-one—together.

"What's the meaning of a ¥55 pay rise? It was insulting; we felt that management regarded us as beggars," one worker who did not take part in the earlier strike said.

An intern at the factory said the Japanese management had been foolish to believe that "the new generation of Chinese workers" could be bribed so easily or intimidated by the sacking of two leaders.

The workers said Honda discriminated against mainlanders, who could rise no higher than deputy department head. They said a Japanese intern told them that he was paid US$380 a day, more than fifty times more than a mainland worker.

"We are doing the same jobs. We know the gap in the cost of living between China and Japan is big, but we don't believe it could be as much as fifty times," one twenty-one-year-old foundry worker said. "They [Honda management] just treat us as cheap labor because more than two-thirds of workers at our factory are interns, who are paid just 800-odd yuan a month."

Independent labor rights activist Liu Kaiming, from the Shenzhen-based Institute for Contemporary Observation, was impressed by this new generation of mainland workers who increasingly know how to protect their rights.

"The young generation of migrant workers is very different from their parents because they are aware of the importance of protecting their human rights," Liu said. The workers at Honda Auto Parts were "pioneers" of the new generation.

"The Honda workers were not only brave but also smart because they knew how to use media power and other external forces to support their strike," he said.

The strike at the parts factory eventually forced Honda, Japan's number-two carmaker, to shut down its four assembly lines on the Mainland.

Many neighboring factories in Foshan's Songgang industrial zone increased salaries to prevent copycat strikes.

Tan kept in touch with his former workmates through QQ, a popular online chat forum, and mobile phone text messages.

"He reminded us to unite, drawing on popular anti-Japanese sentiment," a worker in the factory's foundry department said. "It was very useful because many of us had learned about the anti-Japanese war from our history books and movies."

Also, thanks to Honda's ¥300 lodging allowance, young workers are able to move out of company dormitories, where four to six young people share rooms of ten square meters crowded with bunk beds. That helps keep ties strong and also helped the workers organize the strike.

The unity of the workers was further galvanized on May 31 after two conflicts with hundreds of trade union representatives who had sided with management and were seeking to end the strike.

The first scuffle broke out in the morning when some union staff tried to video workers from the gearbox department who were leading the strike. Workers said they were beaten when they tried to snatch the video camera inside the workshop. Another scuffle, witnessed by reporters and a curious crowd, broke out near the factory's gate in the afternoon when about 70 workers were surrounded by 200 trade union representatives. One female worker was pushed to the ground, a male worker had his hair pulled and the face of another was scratched.

Four days later, after intense negotiation with management, the workers accepted a revised management offer of an extra ¥500 a month—a 34 percent pay rise—ending nearly three weeks of strike action.

Professor Chang Kai, a Beijing-based law scholar who helped the workers clinch the pay rise deal, said he was impressed by those young Honda workers who had managed to find his mobile phone number and seek his help.

"Li Xiaojuan, one of the Honda worker representatives, called me on June 3 asking whether I could be their legal consultant in negotiations with management. I was really surprised when I learned that Li was just nineteen years old and her colleagues were in their early twenties," Chang, director of the Institute of Labor Relations at Renmin University in Beijing and a guest professor at the University of Tokyo, said.

Moved by Li's call, Chang flew the very next day to Foshan to mediate in talks between the young workers and factory management. He did not charge for his services. Chang told the striking Honda workers—bold and assertive but lacking in negotiating skills—to be more flexible.

"I told them their bottom line should be lower than their target of ¥800, because there is no such thing as a fixed price on a negotiating table."

The hastily formed negotiating team—a real blend of youth and experience—worked like a charm. After six hours of negotiations, a deal was reached that resulted in average pay rises of ¥500, no small victory for workers whose average monthly salary was just ¥1,500.

Their success set an example for workers in other coastal cities living from hand to mouth on minimum legal salaries of ¥800 to 1,000.

At the Honda Lock car parts factory in neighboring Zhongshan, 1,500 workers went on strike on June 9 after hearing about the pay rise won by the workers in Foshan. Six leaders, who had originally planned to lead a strike from July 15—after workers received their mid-year bonuses, were shocked by the strength of feeling on the factory floor.

Tan said he never expected that pushing the emergency shutdown button on the Honda Auto Parts production line would have such significant and wide-ranging effects. Strikes led by young migrant workers have since spread from the south to the north, affecting Taiwanese-owned and Japanese-owned factories, including some operated by Toyota, Japan's number-one carmaker.

A Honda Auto Parts worker from Qingyuan, Guangdong, said young workers were tired of being underpaid. Unlike their parents, who were farm workers, they were well-educated technical school graduates.

"We are daring to bargain with management because we have the full support of our parents," he said. "My migrant worker father told me that he doesn't want me to suffer the same unfairness he endured."

罷工

2010 年初夏，罷工浪潮開始在珠江三角洲風起雲湧，後來蔓延至華東和華北。這篇文章介紹這次罷工潮的發起者——在佛山的日本本田汽車配件廠工作的年輕工人們。他們不屈不撓地維護自身應有的權利，促使了罷工，令這個在中國一直被壓抑的威權形式得以健康地組織、開展和擴散。參與罷工的工人大多二十出頭，有別於他們的父輩，這些年輕人更有自信，懂得爭取各方支持，並且能夠運用現代媒體和科技，因而被稱為「新一代的農民工」。作者採訪了參與罷工的工人領袖、普通工人、工人法律代表和勞資問題專家，詳細探討這次罷工的形成和背後因素。

中國的勞資關係、經濟結構和發展模式還在不斷演變，但這次罷工潮令許多中國觀察者對中國工人刮目相看，並對中國經濟起飛的原動力，更有希望和冀盼。

Young Honda workers are the new face of the mainland's migrant workforce, and not content with the status-quo working conditions. Source: South China Morning Post.

Honda workers (in white) confronted a group of people who claimed to be trade union representatives but were unrecognized by the workers. Source: South China Morning Post.

A migrant worker overlooks an urban village demolition site. Migrant workers from western China are frequently employed in the difficult labor of by-hand demolition of houses. Their piecework wages are supplemented by free housing in the evicted homes that they are dismantling. This is a clear example of how socioeconomic disparities are leveraged to underwrite China's urban revolution.

Hukou
Labor, Property, and Urban-Rural Inequalities

Jia Ching Chen
Department of City and Regional Planning
University of California, Berkeley

The hukou divide

Hukou (the household registration system) was developed in its current form during the 1950s to serve as a key tool of demographic control under the command economy. Its present rules were codified in 1958 under the Household Registration Regulation.[1] *Hukou* was used to classify workers into large categories of "rural" and "urban," to allot corresponding socialist entitlements, to regulate the movement of people from villages to urban areas, and to maintain planned control of industrial enterprises in urban *danwei* (work units). Under the *hukou* system,

agricultural households (*nongye hukou*) shared in the collective ownership of rural agricultural land. Urban, "nonagricultural households" (*fei nongye hukou*) shared in the ownership of the state-run enterprises, which channeled entitlements such as housing, education and healthcare through *danwei*. Without *hukou* registration and *danwei* permission, rural migrants to the city could not obtain employment, establish eligibility for food, clothing or shelter, receive education for their children, or even marry or enlist in the army. At the same time, the state took no direct responsibility for providing a parallel set of

entitlements and services in the countryside. *Hukou* was thus a primary instrument of social distinction and control. Without *hukou*, the command economy could not have implemented its rapid urban industrialization while 250 million rural people were in poverty at the end of the Maoist era.

Hukou and labor migration

In the face of such economic disparities, the restrictions of the *hukou* system have paradoxically enabled the development of a cheap and flexible national labor market, arguably one of the most significant social and economic aspects of Deng-era transformations. Beginning formally in 1981, rapid agricultural decollectivization created massive surpluses of rural labor. These workers fueled the booms of rural industrialization during the 1980s and 1990s in township and rural enterprises. The restructuring of state-run enterprises during the 1980s allowed greater leniency in *danwei* hiring practices and the formalization of unemployment status [see "The Danwei" and "From the Iron Rice Bowl to the Steel Cafeteria Tray" in this volume]. Subsequently, the removal of barriers to foreign direct investment and enterprise ownership in the Shenzhen Special Economic Zone unleashed a flood of demand for cheap labor. The corresponding supply has been realized by the massive "floating population" of well over 150 million migrant workers whose household registration gives them no formal status in the cities in which they work. Rural families faced the brunt of "reforms," where agricultural pricing control and a distributional urban bias in government spending and policy contributed to a decline of agricultural resources and productivity and increases in surplus nonfarm labor. At the time of China's accession to the World Trade Organization in 2002, 70 percent of rural households were unable to sustain their livelihoods.[2] The disparities in urban and rural development led many commentators to compare the *hukou* system with apartheid.[3]

In this context, *hukou* enabled industrialization and the national labor market to develop in two important respects. First, by allowing enterprises and local governments to dispense with social benefits such as healthcare and schooling, *hukou* offset the economic cost of industrial labor. The system has gradually loosened over the past decades, particularly in the coastal provinces that have driven economic growth over the reform period. However, rural residents are still not allowed to resettle permanently with the same rights and access to services. In particular, schooling for children and healthcare are very expensive, and are major obstacles to permanent migration.

Second, even in provinces that have gradually relaxed *hukou* enforcement in regards to employment (e.g. Guangdong and Jiangsu), the system has regulated the flow of permanent migration by keeping households tied to their land as their primary safety net. Even as village agricultural output and rural industries have declined over the past decade, village land continues to be a vital source of housing and subsistence. In the case of the PRD, where village land was gradually subsumed by the growth of factory towns, collectives could profit by illegally renting land to private enterprises or by developing housing property. In the factory towns, "urban villages" became a commonplace occurrence, and in some cases, their collective owners became quite wealthy.[4]

Property and new urban inequalities

The state established collective ownership by rural workers through the forced collectivization process beginning in 1952. Under the commune system, the private ownership regime established under the revolutionary Land Reform (from 1949 to 1952) was transformed into collective land ownership. In a parallel structure with urban proletarian *danwei*, land ownership was organized in production teams that coincided with geographic boundaries so that everyone who was born and residing within these boundaries was entitled to equal shares of land and its production surplus.[5] Thus, rural *hukou* has always been tightly bound with concepts of collective property and the distinct relationships rural residents have with the state.

Although the system of *hukou* as a restriction on employment and movement is slowly becoming less important, its salience as a concept of ownership has increased in the context of rapid urbanization and industrialization. With the rapid speed and extent of China's urban revolution, rural areas on the outskirts of cities of all sizes are being converted to state-controlled urban land. This urbanization process requires the undoing of the benefits of agricultural *hukou*— namely, the ownership of land. This is accomplished through monetary compensation and the replacement of village land ownership with the right to purchase subsidized relocation housing, typically in new development districts on the periphery of the expanding city.

In the processes of enclosing rural land for urbanization, village collectives have paradoxically become mechanisms for severing *hukou* relationships and building new institutions of property ownership and belonging. State-led processes of village demolition and relocation are negotiated and channeled through rural collectives. The administrative process of urbanization often goes through stages in which village land and farmland are enclosed separately. During this transitional period, villagers are dispersed and resettled in urban (or suburban) developments. Villagers maintain their *hukou* and ownership over their farmland, but are frequently prevented from continuing cultivation by prohibitive obstacles such as distance or the severing of irrigation infrastructure. Compensation for farmland, when it arrives, is not based on the actual market value of urban land, and does not provide an adequate basis for retirement. Thus, villagers must find new livelihoods while also facing the increased economic demands of an urban life. Employment opportunities for less educated and older villagers are scarce, especially in the high-tech industrial sectors for which rural land is often requisitioned.

In the sense that displaced "collectives" are no longer engaged in production, but are only awaiting compensation for ceded property, agricultural *hukou* status comes to simply signify "not fully urban." It is a transitional placeholder for the millions of rural villagers that are undergoing the social process of urbanization. Though fraught with continuing inequalities, the transition from an agricultural-centric to an urban-centric understanding of *hukou* represents a reorganization of the principal tool through which the state maintained urban-rural social distinction and control over the past six decades. The degree to which *hukou* socioeconomic inequalities become further entrenched by market mechanisms and new forms of segregation such as peripheral relocation settlements remains to be seen.

Notes

1. For more on the history of *hukou* in China, see Flemming Christiansen, "Social Division and Peasant Mobility in Mainland China: The Implications of the Hukou System," *Issues & Studies* 20, no. 4 (1990): 78–91; Chan Kam Wing, "The Chinese *Hukou* System at 50," *Eurasian Geography and Economics* 50, no. 2 (2009): 197–221.

2. State Council Development Research Center, reported in the *China Daily*. October 22, 2002.

3. Among others, see Chan Kam Wing and Will Buckingham, "Is China Abolishing the Hukou System?" *The China Quarterly*, no. 198 (2008): 582–606.

4. See, for example, Lanchih Po, "Redefining Rural Collectives in China: Land Conversion and the Emergence of Rural Shareholding Co-Operatives," *Urban Studies* 45, no. 8 (2008): 1603–23.

5. Christiansen (1990).

戶口：勞工、財產、城鄉間的不均等

1950 年代訂立的「戶口」制度，是中國在計劃經濟時代用以控制人口的重要工具。政府利用法律，把「農業戶口」和「非農業戶口」區分，嚴格限制農民進入城市，就像在城市與農村之間構築了一道高牆，限制人口流動。這項政策把城鄉分離，因而形成「二元經濟模式」。在戶口制度下，中國的工業化快速推進，但在毛澤東時代末期，有 2.5 億農民依然生活在貧窮之中。

隨着改革開放和彈性勞動力市場的發展，人口流動勢不可擋。以深圳為例，高達 1.5 億農民工湧入了其經濟發展的大潮中，可是改革卻帶來了新的問題；農民工在城市裏面對福利待遇不公，但亦同時集體利用土地，這些問題引發了人們對戶口制度的爭議。在工業化的過程中，土地逐漸收為國有，這種新的產權情況造成了很多不公。本文闡述了中國戶口制度的演變歷程，以及這制度現正面臨需要改革卻又舉步維艱的窘境，討論引人深思。

Left-Behind Children in the Countryside

At least 58 million of children in rural China are growing up in households where one or both parents have migrated to the cities in search for work.[1]

The *hukou* system has contributed to this disruption of the traditional notion of the family concept. Parents who choose to migrate are confronted with a difficult choice. If they bring their children without an urban *hukou*, their offspring will not be allowed to enroll in public school. Instead they can go to unregistered urban migrant schools, which offer notoriously substandard education. Children left behind with family members in the countryside will have a more stable learning environment, at the cost of living without their parents. According to researchers, these separated children are at risk of psychological and social problems.

被遺忘在鄉間的孩子

中國農村中至少有 5,800 萬孩童，因父母移居到城市找尋工作，而在城市裡成長。戶口制度加快了傳統家庭概念的瓦解。選擇移居的父母必須面對不同的抉擇。如果他們帶著子女移居，但沒有城市戶口，他們的下一代將無法入讀公立學校，而進入未獲認可的都市民工子女學校，這些學校提供劣質教育。留在家鄉與其他家庭成員生活的孩子，則擁有較佳的學習環境，但是父母卻不在身邊。根據研究，這些留在家鄉的孩子較容易出現心理和社交問題。

1. Stack, Megan. 2010. China raising a generation of left-behind children. *Los Angeles Times*, September 29.

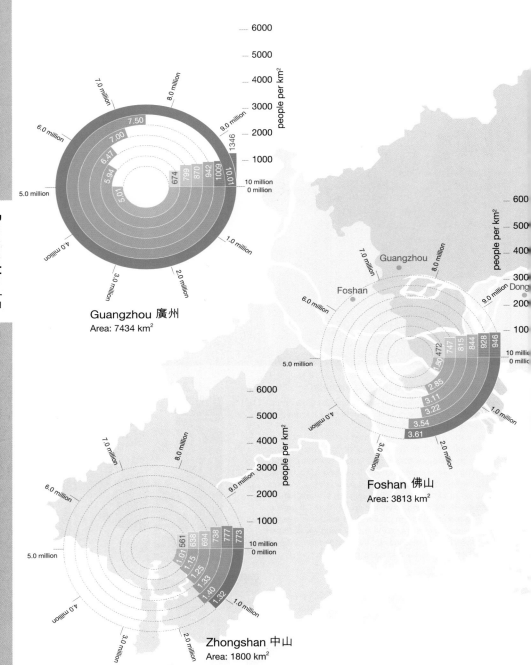

Guangzhou 廣州
Area: 7434 km²

Foshan 佛山
Area: 3813 km²

Zhongshan 中山
Area: 1800 km²

Demographic growth of the Pearl River Delta
珠三角人口統計

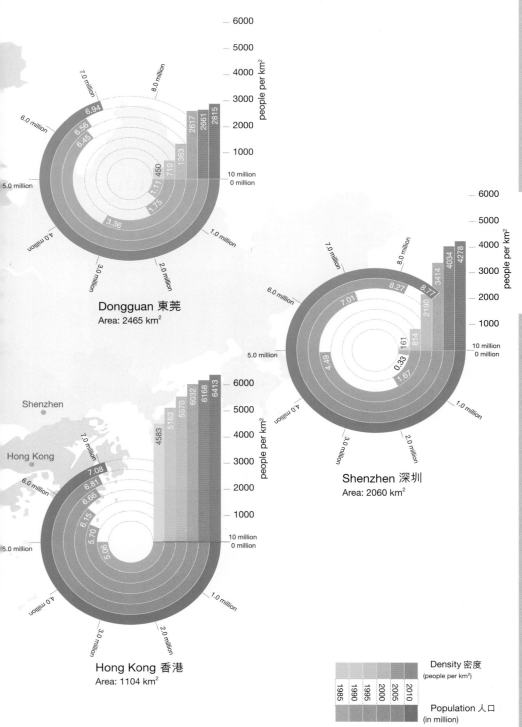

Dongguan 東莞
Area: 2465 km²

6.94
6.56
6.45
450
710
1363
2617
2661
2815
1.11
1.75
3.36

people per km²

6000
5000
4000
3000
2000
1000
0 million

10 million
0 million

8.0 million
7.0 million
6.0 million
5.0 million
4.0 million
3.0 million
2.0 million
1.0 million

Shenzhen 深圳
Area: 2060 km²

8.27
8.77
7.01
161
814
2190
3414
4034
4278
0.33
1.67
4.49

people per km²

6000
5000
4000
3000
2000
1000
0 million

10 million
0 million

8.0 million
7.0 million
6.0 million
5.0 million
4.0 million
3.0 million
2.0 million
1.0 million

Shenzhen
Hong Kong

Hong Kong 香港
Area: 1104 km²

7.08
6.81
6.66
6.15
5.70
5.06
4583
5163
5570
6032
6168
6413

people per km²

6000
5000
4000
3000
2000
1000
0 million

10 million
0 million

7.0 million
6.0 million
5.0 million
4.0 million
3.0 million
2.0 million
1.0 million

1985 1990 1995 2000 2005 2010

Density 密度
(people per km²)

Population 人口
(in million)

37

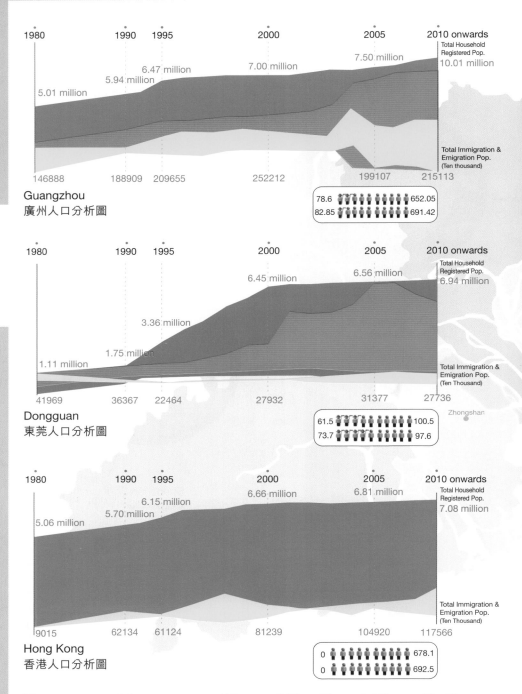

Guangzhou
廣州人口分析圖

Dongguan
東莞人口分析圖

Zhongshan

Hong Kong
香港人口分析圖

Demographic composition of the Pearl River Delta
珠三角人口分析圖

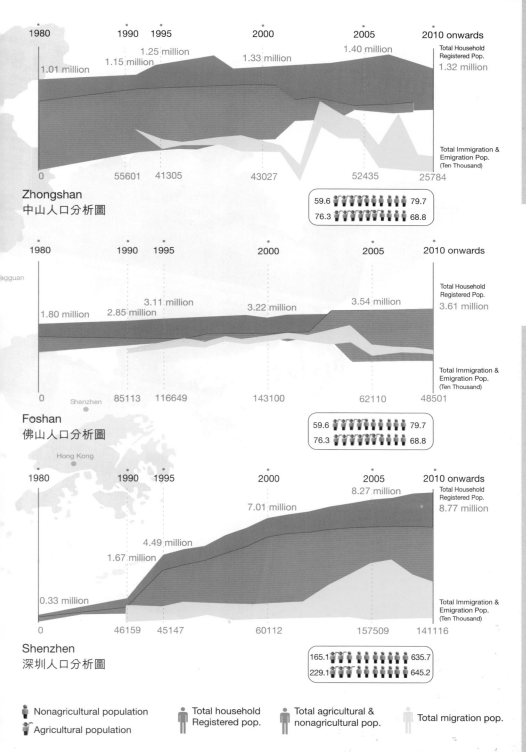

1980 **1990** **1995** **2000** **2005** **2010 onwards**

1.25 million

1.15 million

1.33 million

1.40 million

1.01 million

Total Household
Registered Pop.
1.32 million

Total Immigration &
Emigration Pop.
(Ten Thousand)

0 55601 41305 43027 52435 25784

Zhongshan
中山人口分析圖

59.6 79.7
76.3 68.8

1980 **1990** **1995** **2000** **2005** **2010 onwards**

3.11 million

3.22 million

3.54 million

1.80 million

2.85 million

Total Household
Registered Pop.
3.61 million

Total Immigration &
Emigration Pop.
(Ten Thousand)

0 Shenzhen 85113 116649 143100 62110 48501

Foshan
佛山人口分析圖

59.6 79.7
76.3 68.8

1980 **1990** **1995** **2000** **2005** **2010 onwards**

8.27 million

7.01 million

8.77 million

Total Household
Registered Pop.

4.49 million

1.67 million

0.33 million

Total Immigration &
Emigration Pop.
(Ten Thousand)

0 46159 45147 60112 157509 141116

Shenzhen
深圳人口分析圖

165.1 635.7
229.1 645.2

🚹 Nonagricultural population

👤 Total household
Registered pop.

👤 Total agricultural &
nonagricultural pop.

👤 Total migration pop.

🚹 Agricultural population

Factories: Is this the end of cheap labor?

FROM PAGE 1

"This is the end of the world factory model," said Pan Yi, an assistant professor of social sciences at Hong Kong University of Science and Technology. "Migrant labor is a sin of the times. We need a development model more humane and respectable."

Before operations at the Honda plant were partially resumed on Wednesday, executives at the automaker offered to raise salaries by about 20 percent, taking effect on the production line up to 1,900 yuan ($280) a month — less than the 2,000 to 2,500 yuan they are demanding. The factory union said about 30 people fought with union officials on Monday, leaving some people hospitalized.

"Honda's workers went on strike as the only effective way to negotiate with the company for better treatment. It seems to be their last resort," said Chang Kai, director of Renmin University of China's labor relations institute.

In an unrelated case, Foxconn Technology Group — a Taiwanese-owned contract manufacturer... Sony and other advanced

agencies keep one eye closed. They do not solve problems," added the report. "This has led ... decline in confidence in ...

the Korean automaker's plant in the Chinese capital.
"Strikes in China would jeopardize the company's reputation," he told South Korea newspaper Chosun Ilbo.
Fast forward to last Friday ... at 1,000 workers at ... parts factory

Workers work on circuit boards at the Foxconn factory in Longhua township in southern Guangdong province. Bosses say they will increase salaries by 30 percent.

EDMOND TANG / CHINA DAILY

GLANCE

1,90
workers
Number who wer
at Guangzi Honc
Company in Fo
dong province,
demanding high

1,9
yuan
Typical mo
duction lin
Honda Au
The strik
2,500 yu

3
per
Wag
ing.
Gre
Th
fr

...rikes signal end to cheap labor

...the increase in industrial action mark the beginning of ...
...ng conditions in China? **Li Jing** and **Hu Yinan**...

...ce has finally been ...okered between ...onda bosses and ... striking work...tively shuttered ...ar giant's entire ...hina for almost ... weeks.

...ports emanat... ...rom Foshan ... Guangdong ...dnesday said ...oint venture ...ngqi Honda ... — where ...rs walked ...has agreed

to work for three days while representatives thrash out a deal for higher salaries.

The plant, which makes transmissions and engine parts, is on the upper reaches of the supply chain and Honda's four other assembly factories in China were forced to halt production.

"Our factory in Foshan is back to normal production," said a Honda spokeswoman who would give only her surname, He. "Every worker is back to the normal production line."

A company statement... Honda's four other p... would remain idle until at... Thursday and no date was... for production to resume.

Although the strike... Foshan has seen some strange twists (while the workers pick... eted for better wages, the local trade union was trying to get them to end the stand-off), it is being seen as another example of how Chinese workers are growing impatient with the long hours and low pay culture that has been the bedrock of the country's

Harsh conditions alleged at China factory where Microsoft outsources

BY LINDSAY GOLDWERT
DAILY NEWS WRITER

Tuesday, April 20th 2010, 11:59 AM

Where do you want to go today? If you are a Microsoft exec, you probably don't want to be in the China sweatshop where work is outsourced.

Photos of female workers, their heads resting in their arms, were smuggled out of the KYE Systems factory at Dongguan, China, as part of a three-year investigation by the National Labour Committee, a Pittsburgh-based human rights group which campaigns for workers across the globe.

National Labor Co

Photos of female workers, their heads resting in their arms, were smuggled out of the KYE Systems factory at Dongguan, China.

RELATED NEWS

ARTICLES
Crooks tear off man's pinky to
hands on his iPad
Production of screen causing
launch snafu
Is this the new iPhone? We
claims to have photos of A
prototype

oducts for quality.

of sports shoes prod
Indonesia alone wa
5 percent since 200
ng to the Indonesian
Association.
On the other ha
strike continues an
nationwide, with
may withdraw
rom industries

China last September, the country's Commerce Ministry initially issued a tepid response.
But faced with furious criticism on the Internet, the ministry changed its position later and announced in an...

spring that it would break the r...
his peg to the dollar.
Zoe Zhang, the sales mana
Dongguan Wellcom Electronics
makes portable CD players in
guan, China, said Sunday that h
pany was ready for the rem
move gradually. "Last time the
ment appreciated the renm
... all caught by surprise."...
... ere been c

Inside China's manufacturing machine

12-hour shifts at Foxconn are numbing, fast-paced and highly regimented

BY DAVID BARBOZA

SHENZHEN, CHINA

Inside one of the world's largest electronics factories, Yuan Yandong, 24, sits on a stool 6 nights a week, 12 hours a night, barring meal and bathroom breaks, and assembles computer hard drives for an American company called EMC.

Until a few months ago, he lived in northern China, where he grew up on a farm and worked at a local hotel after finishing middle school. But this year, he traveled 36 hours by train to Guangdong Prnvce in the southeast to find work in Shenzhen. All he took for his journey south on the hard train seat was a sack of clothes, toothpaste, shampoo and his mobile phone.

"Friends my hometown said wages at Foxconn were good," he said. "So I figured I could earn more here."

A series of puzzling suicides at Foxconn and labor strikes at plants in southern China that create auto parts for Honda have put the spotlight on what work is like inside the country's factories. Analysts say rising pressure over wages and demands for better conditions are threatening China's competitive advantage and raising questions about whether its manufacturing model can continue to churn out much of the world's toys, textiles and electronics at rock-bottom prices. To do so, China will need legions of young migrants like Mr. Yuan to continue to make the journey from villages in the interior to the manufacturing hubs along the coast.

And what is life like for a cog in China's labor-intensive factory model? Mr. Yuan, with the approval of his supervisor, described it for The New York Times on June 10 before and after his shift that Thursday. The International Herald Tribune is the global edition of The Times.

6:30 P.M. THE SHIFT BEGINS

Mr. Yuan wakes at 6:10 p.m. at his small apartment, a 20-minute walk from Foxconn's campus. He arrives at the factory at 6:50 for a quick free meal at the canteen, then starts work at 7:30.

His task is to help complete 1,800 hard drives — his workshop's daily quota — and to make sure everyone is perfect. Seated in the middle of the assembly line in his black Foxconn sports shirt, cotton slacks and company-mandated blue plastic slippers, he waits for the next ...

you can become numb," he said. "But I've gotten used to doing this type of work."

10:30 P.M. DINNER BREAK

Time for a subsidized meal at the canteen. This night, he had rice and scrambled egg with tomato and eggplant, well within the 65-cent allowance for the meal. Then he went for a short walk.

11:30 P.M. BACK ON THE LINE

Foxconn, owned by Taiwan's Hon Hai Group, is one of the world's biggest contract manufacturers, building and assembling for leading brands like Apple, Dell and Hewlett-Packard.

Luo Jar Der, a sociology professor at Tsinghua University in Beijing and an authority on the Chinese manufacturing model, says contract manufacturers like Foxconn have borrowed techniques ...

If his team members do not meet the daily quota, they are asked to keep working.

from the United States and Japan.

"Foxconn has a team of 500 people to analyze each action a worker makes," Professor Luo said. "They want to be the most efficient actions of a worker."

Professor Luo says that work can be intense and that workers are treated like machines at some plants. This is the marvel of the manufacturing boom in the na... factories are known ... with machines that an... but in China factories ... trend and replace co... workers like Mr. ... sometimes prefer...

Strike ... at Toyota in ...

BEIJING

FROM NEWS REPORTS

員工「連11跳」危機

---

sueddeutsche.d

Politik | Wirtschaft | Geld | Kultur | Sport | Leben | Karr

Home > Wirtschaft | Arbeit und Soziales | Unternehmen

China

Aus für Billiglöhne

Von Marcel Grzanna, Peking

Gehofft, gekämpft - und gewonnen: Chinas Fabrikarbeit Bezahlung durch. Aber verlagern jetzt ausländische Inv Drittländer?

Streiks und Unzufriedenheit unter Arbeitern haben Arbeitgeber z höhere Gehälter zu zahlen. Die Steigerungen der Mindestlöhne rückständigen Provinzen und erhöhen den Druck auf die Zentral von 31 Provinzen und Regionen im Land haben sich bislang den September anheben. Zuletzt verkündete die Provinz Qinghai, auch sie werde entzogen. Die steigenden Lohnkosten bereiten Peking, weil der Exportsektor besonders von billigen Arbeitskräften profitier ein Stützpfeiler des chinesischen Wachstumsmodells; sie drohen e Arbeit in China zu teuer wird.

Feier mit dem besten Netz.

sueddeutsche.de

Home > Wirtschaft > Unternehmen

130 Überstunden, unbezahlt - Monat für Mo

Von Silvia Liebrich

Aldi, Adidas und Metro am Pranger: Menschenrechtler kritisieren die katastrophalen Arbeitsbedingungen in China. Selbst Ethikprogramme taugen kaum um die Missstände zu beseitigen.

90 Überstunden und mehr pro Monat sind offenbar nichts Ungewöhnliches. Doch selbe chinesische Verhältnisse überschreitet das oben die Grenzen des Erlaubten. Erschreckend dass sich deutsche Unternehmen immer wieder in der Kritik geraten. Bei Lieferanten des China wegen Verstö gegen das Arbeitsrecht immer wieder in die Kritik geraten. Bei Lieferanten des China gründenden Rechtsverletzungen und ihre Zulieferbetriebe in China wegen Versto Als und des Sportartikelherstellers Adidas kommt es laut einer neuen Studie teilw Metro in China. Eine am Donnerstag veröffentlichte Studie des Südwind-Instituts Ökonomie und Ökumene zeigt, dass selbst aufgelegte Ethikprogramme der Fir dazu beitragen, diese Missstände zu beseitigen.

"Am schlechtesten sind die Bedingungen bei Aldi-Zulieferern", h der Studie. Bei einem Textilbetrieb in der Provinz Guangdong bis zu 130 Überstunden im Monat, meist ohne Bezahlung, so Lieferanten in der Provinz Fujian seien exzessive Überstund 92 Überstunden im Monat überschreitet das Erlaubte laut d in klarer Verstoß gegen die Bestimmungen.

Das christliche Südwind-Institut moniert außerdem, auch Mindestlöhne liegen. Die deutsche Mindestlohn seien ..., während die Unternehmen ... um 1640 Renmin...

士康昨深夜
爆第12跳

Divergent Workshops of the "World Factory" in the Pearl River Delta
A Comparison of Hong Kong and Taiwanese Manufacturing

Chun Yang
Department of Geography
Hong Kong Baptist University

In the last three decades of reform, the Pearl River Delta in South China has benefitted from massive inflows of foreign investment, particularly overseas/ethnic Chinese investment from Hong Kong and Taiwan. Hong Kong and Taiwanese investments have generally been treated without much differentiation because both have involved cross-border transplantation of labor-intensive and export-oriented manufacturing to the PRD since the 1980s. However, taking Dongguan, the famous workshop of the world factory as a case, divergent transformations have been found between the two forms of investment since the 1990s, especially after China's accession to the World Trade Organization in 2001. Industrialization in Dongguan has transformed from being predominantly driven by Hong Kong investment in the 1980s to being increasingly dominated by Taiwanese investment since the 1990s. The latter has contributed significantly to the sectoral upgrading of Dongguan's local economy and to a gradual shift from an export orientation based on cheap labor to a domestic market orientation since the late 1990s. Investors from Hong Kong and Taiwan have followed different strategies of adaptation to the institutional changes in the host-region, due to their distinct home advantages and the nature of interactions between the host and home regions.

One Hong Kong entrepreneur, who established his toy firm in Dongguan in the late 1980s, noted:

> Hong Kong investment is no longer regarded as highly as in the early 1980s. The status of Hong Kong investment in Dongguan is declining. Instead, investments from Taiwan, South Korea and Japan, particularly those in high-tech industries, are more welcomed by the local government. Previous privileges granted to Hong Kong investors are disappearing. (Interview by the author)

Reflecting this shift, local governments in Dongguan, such as in Qingxi Town, had in 2004 adopted an FDI policy with explicit directives for dealing with investments from different regions, such as "setting Taiwanese investment" (*zhuajin taizi shi fangxin*), "fastening Japanese investment" (*wojin rizi bu fangsong*), "attracting European and American investment" (*yinru oumei xia hengong*), and "observing Hong Kong investment" (*guancha gangzi xing buxing*).

Both Hong Kong and Taiwanese investments in the 1980s and early 1990s in Dongguan were characterized by export-oriented and labor-intensive manufacturing sectors (toys, footwear, textiles, and so on). Differences began to emerge in the late 1990s, as an influx of investment in information technology (IT) came from Taiwan, particularly in the manufacturing of personal computers and related peripherals. As a result, Dongguan became a "global manufacturing factory" of IT products, especially desktop computer-related products. Dongguan-made computers and peripherals accounted for a large share of the international market; nearly one in three disk drivers and one in five scanners and mini-power switches are now made in Dongguan. Nearly all computer components can be obtained in towns within an hour and a half's distance from Dongguan. The city is capable of supplying about 95 percent of the parts and components for its computer manufacturing plants.

In contrast, after the relocation of manufacturing activities to the PRD was completed in the late 1990s, Hong Kong investors began to turn to the service sectors, especially in the early 2000s, benefiting from the newly established Closer Economic Partnership Arrangement (CEPA) between Hong Kong and China in 2003. Under CEPA, small-and medium-scale service companies in Hong Kong could enter the Mainland's domestic market with lower thresholds. The differences between Hong Kong and Taiwanese investments were clearly summarized by an experienced local government official who has served in the Bureau of Foreign Trade and Economy in Dongguan for more than twenty years:

The main reason for the differences lies in the different economic, especially industrial policies of Hong Kong and Taiwan. Hong Kong has long implemented a "proactive nonintervention" policy in the pre-1997 period and there has been no substantial change after 1997. I have participated in many meetings with Hong Kong officials to discuss cooperation in sectoral upgrading of Hong Kong investment in Dongguan. Their responses were that the government could not do anything except follow the rules of the market. (Interview by the author)

The different home-base advantages of Hong Kong and Taiwan have contributed significantly to the dissimilar transformation patterns. The critical difference between Hong Kong and Taiwan is the failure of Hong Kong manufacturers to upgrade local industrial activities. Hong Kong's manufacturing sector has continued to focus on low-value-added manufacturing, while Taiwan has dramatically upgraded its industrial base since the mid-1980s. Taking the electronics industry as an example, entrepreneurs of the three Newly Industrializing Economies (NIEs) in Asia, i.e. Taiwan, Singapore, and South Korea, have responded to the challenges of global restructuring by a combination of two strategies—outward investment and relocation of production facilities to other developing countries, and upgrading their domestic industrial structure and increasing the value-added component of exports. However, Hong Kong's electronics industry responded almost exclusively by relying on relocation and failed to move beyond producing consumer and low-end electronics. Most of the Hong Kong firms I interviewed relied on designs provided by their customers, whereas Taiwanese firms were in a position to utilize their own research and development specialists who are primarily based in Taiwan.

Despite these differences, the motivations underlying cross-border investment from Hong Kong and Taiwan have changed dramatically over the last decade. At the early stage of transplantation to the PRD, "reducing labor costs" was listed as a top motivation by both Hong Kong and Taiwanese investors. It is worth noting that the driving forces have been changing since 2000. As a Taiwanese entrepreneur who set up his first furniture plant in 1991 in Dalingshan Town of Dongguan remarked:

> Export-oriented investments have become increasingly less attractive compared to the lure of the enormous and expanding domestic market of the Mainland. (Interview by the author)

Similar changes involving diversification have occurred in enterprises with investment from Hong Kong, while with a pronounced gravitation toward the service sectors. For example, a Hong Kong entrepreneur who started a furniture processing and assembly plant in the late 1980s has now expanded his operations to retail, real estate and other services. Thus, opportunities "to exploit China's domestic market" and "move closer to customers and business partners" have become prime forces motivating cross-border investment for both Hong Kong and Taiwanese investors since the 2000s.

Hong Kong, the largest source of foreign investment in the PRD and Dongguan in the last three decades, has played a crucial role in the region's rapid industrialization and urbanization. But since the turn of the millennium, Taiwanese investment has accelerated and become the major driving force in the region's economic development. However, due to insufficient local support and the changing business environment in recent years, particularly, the shortage of migrant labor and the upsurge of labor costs, Taiwanese investments have transplanted and expanded to the Yangtze River Delta and other inland provinces, such as Chengdu in Sichuan Province, Zhengzhou in Henan Province, and so on. The workshop of the "world factory" in the PRD has undergone dramatic transformation in a remarkable trajectory that warrants further investigation and intensive monitoring.

香港與台灣製造業的比較

隨着中國近三十年的改革開放，珠三角地區已從大量外國投資中受益，其中來自香港和台灣的投資，佔了百分之八十以上。自 1980 年以來，香港和台灣均有參與勞動密集型和出口導向型製造業的發展，並向珠三角地區跨境遷移，因此兩地的投資被認為並無差別。然而，本文作者根據過去五年在東莞的實地考察和實證研究，論述了東莞這個世界知名的「世界工廠」的產業格局的轉變，並指出在 1990 年後，尤其在中國加入世界貿易組織後，香港和台灣的投資之間出現的差異。

From the Iron Rice Bowl to the Steel Cafeteria Tray

Jia Ching Chen
Department of City and Regional Planning
University of California, Berkeley

The "iron rice bowl" (*tiefanwan*) was once the symbol for the lifelong employment and welfare given through many state-run enterprises during Maoist-era socialism in China (as well as Taiwan's clientelist, developmental state era). These benefits were channeled and managed through state-controlled *danwei* (commonly translated as "work unit"), which provided everything from housing to health care and schooling within its compounds [see "The Danwei" in this volume]. The colloquial term "rice bowl" means a job and livelihood. Thus, to fire someone is to "break his/her rice bowl" (*dapo tade fanwan*).

The iron rice bowl became brittle during the reform period under Deng Xiaoping (1978–1990s), and was finally shattered with the implementation of the socialist market economy and full repudiation of the Maoist planned economy. Under the Hu-Wen administration, full integration into the global market economy under the norms and "harmonization" of the WTO regime has unfolded along with intensive privatization, fiscal decentralization and state retrenchment since the early 2000s.

Before Shenzhen was formally recognized as the flagship of the new economy following Deng Xiaoping's famous Southern Tour in 1992, it had already flourished for over a decade as a special economic zone by utilizing migrant workers who received none of the guarantees covering industrial workers in a state-run *danwei*. Without the burden of having to provide iron rice bowls to their workers, new export manufacturers took advantage of the emerging national labor market that continued to be segmented into rural and urban populations by the operation of *hukou*—the household registration system [see "Hukou" in this volume]. Over the past twenty years, China's rapid growth rate has been fed by footingless labor as well as footloose capital. Major restructuring of the economy and the development of flexible labor have meant that jobs have been increasingly fragile and subject to bare economic imperatives. In 1980, state-owned, state-controlled, and collective enterprises accounted for over 99 percent of industrial output (Industrial Census, 1995). By 1990, the percentage had eased down to just over 90 percent. Throughout the 1990s, economic stagnation in the state sector helped to justify the massive wave of privatization that followed. Now, twenty years after the dismantling of the iron rice bowl system, the state sector share of industrial output has fallen below 40 percent, and under 17 percent for SOEs, according to the National Statistics Bureau. The restructuring of the labor market—especially the creation of a 150-million strong migrant worker population— was fundamental to the country's incredible double-digit GDP growth rates in the 1990s (averaging over 18 percent from 1991 to 1994, according to the World Bank).

Although China continues to be characterized by many writers as "the world's factory" with limitless labor, a paradoxical outcome has resulted from the restructuring that first enabled the country's rise to that standing. The rapid growth of a flexible national workforce— including a massive "floating population" of well over 100 million migrant workers—has also made annual labor shortages typical in the coastal provinces. As workers return to their homes during the Spring Festival holidays, they also search for their next jobs. Beginning in the 2000s, labor shortages of 10 to 20 percent were reported in many factories in Guangdong at the same time as national underemployment increased.[1] In 2010, the manufacturing hub of Dongguan was short of over 150,000 workers after the Spring

Festival, according to the local labor bureau. This occurred despite increased unemployment and the fact that over 400 factories closed in Dongguan during 2007 and 2008.[2] How do we make sense of this apparent paradox of high unemployment and high labor shortages? And how have workers and employers responded?

Along with the rural-urban labor segmentation created by the *hukou* system, the concept of *danwei* is crucial to understanding how workers have been employed and retained, as China's development models and corresponding modes of organizing production and social reproduction have transformed. The Maoist *danwei* comprised a complete utopian model encompassing most aspects of urban workers' lives. But rural workers did not have the guarantees and organized social benefits enjoyed by their urban counterparts. None of the prevailing models of post-Maoist rural development and transition provided similar forms of security and benefits to those of state-owned *danwei*. Even in Jiangsu Province—the heartland of state-led rural industrialization, where esteemed sociologist Fei Xiaotong described the "Sunan model" of state-run town and village enterprises (TVEs)—collective ownership of assets (i.e., land) provided no guarantees. Although such industries provided a major engine for China's growth and industrialization from the 1980s to 1990s when rural industrial output eclipsed that of state-owned enterprises (Naughton, 2007), they could not keep pace with the steady growth of the rural labor force (Kung and Lin, 2006).[3] At the same time, villagers faced a major decline in prices of farm produce, which drove greater numbers of younger people to non-farm labor. Although family plots are often maintained by the generation of

older able-bodied villagers in order to supplement family incomes by providing subsistence, many more rural workers are forced to enter the migrant labor force while still being tied to their villages.

The current models of development in the PRD are much more complex and responsive to global capital, leveraging previous modes of state intervention while allowing for flexibility and private corporate governance. Employers are likewise responding to current conditions with hybrid models of management that take advantage of state-run labor recruitment and infrastructure. While lifelong employment is no longer a consideration, non-wage benefits are an important factor in retaining labor, especially in rapidly growing industries that demand skilled workers.

In the example alluded to in this essay's title—I call it the "steel cafeteria tray" (*buxiugang canpan*)—workers are housed and boarded in facilities that are actually owned, managed, and subsidized by state-run entities such as various special economic zones (SEZs). For example, the use of the SEZ's cafeteria is shared by private enterprises, state joint ventures, state-owned private enterprises, and state units such as the zone administration itself. This model encourages investment by reducing labor management costs and helping to retain labor for longer periods. Private enterprises also use hybrid state-owned private human resource companies that help recruit and even manage and train workers through temporary worker dispatch systems. For a start-up company with simple labor needs, this system can save up to 80 percent in human resources and management costs.

The "steel cafeteria tray" model is thus tailored to the needs of rapidly growing private enterprises, while addressing some of the pitfalls of employing a flexible labor force of migrant workers. In contrast to the "iron rice bowl," the durability of the "steel cafeteria tray" is not a reflection of permanent employment conditions. Rather, its durability lies in its ability to persist as a form of organization in the face of an ever-changing and fungible labor pool.

Notes

1. According to the National Statistics Bureau, adjusted unemployment numbers for urban areas persisted at over 4 percent from <3 percent throughout the 1980s and early 1990s. This number is recognized as a gross underestimate as it excludes migrant workers with rural *hukou*, and is based exclusively on workers who have applied for unemployment benefits. Using an international definition of unemployment, a survey conducted by Giles et al. (2005) found gross underestimates in official data for both permanent residents as well as migrant workers; see John Giles, Albert Park, and Juwei Zhang, "What Is China's True Unemployment Rate?" *China Economic Review* 16, no. 2 (2005): 149–70. See also *People's Daily and Xinhua News* archives for regular reports.
2. Jin Jiangbo has documented the Dongguan crash in a striking series of photographs.
3. Barry Naughton, *The Chinese Economy: Transitions and Growth* (Cambridge: MIT Press, 2007). James Kai-sing Kung and Yi-min Lin, "The Decline of Township-and-Village Enterprises in China's Economic Transition," *World Development* 35, no. 4 (2007): 569–84.

從鐵飯碗到鋼製食堂餐盤

「鐵飯碗」曾被用來形容計劃經濟體制下「單位制」這種終身的聘用和福利制度，隨着社會主義市場經濟的建立，這制度也逐漸瓦解。在改革開放之後，以深圳為首的多個中國城市，實現了飛速的工業化和經濟發展，大量的流動農民工在其中起到重大作用。但由於戶口制度的限制，他們成為了遊離於社會邊緣的弱勢群體。農民工的大量流動更帶來了高失業率和勞動力匱乏的雙重局面。在戶口制度下，單位制度將城市工作者生活的多方面聯繫起來，給城市居民提供了一種烏托邦式的生活模式。然而，不論過去或現在，農民工卻從未享受過任何社會福利保障。他們為了求生計，不得不湧入流動工潮中，卻又被戶口制度牢牢地禁錮在自己家鄉。

在這種情境下，珠三角探索出了一種新模式，也就是本文題目中所提到的「不銹鋼餐盤」。工人們住在配有自己所屬、自行管理、政府資助的地方。這種原為私人企業量身訂做的模式，雖然不能像「鐵飯碗」般提供永久的聘用，卻不失為應對流動性極大的勞動力市場的一劑良藥。

Top seven export and import countries
前七名進出口國家 @2009

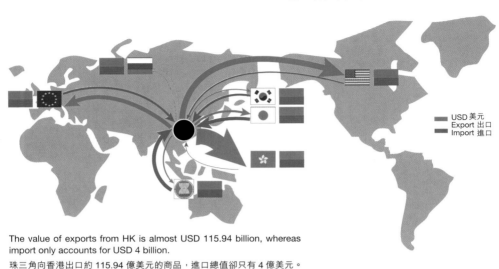

- USD 美元
- Export 出口
- Import 進口

The value of exports from HK is almost USD 115.94 billion, whereas import only accounts for USD 4 billion.

珠三角向香港出口約 115.94 億美元的商品，進口總值卻只有 4 億美元。

Most of the investment comes from Asia, especially from Hong Kong, Taiwan, and Macao. The investment funding from these three regions takes up two-thirds of the total investment.

大部分投資來自亞洲，主要是香港，台灣和澳門，佔據三分之二的總數。

Flag	Ranking Number of agreements signed Foreign captital utilized

Top investments
主投資方 @2009

Name — ASIA 亞洲 — SOUTH AMERICA 南美
— NORTH AMERICA 北美 — EUROPE 歐洲
— OCEANIA 大洋洲 — AFRICA 非洲

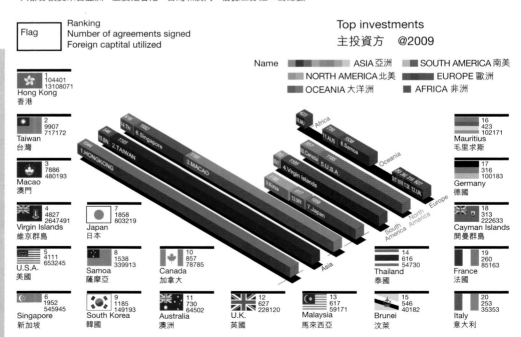

Hong Kong 香港	1 104401 13108071
Taiwan 台灣	2 9907 717172
Macao 澳門	3 7886 480193
Virgin Islands 維京群島	4 4827 2647491
U.S.A. 美國	5 4111 653245
Singapore 新加坡	6 1952 545945
Japan 日本	7 1858 803219
Samoa 薩摩亞	8 1538 339913
South Korea 韓國	9 1185 149193
Canada 加拿大	10 857 78785
Australia 澳洲	11 730 64502
U.K. 英國	12 627 228120
Malaysia 馬來西亞	13 617 59171
Thailand 泰國	14 616 54730
Brunei 汶萊	15 546 40182
Mauritius 毛里求斯	16 423 102171
Germany 德國	17 316 100183
Cayman Islands 開曼群島	18 313 222633
France 法國	19 260 85163
Italy 意大利	20 253 35353

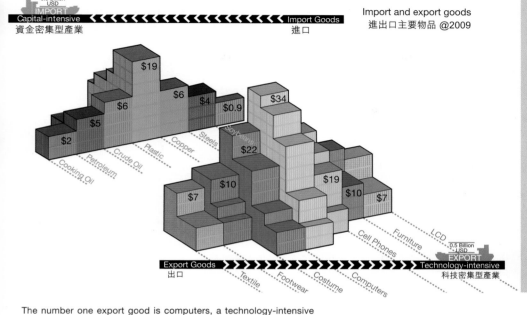

Import and export goods
進出口主要物品 @2009

The number one export good is computers, a technology-intensive industry worth USD 34 billion. The number one import good is plastic, a capital-intensive industry of USD 19 billion.

出口量第一的產品是電腦，達到 34 億美元。進口的最大量是塑料，屬於資金密集型產業，達 19 億美元。

Comparison with other provinces
進出口比較 @2009

Five provinces accounted for 81% of China's export in 2000, and 92% in 2009. However, the PRD's export rate decreased by 25%.

2000 年，以下五省市佔了中國經濟出口總量的 81%，2009 年達到 92%。然而，珠三角進出口率卻在這幾年間下降了 25%。

40%	13%	12%	9%	7%

CHINA

YEAR 2000

-25%	+31%	+125%	+22%	0%

YEAR 2009

| Guangdong | Jiangsu | Shanghai | Zhejiang | Shandong |
| 廣東省 | 江蘇省 | 上海市 | 浙江省 | 山東省 |

Battle for the land 土地之爭

Comparison of the growth of
LAND PRICE, GDP & INVESTMENT in 2003 and 2009
地價、GDP、投資增長率比較 2003–09

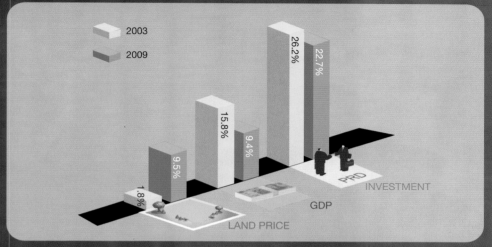

2003
2009

26.2%
22.7%
15.8%
9.4%
9.5%
1.8%

INVESTMENT
GDP
LAND PRICE
PRD

Nowadays, the rapid increase of land prices in the PRD has become disassociated with the growth of GDP and investment. The battle for land pushes up the cost of manufacturing.

珠三角地區地價的快速增長與 GDP 和投資增長不成比例，對土地爭奪的熱情遠高於製造業的發展。這也導致了工業發展土地成本的增加。

Comparison of LAND PRICE in the PRD
珠三角土地價格比較

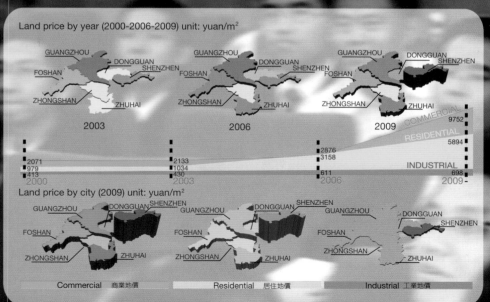

Land price by year (2000-2006-2009) unit: yuan/m²

GUANGZHOU DONGGUAN SHENZHEN FOSHAN ZHONGSHAN ZHUHAI

2003   2006   2009

COMMERCIAL 9752
RESIDENTIAL 5894
2876
3158
INDUSTRIAL 698
2071
979
413
2133
1034
430
611

2000   2003   2006   2009

Land price by city (2009) unit: yuan/m²

GUANGZHOU DONGGUAN SHENZHEN FOSHAN ZHONGSHAN ZHUHAI

Commercial 商業地價   Residential 居住地價   Industrial 工業地價

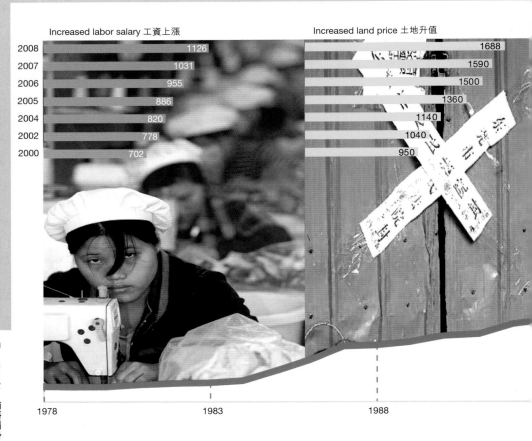

Increased labor salary 工資上漲

2008	1126
2007	1031
2006	955
2005	886
2004	820
2002	778
2000	702

Increased land price 土地升值

	1688
	1590
	1500
	1360
	1140
	1040
	950

1978   1983   1988

GDP Growth by City in the Pearl River Delta 2000–08
珠三角各城市 GDP 增長比較

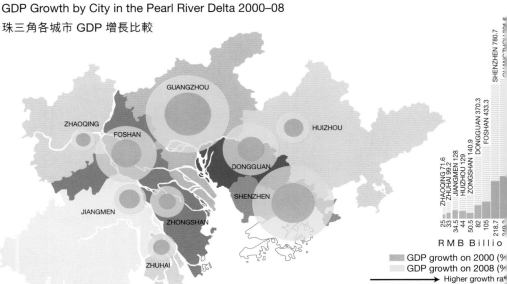

GUANGZHOU

ZHAOQING

FOSHAN   HUIZHOU

DONGGUAN

SHENZHEN

JIANGMEN

ZHONGSHAN

ZHUHAI

SHENZHEN 780.7
DONGGUAN 370.3
FOSHAN 433.3
ZHONGSHAN 140.9
HUIZHOU 129
JIANGMEN 128
ZHUHAI 99.2
ZHAOQING 71.6

25
33
34.5
44
50.5
82
105
218.7

R M B Billio

GDP growth on 2000 (%
GDP growth on 2008 (%
→ Higher growth ra

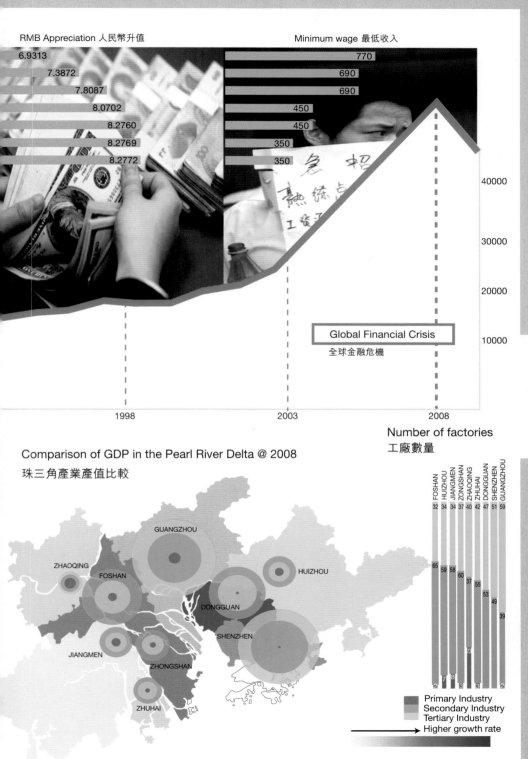

RMB Appreciation 人民幣升值

6.9313
7.3872
7.8087
8.0702
8.2760
8.2769
8.2772

Minimum wage 最低收入

770
690
690
450
450
350
350

40000

30000

20000

Global Financial Crisis
全球金融危機

10000

1998
2003
2008

Number of factories
工廠數量

Comparison of GDP in the Pearl River Delta @ 2008
珠三角產業產值比較

GUANGZHOU
ZHAOQING
FOSHAN
HUIZHOU
DONGGUAN
SHENZHEN
JIANGMEN
ZHONGSHAN
ZHUHAI

FOSHAN 32
HUIZHOU 34
JIANGMEN 34
ZONGSHAN 37
ZHAOQING 40
ZHUHAI 42
DONGGUAN 47
SHENZHEN 51
GUANGZHOU 59

65
59
58
60
37
55
53
49
39

2
7
8
3
3
2

Primary Industry
Secondary Industry
Tertiary Industry
→ Higher growth rate

53

Early nineteenth-century print showing the precursor of a factory in Britain

The Power of Factories

Paul Chu Hoi Shan

Pre-factory practice

Prior to and during the early period of the Industrial Revolution, entrepreneurs provided poor families with raw materials for spinning, weaving, and garment making in their own homes. The above early nineteenth-century print shows an English family sewing uniforms for the British army. In a domestic environment preceding modern factories, family members gathered around the window, seizing the daylight as an opportunity for work. Male relatives were responsible for the transportation of heavy materials and products, while female members assembled parts. As such, the physical power of human bodies and the availability of daylight determined productivity. Spatial and location requirements for production were simple in this pre-factory model: as long as daylight was available and raw materials and products were located in proximity. There was relatively little supervision as coworkers were either relatives or neighbors.

Later advancement in textiles spinning, steam power and iron founding brought about by the Industrial Revolution gave rise to a new working environment. Mechanical power replaced manual labor, and purposely-built workplaces provided artificial lighting for work in the absence of daylight. Factories started to emerge as a new form of living and manufacturing.

Utopian model: Saline de Chaux, Saltworks and town of Chaux, France by Claude-Nicolas Ledoux, 1775

Perhaps the Royal Saltworks of Arc-et-Senans (a factory for the production of salt, glass, silverware, agriculture and medicine) located near Besançon in the Franche-Comté region of France was the first model to establish a relationship between economical organization and social living in the factory complex. Salt was of fundamental economic importance as it was subject to a heavy and unpopular sales tax, the *gabelle*, which formed a major contribution to state finances. Under orders of Louis XV, the French architect Claude-Nicolas Ledoux set about to build a utopian work environment at the beginning of the Industrial Revolution. It was never completely finished, but the vast, semicircular salt complex was designed as a hierarchical and rational organization for work and life. Ledoux chose a site that was not right next to the saltwater springs, but next to the wood forest, which provided the fuel necessary for salt production. Locating the complex in proximity to energy resources in a completely remote living environment was a totally innovative idea at that time. "It was easier to control the water flow than to transport a whole forest," wrote the architect.

Rather than constructing an obvious observation tower, the power to supervise and command—in the form of the centrally located directors' house— was rather symbolic by nature. The factory was arranged in a symmetric way so that everybody saw the center of the circle, and hence everybody understood his or her positioning and role in the factory. With the rise of modern technologies, the factory fell into obsolescence and closed down in 1895. It was eventually declared a UNESCO World Heritage Site.

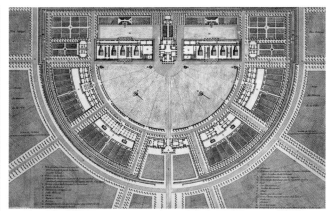

Arc-et-Senans. The Royal Saltworks, 1775–79; plan of second project.

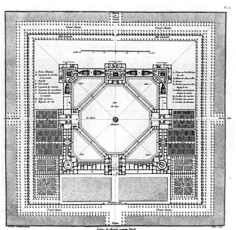

Plan of the third project. Source: Ledoux, 1804.

Arc-et-Senans. The Royal Saltworks, 1775–79; plan of first project: all buildings (residential, factory, and others) were surrounded by trees, leaving a 4000-square-foot plaza in the middle.

Social Model: New Lanark Cotton Mill, Scotland by Robert Owen, 1816

From 1800 to 1825, under the management of social reformer Robert Owen, the cotton mills and village of New Lanark in Scotland became a model factory community, in which a caring and humane regime took over the conventional drive toward progress and prosperity through new technologies of the Industrial Revolution. The mill enjoyed the hydrological power afforded by the falls of the River Clyde; the social buildings were placed in the middle, surrounded by residential towers at the edges; gardens were in between the residences, and roads were outside gardens; factories stood at the outermost ring.

The hall for socialization and learning in the New Lanark Mill

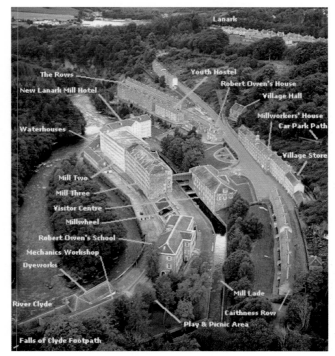

New Lanark Mill factory nowadays: A World Heritage Site

Under Robert's philanthropic philosophy, the New Lanark built the first factory infant school in the world in 1816 for children from three to ten years old, or to thirteen if their parents could afford for the children not to work. The objective was to inculcate students with good habits and dispositions during childhood according to the practice of the utilitarian theory of education. Dances, music and drills were deemed essential to cultivate a cooperative manner and upright personality. The philanthropic approach also led to the introduction of a crèche for working mothers, free medical care, a comprehensive education system for children, and evening classes for adults. Instead of mechanical and physical power, the functional spaces and the teaching of attitudes became new forms to promote not only productivity but also subject formation in workers. The productive power of the factory came from social and educational aspects apart from managerial surveillance.

"What ideas individuals may attach to the term 'Millennium' I know not; but I know that society may be formed so as to exist without crime, without poverty, with health greatly improved, with little, if any misery, and with intelligence and happiness increased a hundredfold; and no obstacle whatsoever intervenes at this moment except ignorance to prevent such a state of society from becoming universal ... " said Robert Owen in his *Address to the Inhabitants of New Lanark* on New Year's Day, 1816.

Mechanic model: *Modern Times* by Charlie Chaplin, 1936

It was never common for factory owners to adopt the Robert Owens approach. Charlie Chaplin's movie *Modern Times* (1936) depicts how

Still from the movie Modern Times *(1936)*

repetitive working procedures and intensive surveillance by managerial personnel drive a steel factory worker crazy. In the movie, the straight and unstoppable assembly line, the labeling of different social classes (the factory owner, the supervisor, and the workers are clothed in different costumes) and the unreasonable supervision push worker Charlie into collapse. For instance, a feeding machine forces Charlie to eat and clean within a short time to maximize production efficiency.

The movie exaggerates the machinery-like factory environment in the modern era and the pragmatic attitude of the entrepreneur. The cold, efficient heavy machines contrast with the humanistic, artistic ballet dance by Charlie as he succumbs to a mental breakdown.

Still from the movie Modern Times *(1936)*

Factories nowadays:
Foxconn, China, 1974–

With further advances in technology, sophisticated manufacturing machines replaced labor in the production of precision products like electronic and computer components. Factory production has become more and more specialized. With much easier and cheaper transportation means, an electronic product may be composed of components manufactured in different parts of the world and then assembled in another country. A single factory is no longer producing an industrial product from head to toe.

For factories like Foxconn in China, the proximity to cost-effective labor outweighs the availability of natural resources. The factory takes advantage of the Open Door Policy in China, and has become a destination for migrant workers mobilizing from villages in other provinces to "Foxconn City." The Foxconn factory in Shenzhen, for example, employs migrant workers from all over China. The factory complex can employ up to 450,000 workers, and functions as a town in itself. Apart from worker dormitories, provision also includes a fire brigade, a bank, grocery stores, bookstores, hospitals, recreational facilities such as swimming pool, and even its own TV broadcasting station.

With the widespread publicity due to advancements in information technology and the media, Foxconn came to be held accountable by internet discussions and public forums for workers' well-being. The extensive media reports of workers' suicide cases in 2009 have forced Foxconn's owner to improve the working hours, and to attend to issues of workers' mental health and the working and living environment. The factory now takes on the social responsibility of ensuring better lives for its large number of migrant workers. As a result, the design of the factory is not only based on efficient assembly lines, but also according to the workers' mental and physical necessities. The design of the factory not only aims to realize architects' artistic vision and factory owners' requirements (as in other models discussed), but would also take into consideration workers' needs.

工廠的力量

本文回顧從工業革命時期到現代，在不同社會背景下，全世界工廠模式的演變歷程。工業革命推動了工業生產的發展，以家庭作業為主的工業形式被正式的工廠所取代。建於 1775 年的阿爾克－塞南（Arc-et-Senans）皇家鹽場，在工廠綜合建築中，創新地混合了經濟生產和社交生活。本文亦探討以新拉納克（New Lanark）為代表的社會模型，歐文（Owen）在這裏實現了他心目中的理想社會。1930 年代卓別林演繹的《摩登時代》，勾勒了當時資本主義社會大量生產之下的機械模式；最後本文以富士康為例，探討現代工廠模式。富士康是一家在中國僱用大量農民工、從事產品裝配的公司，在 2009 年被接二連三的自殺事件推上了輿論的頂峰。現今的工廠已不再僅僅為廠主賺取收益，更應關注員工的精神健康，為他們提供更好的生活及工作環境，以擔負起更重的社會責任。

Foxconn workers at work

Will Design Play a Role in "Postindustrial" PRD?

Rex Wong
Member of the Guangzhou City Committee
Chinese People's Political Consultative Conference

Recently, I met a young American architect and novice developer who was working on his first project in Guangzhou. Our conversation quickly focused on the latest government planning policies for the PRD, the function of design, and the role of urban designers and architects working with developers in this region. Looking back, we were asking ourselves the following question, "Will design play a role in 'postindustrial' PRD?"

We spoke at length about the difference between the postindustrial nature of the PRD and that of Western cities such as Manchester in the United Kingdom. Manchester has been widely discussed as a typical case of cities affected by changing economic structures primarily driven by the export of manufacturing activities to other lower-cost locations overseas. China, in particular the PRD, has for years been a destination of these exported industrial activities, thus acquiring its reputation as the "global factory." Yet the postindustrial nature of the PRD is a distinctly different and recent phenomenon. It is in effect a situation caused by the strategic planning policies of Beijing and the regional government, rather than economic forces alone.

Policies toward a "postindustrial" PRD

The central government has long defined the PRD as a strategic economic experimental zone. During the first thirty years of the Reform and Open Door Policy since 1979, the PRD was the first to be given the green light to bring in foreign investment and new production models. The current industrial landscape is a direct result of this positioning. Yet in recent years, to continue to serve as the frontier for economic experimentation, the PRD has been given a new task by Beijing to become the "center of advanced manufacturing and modern service industries" and a "center for international shipping, logistics, trade, conferences and exhibitions and tourism" according to *The 2008–2020 Plan* released by China's National Development and Reform Commission.

In order to realize this goal, the government of the PRD has introduced a policy called 腾籠換鳥 , literally translated as "empty the cage to make way." The cage refers to the PRD's industrial area. "To empty" suggests the intention of driving out the existing labor-intensive production to make way for high-value forms of production, such as high-tech manufacturing and its supporting service industries. For example, it involves a series of directives such as a more stringent execution of labor protection and environmental laws aimed at discouraging industries from continuing their manufacturing operations in the PRD. At the same time, the government introduces favorable terms for these same companies to attempt to retain their administrative, research and development workforce in the PRD.

Also at work is another policy called 三舊改造 , literally translated as "renewal of the three 'olds'" — old towns, old factories, and old villages. A land renewal policy, it is a governmental measure to encourage regeneration of the previously industrial landscape into higher-value commercial and residential properties, by providing incentives to developers in the form of lower land premium. It also simplifies administrative procedures to allow projects to be executed more effectively. This policy gives the existing factory owners another incentive to relocate to inland provinces so that their industrial land can make way for higher-value development.

Not everyone may be interested to see these factories leave the PRD. The original inhabitants of the region have gained tremendous wealth during the last three decades primarily due to the increase in land value. By leasing their collective land for industrial use, the native villagers were able to secure a steady income stream that allowed them to sustain a middle-class lifestyle, including such activities as shopping and leisure. They may be the first to experience changes to their living quality as a result of decreasing industrial activities.

The local governments may also be reluctant to see the industries leave the PRD because of the steady tax income that they bring in. Much of the valuable infrastructure in the PRD is a direct result of this money. The rapid growth of the PRD relies heavily on infrastructure development that not only meets practical needs, but also helps to build an urban, progressive image for the region. For instance, the landscaping along the main roadways of Guangzhou has helped to shape a green and livable image for the city in the past years. Can these elaborate plantations be sustained in the face of substantial reductions in tax revenue?

The new role of design

Due to this "postindustrial" condition, the PRD's earliest residents have already been seeking ways to sustain the value of their accumulated wealth in order to confront inflation. Some consider purchasing properties with different architectural styles as a worthwhile investment. A design that was once thought to be too progressive suddenly may be a lot more acceptable, even if it challenges the notions of *fengshui*. Potential buyers are also increasingly seeking properties that are ecologically sustainable. With the recent introduction of a policy to limit the number of properties that one can own, the process of choosing the right property has become even more refined.

In the public realm, there is an attempt to have the private sector invest in public space. As evident in the current urban renewal policy, a third of the land is required to be surrendered to public use. The developers have every incentive to make sure that this space works with the design of the property. This not only reflects an increasing concern regarding public space in the society, but also allows for the project to better fit into the larger context of the neighborhood. Urban designers can have a key role in this process in order to ensure the vibrancy of these places, making sure that they are accessible and well connected to urban infrastructure—not only building an image for the neighborhood but also animating the community.

These new trends answer the question about the role of design in the "postindustrial" PRD. Design can serve as a way of making a development project more profitable by increasing its value through providing an alternative product. At the urban scale, design can also help the property to fit more harmoniously in its setting, thus projecting a greater sense of livability. This statement, I suspect, also encapsulates my acquaintance's vision for his latest development project in Guangzhou, which attempts to transform an industrial site into a residential community.

設計產業將在珠江三角洲「後工業化」佔有一角嗎？

珠江三角洲曾經被稱為「世界工廠」，是中國改革開放的先行地區，也是中國重要的經濟中心區域，在全國經濟社會發展和改革開放大局中，具有突出的帶動作用和舉足輕重的戰略地位。然而，隨着其後工業化時代的來臨，珠三角無法再在「低成本擴張」的道路上繼續前行。珠江三角洲被賦予了新的發展定位，面臨着產業調整的重任。為實現產業結構的升級，珠三角政府推出了「騰籠換鳥」、「三舊改造」等政策，以推進勞動密集型產業向高級製造業和現代服務業的轉型。不過，工廠的遷出卻為地方民眾和地方政府帶來了前所未有的壓力。本文旨在探討於後工業化時代的珠三角，為保障當地居民的利益及為他們帶來更舒適的生活環境，擔當了怎樣的新角色。

A generous setback ensures sufficient reception of natural lighting in each building.

The Adwin Factory
The Design of Industrial Buildings

Paul Lin
Architect and owner, The Adwin Dongguan Factory

The Adwin Dongguan Factory, a textile factory, is located in Hengli Town, one of the most concentrated factory towns in Dongguan. As in other factories, the company employs workers from other provinces. Therefore, the factory needs to provide accommodation and other facilities for the workers. In this factory, greenery is an important element. Trees are planted around each factory building. Generous and landscaped open spaces are incorporated into the master plan.

Labor shortage has become acute and it has been more difficult to run a factory in the Pearl River Delta. Apart from salary, the factories in the region need to provide a comfortable environment to attract and retain their staff.

Generally speaking, factory buildings in the Pearl River Delta are gradually evolving from conventional, monotonous generic blocks toward worker-oriented factory types. More attention is now given to the environment, the living standards of the workers, as well as corporate images.

The main concerns of conventional factory buildings are with the construction economy and basic practical requirements. Structural span and headroom are optimal to suit the needs of the most common industries, as a set of dimensions are standardized and adopted by building plans that can be reused. The usual choice of external wall tiles also helps to keep the construction cost low. Factory owners can benefit from a short construction period as building contractors can duplicate buildings more easily. The preparation time for creating blueprints can also be shortened by simply modifying the standard plan for each new site. Since the generic factory buildings look similar and can be mass-produced, local architectural firms often refer to them as "matchboxes." The variation in workmanship, the low level of construction skills required, and the inconsistency in construction management and supervision often result in early-appearing defects and shortened building life.

The primary interest of factory owners is to make profit. Generic factory buildings help meet this fundamental need by effectively reducing initial costs. Factory operators are also inclined to adopt management systems that provide greater control over workers, and to execute stricter policies on security and access. Larger factories appear more effective in the management of workers and the owners are therefore more inclined to violate workers' rights. Recent tragic incidents due to draconian factory management have led to greater awareness of workers' quality of life. Social issues within factories have drawn media and public attention. As a result, factory operators are more concerned with the long-term well-being of their workers.

The pressure that the manufacturing business faces is greater than ever. Factory operators are confronted with various challenges; these include limited land resources in the Pearl River Delta region, discouraging local government policies, fluctuations in the global economy, competition from surrounding countries, increasing labor costs and currency costs for exports. As a result, factories in the region have a high rate of shutdown. The vacated premises raise further concerns in terms of the factories' sustainability.

While factory owners recognize the importance of sustainable development, it is the role of architects and planners to contribute to a more sustainable factory evolution. They should think of ways to help prolong the lifespan of factory buildings and provide a more pleasant working environment.

向榮紡織：工業建築的設計

本文以東莞橫瀝鎮艾迪威（Adwin）棉紡廠為例，講述了工廠在為外來員工提供基本的住宿及生活設施的同時，工廠的建築更是美觀大方，廠區環境優美舒適。

珠三角地區正面臨種種困難，當中包括土地匱乏、政府政策收緊、全球經濟動盪、產業競爭激烈、製造業工人壓力升高等。在這些不利因素下，不少工廠被迫關閉，而勞動力匱乏已經成為珠江三角洲工廠運營的主要難題。工廠為員工提供的舒適生活環境，已成為薪水之外吸引員工的重要因素，而工廠建築已逐漸從傳統、單調的經濟型設計，轉變成內部環境舒適、着重提升生活水平的建築形式；它們更成為了樹立公司形象的旗幟。當工廠正為如何在未來實行可持續發展，努力尋找出路的時候，建築師和規劃師也應思考如何在其中貢獻一己之力。

The factory floor is designed to meet requirements in production efficiency, lighting and ventilation.

High ceilings, garden views, cafe settings, and natural and artificial climate control attempt to create a pleasant office environment.

The work spaces and dormitories have access to roof terraces with gardens.

The dormitory rooms attempt to provide a homely environment for staff coming from other provinces.

The factory's product showroom

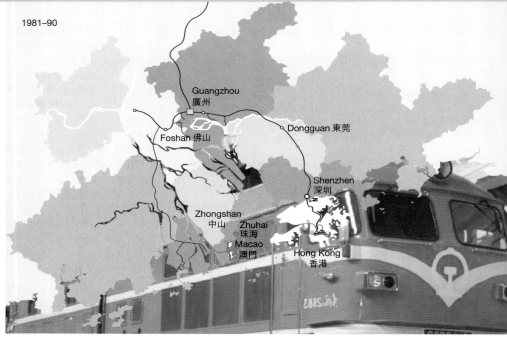

1981–90

Guangzhou
廣州

Dongguan 東莞

Foshan 佛山

Shenzhen
深圳

Zhongshan
中山   Zhuhai
珠海
Macao
澳門

Hong Kong
香港

Photo: Dongfeng 4 Locomotive 東風四型機車

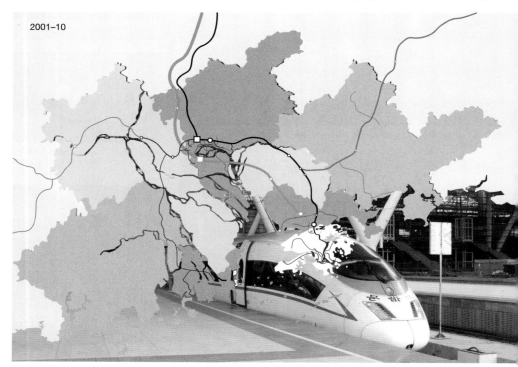

2001–10

Photo: Guangzhou South Station and CRH Train 廣州南站與和諧號列車

1991–2000

Photo: Guangzhou Metro Line 1 Train 廣州地鐵一號線列車

2001–10

Photo: Guangzhou-Shenzhen-Hong Kong Express Rail Link West Kowloon Terminus (under construction)
廣深港高速鐵路西九龍總站 (興建中)

1981–90

Guangzhou
廣州

Foshan 佛山

Dongguan
東莞

Shenzhen
深圳

Zhuhai
珠海

Macao
澳門

Hong Kong
香港

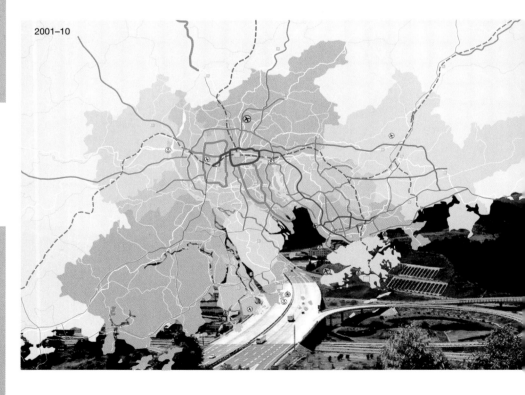

2001–10

1991–2000

2001–10

HONG KONG
香港

Administration 分區

Hong Kong has five major regions: Hong Kong Island, Kowloon East, Kowloon West, New Territories East and New Territories West.

香港有五個主要區域，分別是香港島，九龍東、九龍西、新界東及新界西。

Subdistricts 城鎮體系

There are 18 subdictricts in Hong Kong, each of them has its own district council.

香港總共有十八個分區，各自擁有獨立的區議會。

68

Hong Kong is located in South China. It was first incorporated into China during the Qing Dynasty (221 BC – 206 BC). The British Hong Kong period began in the nineteenth century when the British, Dutch, French, Indians and Americans saw China as the world's largest untapped market. The British empire launched their first and one of the most aggressive expedition to claim the territory under Queen Victoria in 1840, three years after she became queen of the United Kingdom of Great Britain and Ireland. The territory that would later be known as Hong Kong was gained from the last dynasty of imperial China. In 1984, about 24,000 people lived in Hong Kong Island which measured about 72 square kilometers.

During the history of occupation, Hong Kong Island and Kowloon were ceded to the United Kingdom in perpetuity, but the control of the New Territories was governed by 99-year lease. At the end of the lease period in 1997, all of Hong Kong was handed over to be administered by the People's Republic of China under the one country two systems policy. The total area of Hong Kong was (at the time of handover) approximately 1,104 square kilometers with a total population of 7 million.

香港位於南中國沿岸。前秦時期（公元前 221 年 - 公元前 206 年）首次納入為中國的一部分。港英殖民統治時期開始於 19 世紀，英國人、荷蘭人、法國人、印度人和美國人認為中國是世界上最大的未開發市場。1840 年，維多利亞女王登基三年後，大英帝國發動了首次，亦是野心最大的遠征。這後來被稱為香港的地區，當時為中國末代王朝統治。到 1984 年，約有 24,000 人居住在面積約 7 2 平方公里的香港島。

英佔期間，香港島和九龍是永久割讓給英國，而新界則租予英國 99 年。1997 年，租約期滿，香港回歸中華人民共和國。當今，香港的總面積為 1104 平方公里，人口為 700 萬。

Land Use 土地利用

Hong Kong has a relatively mixed land use pattern combining commercial, residential and institutional land as some districts are exclusively for industrial use. Only some districts have industrial use exclusively.

香港的土地多為混合式（商、住、院舍類）用地，只有部分地區有專用的工業用地。

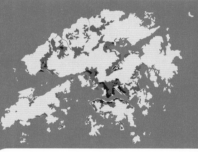

Urbanization 城市化

The urban area of Hong Kong was originally focused around Victoria Harbour until planning policy initiated the construction of "New Towns" within other parts of the territory.

香港的城市化進程始於維多利亞港，從香港島和九龍一直向南、東、北、西四周發展。

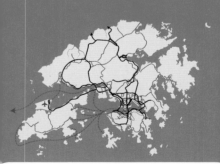

Transportation System 交通系統

Major infrastructures in Hong Kong include the international airport, highways, roads, railways, tramways, and piers.

香港主要的交通基建包括國際機場、高速公路、道路、鐵路、電車和碼頭。

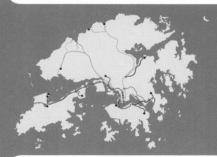

Railway System 鐵路系統

Hong Kong has 10 MTR lines in total.

香港共有十條地鐵線路。

First Generation of Industrial Towns; Tsuen Wan District
第一代的工業城：荃灣區

Tsuen Wan 荃灣

Sha Tin 沙田

Hong Kong's industrialization dates from the 1950s and was initially centered around the textile industry. In the 1960s the economy gradually started diversifying into clothing, electronics, plastics and other labor-intensive products, most of which were for the export market.

1950 年代的禁運催生了香港的工業發展。早期最蓬勃的是紡織業，後來於 1960 年代，香港的工業逐步邁向多樣化，出口主要包括服裝、電子、塑膠及其他勞工密集的產品。

Hong Kong Island before reclamation 填海工程前的香港島

Early Reclamation during the Victorian Era 在維多利亞時代初的填海工程

Land reclamation started in the early 1850s. During the early years of the urbanization of Hong Kong Island the north shore was very narrow. Since there was insufficient land along this coast to meet the housing demands of an increasing population, reclamation was carried out from Kennedy Town in the west all the way along to Wanchai to the east.

香港的填海工程開始於 1850 年代初。在發展初期，香港島的北岸非常狹窄。由於人口越來越多，香港缺乏土地去滿足居住需求，填海工程遂展開，東至灣仔，西至堅尼地城。

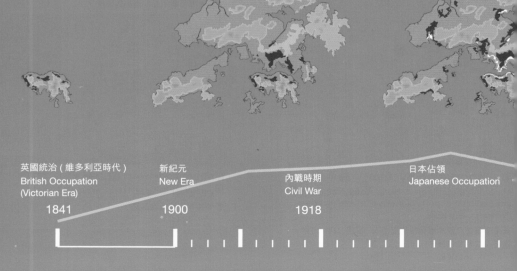

英國統治 (維多利亞時代)
British Occupation
(Victorian Era)

新紀元
New Era

內戰時期
Civil War

日本佔領
Japanese Occupation

1841   1900   1918

Second Generation of Industrial Towns Sha Tin District
第二代工業城：沙田

In the late 1960s, the government did not engage in active industrial planning. This was partly because the government was preoccupied with housing large flows of immigrants.

在 1960 年代後期，政府沒有進行積極的工業規劃。其中原因是政府忙於應付移民潮產生的房屋需求。

Hong Kong started developing new towns in the 1950s to accommodate the booming population. The first towns included Tsuen Wan, Sha Tin and Tuen Mun which started to be populated in the early 1970s.

香港在 1950 年代開始發展新市鎮，以配合蓬勃發展的人口。最早期的新市鎮包括荃灣、沙田及屯門，都在 1970 年代初建成。

Tung Chung was the last new town to be developed, being constructed during the 1990s. The town's development was planned along with the neighboring construction of the new Chek Lap Kok airport.

東涌是最近一個開發的新市鎮。興建於 1990 年代，與鄰近的香港國際機場同步發展。

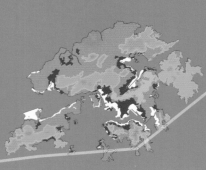

1962 — Tram Road, Sheung Wan (Des Voeux Road Central)

Des Voeux Road Central was commonly known in the 1950s as Tram Road. Where it extends west into the district of Sheung Wan the street was historically known as something of a red light district.

德輔道中在 1950 年代被俗稱為「電車路」。西廷至上環的地區是從前廣為人知的紅燈區。

People (million)
人口（百萬）

Total Population
總人口

1997 - Handover Hong Kong to China
1997 年香港回歸中國

The handover ceremony was held at the new wing of the Wanchai Convention and Exhibition Centre in Wanchai on the night of 30 June 1997.

香港回歸中國的交接儀式在 1997 年 6 月 30 日晚上於灣仔香港會議展覽中心新翼舉行。

時期
sition
od

新里程
A New
Beginning

50　　　　　1960　　　　　　　　　　　　　　　2000　　　2010

7
6
5
4
3
2
1
0.5

Hong Kong 香港 Kwun Tong Industrial Town 觀塘工業城

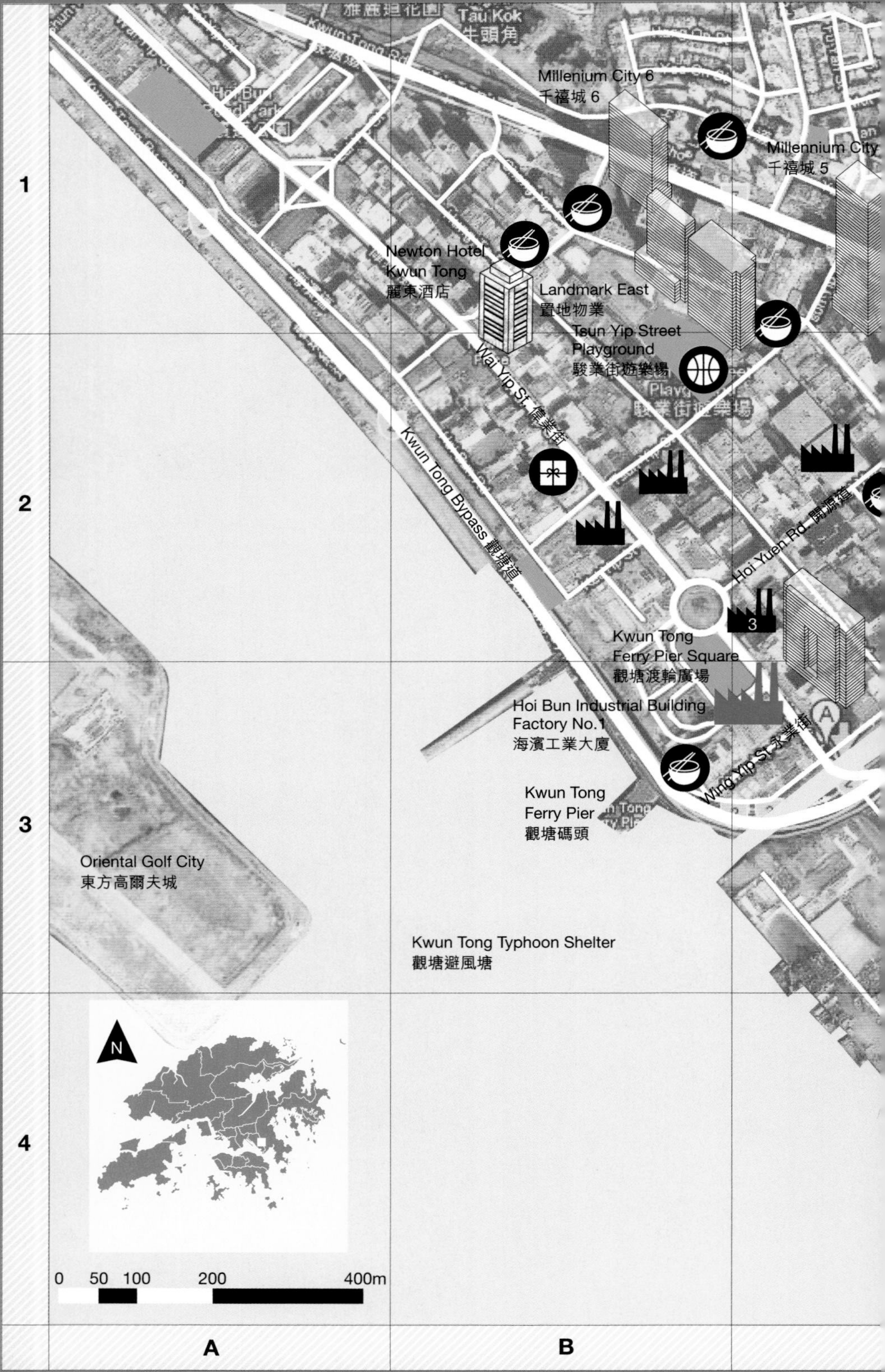

Tau Kok
牛頭角

Millenium City 6
千禧城 6

Millennium City
千禧城 5

Newton Hotel
Kwun Tong
麗東酒店

Landmark East
置地物業

Tsun Yip Street
Playground
駿業街遊樂場

Wai Yip St. 偉業街

Kwun Tong Bypass 觀塘繞道

Hoi Yuen Rd 開源道

Kwun Tong
Ferry Pier Square
觀塘渡輪廣場

Hoi Bun Industrial Building
Factory No.1
海濱工業大廈

Kwun Tong
Ferry Pier
觀塘碼頭

Wing Yip St 永業街

Oriental Golf City
東方高爾夫城

Kwun Tong Typhoon Shelter
觀塘避風塘

N

0   50 100   200   400m

1

2

3

4

A   B

Hoi Bun Industrial Building
海濱工業大廈

Located next to the Kwun Tong Ferry Pier, this industrial building built in the 1960s has easy access to the MTR, buses, ferries and also to highways. Reaching fifteen storeys, it hosts several factories inside, one of them being the printing factory located on the podium level.

海濱工業大廈毗鄰觀塘碼頭，乘搭港鐵、公車、渡海海和使用高速公路前往都很便利。這棟15層的大樓建於1960年代，容納了多家工廠。觀塘印刷廠就位於這長型大樓的平台層。

Kwun Tong Industrial Center (abandoned)
建國陶瓷廠 (已結業)

This industrial center occupies four city blocks next to the Kwun Tong MTR station, the busiest point of the district.

建國陶瓷廠毗鄰觀塘港鐵站，由四棟大廈組成。

Mai Tak Industrial Centre
麥德工業中心

A few industrial buildings in Kwun Tong have recently begun to incorporate commercial functions since most industrial activities have been relocated to China and elsewhere. One such building is the Mai Tak Industrial Centre.

隨着大部分工業從香港遷出，觀塘的一些工業大廈近年來逐漸引入商業功能。其中的一個例子就是麥德工業中心。

Kwun Tong Printing Factory 觀塘印刷廠

In the 1950s the British government developed Kwun Tong as the first satellite city to settle large numbers of immigrants from mainland China. Due to space constraints, the industrial buildings were high-rise, like most of Hong Kong's buildings. Hong Kong's manufacturing industry started to decline in the 1980s after the "opening up" of China saw most industrial functions move to the Mainland, and many industrial buildings were left at least partially empty. Many of these buildings were renovated and converted to accommodate other uses such as warehousing and offices. One such example is Hoi Bun, which accommodates a number of uses.

於 1950 年代，英國政府將觀塘發展成第一個衛星城，以安置從內地來港的大量移民。由於受空間所限制，建成的工業大廈大多是高層建築。隨着 1980 年代工廠開始往內地遷移，香港再造業日漸衰落，大量工業大廈空置。其中一些工業大廈經翻新後改為如倉庫和辦公室等其他用途。以海濱工業大廈為例，它包含了電子、玩具、家具、印刷廠等多個用途。

Ⓑ Kwun Tong Ferry Pier 觀塘輪渡碼頭

Ⓒ Wing Yip Street 永業街

Ⓓ Building facade 建築物外觀

Factory name: Kwun Tong Printing Factory
Factory address: Wing Yip Street, Kowloon
Plot size: 6500 sqm
No. of workers: 100
Construction era: 1980s

工廠名稱：觀塘印刷廠
工廠地址：九龍永業街
用地面積：6,500 平方米
工人數量：100 人
建設年代：1980 年代

The whole building is used for industrial activities such as printing and manufacturing. Each use typically occupies one or two stories of a particular block and they are often referred to as "flatted factories."

整棟建築用於如印刷廠和產品製造等工業生產，產品包括電器、塑料、家具等。這些工廠通常會佔用特定樓面的一至兩層。這種方式通常被稱為分層工廠大廈。

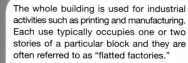

The printing factory is located on the 3rd and 4th floors of the podium level, operating its production lines, storage and office functions in around 6,000 sqm of double height floor space.

印刷廠位於平台層的三至四樓。這種雙樓層空間的工業形態在大約 6,000 平方米的面積內滿足了生產、儲藏和辦公的功能要求。

Covered walkway
有蓋行人道

At the Kwun Tong Cooked Food Market, workers get their daily meals. It is located on the ground floor of the attached building.

工人們可以在觀塘熟食市場用膳。這個市場位於附屬建築物的地面層。

Kwun Tong Bypass
(Elevated Road)
觀塘道（高架路）

Production Line 生產流程

Materials:
White paper roll
Plastic sheet
Color ink for printing
原材料：
白紙、塑膠片、顏色油墨

Stage 1
Color and Page Settings
Designers work on the color adjustment and print settings.

第一階段
顏色和頁面設置：
設計者校訂顏色和打印設定。

CLICK
CLICK ...

Stage 2
Printing
The printing machine prints many pages at once and cuts the paper to the appropriate size.

第二階段
印刷：
印刷機能一次打印多頁，並將紙頁裁成特定尺寸。

ZING ZING...

Stage 3
Sorting
The printed pages have to be sorted before they are bound.

第三階段
排序：
在釘裝成冊前，須將印刷好的紙頁按次序排列。

TAP TAP...

Stage 4
Binding
The binding machine compiles the completed pages into books.

第四階段
裝訂：
釘裝機將印刷成的紙張裝訂成冊。

ZICH ZICH...

Shopping Guide 購物指南

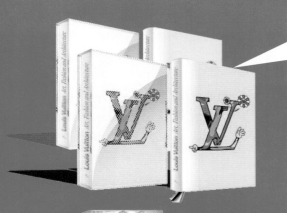

Best Seller!
Product 1
Name: Lifestyle and Fashion Books
Features: 1. hardcover
2. addresses, brand history and designers
3. contains illustrations and photos
Language: French, English and Italian
Mass produced since: 2010
Price: USD 85

名稱：生活和時尚手冊
特點：1. 硬皮封面
2. 品牌的歷史和設計
3. 插圖
4. 照片
語言：法語、英語和意大利語
生產年代：2010 年
價格：85 美元

Product 2
Name: Children's Books
Features: 1. hardcover
2. riding guide
3. riding facility
4. riding equipment
5. riding vocabulary
Mass produced since: 2003
Price: USD 13.50

產品 2
名稱：兒童書
特點：1. 硬皮封面
2. 騎馬指南
3. 騎馬設施
4. 騎馬裝備
5. 騎馬詞彙
生產年代：2003 年
價格：13.50 美元

Product 3
Name: Notepad
Features: full-colored papers
Mass produced since: 2004
Price: HKD 35

產品 3
名稱：便條本
特點：全彩色
生產年代：2004 年
價格：35 港元

Product 4
Name: Reading books
Features:
1. colorful photographs and illustrations
2. historical facts about famous aircraft
3. aviation history
4. 24 paper airplane models
Mass produced since: 2007
Price: USD 25

產品 4
名稱：書籍
特點：1. 彩色照片和插圖
2. 關於著名飛機的歷史事實
3. 航空歷史
4. 24 個紙飛機模型
生產年代：2007 年
價格：25 美元

July 2008						
Mon	Tue	Wed	Thu	Fri	Sat	Sun
	1	2	3	4	5	6
7	8	9	10	11	12	13
14	15	16	17	18	19	20
21	22	23	24	25	26	27
28	29	30	31			

Product 5
Name: calenders
Mass produced since: 2008
Price: HKD 50

產品 5
名稱：月曆
生產年代：2008 年
價格：50 港元

Product 6
Name: Greeting cards
Mass produced since: 2005
Price: HKD 30

產品 6
名稱：賀卡
生產年代：2005 年
售價：30 港元

Wining and Dining 工人的飲食

Exterior facade of the food market 食品市場外牆

Interior of the food market 食品市場

Menu of the day 是日餐牌

Lunch 午餐

Name: Food market lunch set
Features: meat, vegetables, and soup
Lunch time: 12.00 pm

Taste ranking: ★★★

名稱：食品市場午餐套餐
特點：肉類、蔬菜和湯
午飯時間：上午 12:00

美味指數：★★★

Dinner 晚餐

Name: Food market dinner set
Features: meat, vegetables, and milk tea
Dinner time: 6:00 pm

Taste ranking: ★★★

名稱：食品市場晚餐套餐
特點：肉類、蔬菜、奶茶
午飯時間：下午 6:00

美味指數：★★★

Accommodation 工人的住宿

Early public housing estate in Kwun Tong
早期的觀塘公共屋邨

Yuet Wah Street
月華街

Wo Lok Estate, 1960s 和樂邨，1960 年代

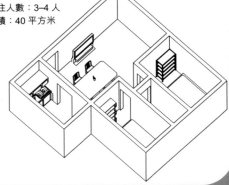

Family suite
Capacity : 3–4 persons
Size of the accommodation: 40 sqm

家庭戶型宿舍
居住人數：3–4 人
面積：40 平方米

Employee of the Day 今日之星

Nickname: Willie
Age: 30
Hometown: Hong Kong
Marital status: Single
Post: Binding worker
No. of years in the factory: 6
Monthly income: HKD 8,000

暱稱：威利
年齡：30
居住城市／出生地：香港
婚姻狀況：單身
職位：裝訂工
在此工廠的年資：6 年
月薪：8,000 港元

Workers' uniform in the factory 職員制服

About my life

I am a Hong Kong citizen. As I am single, I still live with my parents in the New Territories; this way, I am able to save more money for my future.

我的生活

我是香港公民，單身人士，與父母在新界居住，這樣，更能省錢。

My career

After I graduated from high school, I worked in othe industrial jobs before I started here. It was nearly years ago that I joined this company. I think that this i a good opportunity for me. Working in a medium-size factory allows me to learn more from my colleague as we are quite close and get on well with each other

我的事業

高中畢業後，我曾在其他工廠行業就業，六年前加入這公司。我認為在中型模式工廠工作是一個難得機會，既和同事們關係親密，又能從他們身上學習。

Living with my parents

I live in a common flat with my family where I feel very comfortable. I am not thinking of moving out of the house, at least for now. First, because I have no plans to get married yet, and second, because I have to save money in order to be able to achieve my dream.

我的願望

我和家人住在一個普通的單位內，居住環境很舒適。我並沒有打算搬出來住：一，我並未有計劃結婚；二，我要為我的理想省錢。

About my dream

I have a desire to be able to get a degree. One day, when have saved enough, I will star a part-time degree.

我的夢想

我的夢想是終有一天能夠取得一個學位。當我有足夠的積蓄，我打算報讀兼讀學位課程。

A one-hour commute

Overall the transportation in this area is convenient enough. I usually travel from home to work in approximately one hour by bus.

一小時往來

總括而言，在這裏上班交通大致上很方便，我從住所乘搭巴士上班約需一小時。

My colleagues live all over town

What I really like best about this job is getting to know my colleagues, they're very kind people. We share many interests such as karaoke. We always have lunch and dinner together, but we all live in different parts of Hong Kong, so we can only hang out at work or right just after we get off.

我的同事

我很喜歡我的工作，因為我的同事都很友善，我們都喜歡唱卡拉 OK。不過，由於大家住在香港不同地區，只能在上班或下班後一起閒聊。

Around the Clock 他／她的一天

Start

Lunch

13:00

09:00

I usually arrive at the factory at 8.50 am. I start working after getting changed.

我通常在上午 8 時 50 分到達工廠，換衣服 後就開始工作。

10:00

12:00

Since our lunch is not provided by the factory, I usually have my meal together with my colleagues in a nearby food market. The food tastes quite good and is affordable.

工廠沒有提供午 餐，我多數會和同 事一起吃飯，附近 食品市場的食物不 但便宜，而且味道 很不錯！

Sleep

22:00

13:30

Work

21:00

I have to come back to work after dinner. If I am lucky enough, I can join my colleagues for karaoke.

晚餐後我常常要回到工廠工 作。但偶爾可以跟同事 一起唱卡拉 OK。

18:00

Even though we do not really communicate while working, I love working in a team rather than working by myself.

雖然工作時大家說話不多，但我 比較喜歡團隊工作，而不 是獨自的工作。

11:30

11:00

81

SHENZHEN
深圳

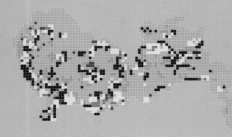

Land use 土地利用

Shenzhen has a mixed land use pattern, however, industrial and residential uses dominate.

深圳的土地用途雖然繁多，但以工業和住宅為主。

Administration 分區

Shenzhen consists of 3 main zones: the SEZ, Bao'an and Longgang. These 3 zones are further broken down into 23 smaller districts that shape the city of Shenzhen.

深圳市擁有 3 大地區：經濟特區、寶安區和龍崗區。這三個地區再劃分為 23 個小區。

Shenzhen, located in southern China, is a district city of the Guangdong Province. The city is bordered by Hong Kong to the south, Dongguan to the north and Huizhou to the northeast. Being the neighboring city to Hong Kong, Shenzhen economically benefits from its close ties with Hong Kong's well-established economy.

Historically, Shenzhen was a small fishing village; this however changed at the end of the 1970s when Mao Zedong decided to designate Shenzhen as the first, and now largely considered the most successful, Special Economic Zone (SEZ) in China. The city's population today is roughly 14 million people, of which only around 2 million are considered to be local residents. The majority of the remaining people are migrant workers from other parts of China, who mostly come to Shenzhen to work in the manufacturing section.

深圳位處於中國南部，是廣東省的一個經濟特區城市。深圳以南是香港，以北是東莞，東北面是惠州。由於地理位置關係，深圳得到來自香港的經濟支持和好處。

自從 1970 年代毛澤東決定將深圳定為經濟特區後，深圳由一小漁村變為中國現今最成功的經濟特區。今天深圳約有 1,400 萬人，其中有 200 萬人為本地人，其他均為移動人口，在深圳工廠當工人。

Industries 工業類型
The majority of industries in Shenzhen is focused around electronic and assembly-based products.
深圳市的主要工業類型是電子產業和安裝產業。

Urbanization 城市化
Shenzhen used to be a very small fishing village (dots in red), and it is now urbanized in every corner within the city boundary.
深圳從一個小漁村（紅點）變成現在的大城市。

Transport System 道路系統
Shenzhen, as the only neighbor of Hong Kong, offers a variety of transit modes to cross the border.
深圳是香港唯一的內陸連鄰。深圳與香港都提供不同類型的交通工具，如鐵路、公車和渡船等，方便市民往返兩地。

Map of Shenzhen in the time of the Ming Dynasty
明代的深圳

Setting up a barrier to protect the Shenzhen Special Economic Zone
在特區邊界設圍欄

Shenzhen Special Economic Zone established

The Qing Dynasty leased the New Territories to the British in 1899.
1899 年，清政府把新界租讓給英國。

Mainland citizens trying to immigrate illegally are caught and sent back to Shenzhen
被遣返深圳的大陸偷渡者

People moved to Shenzhen to support the large amount of construction work
人們搬到深圳支援特區的建設工作

Opening of the Kowloon - Canton Rail
九廣鐵路開通

1640   1911   1949   1979

Deng's statue was regarded as one of Shenzhen's most famous monuments
鄧小平雕像被評為深圳最重要的建築之一

Deng Xiaoping's first visit to Shenzhen in 1984
1984 年鄧小平首次訪問深圳

China's first stock market was founded in Shenzhen
中國的第一個證券交易市場在深圳成立

"Window of the World" opening - one of the many theme parks in Shenzhen
世界之窗 - 深圳多個主題公園的代表之一開張

Shenzhen became one of the most important cities in mainland China
深圳現已成為中國其中一個重要的城市

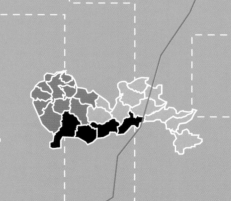

10

9

8

7

6

5

4

3

Total Population
2
Persons
(Million)

1990 1992   2000 2002   2005   2007   2008   2010

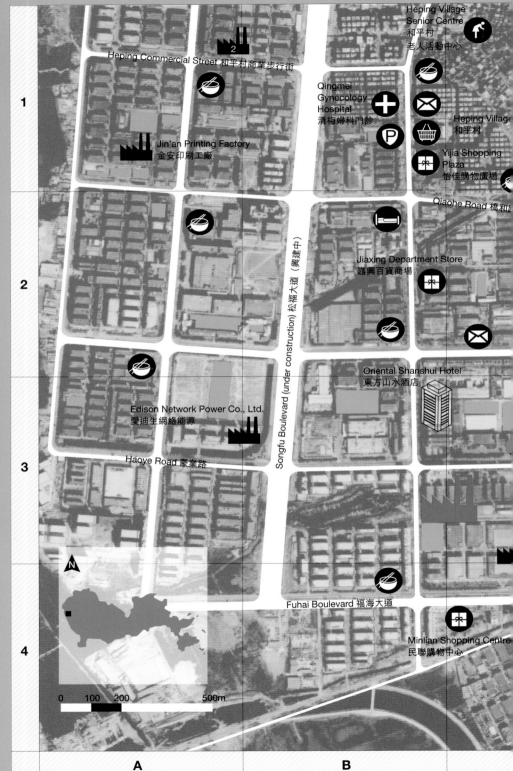

Heping Village
Senior Centre
和平村
老人活動中心

Heping Commercial Street 和平村商業步行街

Qingmei
Gynecology
Hospital
清梅婦科門診

Heping Village
和平村

Jin'an Printing Factory
金安印刷工廠

Yijia Shopping
Plaza
怡佳購物廣場

Qiaohe Road 橋和

Jiaxing Department Store
嘉興百貨商場

Songfu Boulevard (under construction) 松福大道（興建中）

Oriental Shanshui Hotel
東方山水酒店

Edison Network Power Co., Ltd.
愛迪生網絡能源

Haoye Road 豪業路

N

Fuhai Boulevard 福海大道

Minlian Shopping Centre
民聯購物中心

0   100   200   500m

A

B

1

2

3

4

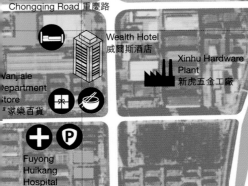

uzhou
imary School
洲小學

Qiaotou Village
橋頭村

Yongfu Road 永福路

Chongqing Road 重慶路

Wealth Hotel
威爾斯酒店

Xinhu Hardware
Plant
新虎五金工廠

Vanjiale
Department
tore
家樂百貨

Fuyong
Huikang
Hospital
萬福永惠康
綜合門診

Xinhe Village
新和村

D

Shenzhen Newcolor Optoelectronics Co. Ltd.
深圳市新彩光電有限公司

This company produces LED products, including LED displays and lighting. The company specializes in R&D, production and marketing of LED products. The 30,000-sqm-factory is equipped with automatic production lines, advanced manufacturing equipment and high-end testing devices, guaranteeing a monthly LED production capacity of 5000 sqm.

專業從事 LED 顯示屏及 LED 照明產品（LED 路燈、LED 日光燈等）開發、生產、銷售為一體的綜合運營服務商。新彩工業園佔地面積 30,000 多平方米，配備了高度自動化、設備最齊全的生產線，月產能達 5,000 平方米，是華南地區三家全自動 LED 顯示屏企業之一。

Shenzhen Creative Future Electronic Co. Ltd.
深圳創意未來電器有限公司

Shenzhen Creative Future Electronic Co. Ltd., founded in 2004, is a professional manufacturer of multimedia speakers and headphones. The company is devoted to R&D, production and sales of Hyundai brand speakers in the Chinese market.

深圳市創意未來公司是一間集生產、研發與銷售為一體的生產商。創意公司在現代集團的多方位支持下，本着精益求精的設計理念，打造多種視聽產品和 IT 產品。

Lincoln Alemex (Shenzhen) Co. Ltd.
林肯阿麗瑪（深圳）科技有限公司

This company is located at the Fuyong Town Hi-tech Industrial Campus. With a site area of 60,000 sqm, the company produces peripheral equipment for photocopiers such as automatic sorters, etc.

林肯阿麗瑪（深圳）科技有限公司位於福永高新技術園區，佔地面積 6 萬平方米。主要生產自動選紙機、分頁器等複印機外部設備。

Newcolor Optoelectronics Co. Ltd. 新彩光電有限公司

A1 **A2** Factory & office building 廠房與辦公綜合大樓

B1 **B2** Worker dormitory 工人宿舍

C Signpost 路標

D Basketball court 籃球場

Showroom 展示廳

Assembly workshop 組裝工場

Warehouse & showroom 倉庫與展示廳

Factory name: Newcolor Optoelectronics Co. Ltd.
Factory address: Yonghe Road, Shenzhen, China
Plot size: 3 hectares
No. of workers: 250–300
Construction era: 2006

工廠名稱：新彩光電有限公司
工廠地址：深圳市福永鎮永和路
用地面積：3 公頃
工人數量：250–300 人
建設年代：2006 年

The main factory building has a floor area of approximately 3,000 sqm with a floor height of six to seven meters. Located on the ground floor are the assembly workshop, warehouse, showroom and the reception hall. Dust-free workshops and offices occupy the first and second floors of the building.

工廠主樓佔地面積約 3,000 平方米，層高達到 6-7 米。一樓為組裝工場、倉庫、展示廳以及公司接待大堂等。二至三樓是無塵工場和辦公室。

Amenities
生活娛樂區

A1
B2
C
B1
D
A2

Office and factory
辦公室與生產工場

Tongfu Road 同富路

The dormitory and canteen are located in the same building which is of a similar architectural style to the main building. The canteen is on the ground floor with the activity center on the first floor, and staff dormitory accommodation is on the levels above. There is also a basketball court for workers to enjoy outdoor activities.

員工宿舍與餐廳在同一棟樓，建築形式與工廠主樓一致。一層為餐廳，二層是活動中心，三樓以上是員工宿舍。另設有一籃球場提供工人活動。

Production Line 生產流程

Shenzhen 深圳

Newcolor Optoelectronics Co. Ltd. 新影光電有限公司

Materials:
Phosphor for LED
Circuit board
LED chip

原材料：
墨螢光粉、電路板、LED 芯片

TSI TSI...

Stage 1
Light Emitting Diodes (LEDs) are inserted onto printed circuit boards (PCBs), each forming a pixel point.

第一階段
將不同顏色的二極管燈插入 PCB 板孔中，構成像素點。

Stage 2
Drive plates are completed by the fixing of components such as Integrated Circuits (ICs), electrical resistors and capacitors.

第二階段
先將集成電路、電阻、電容等元器件貼到驅動板上。然後將 PCB 燈板和驅動裝入塑料套件（模殼），用排針固定。

嚓嚓！

Stage 3
The electrical supply system is installed and is injected with silica gel as the outdoor modules are required to be water resistant. These semi-finished modules are then ready to be placed within their protective covers.

第三階段
為模組安裝電源。戶外模組需要防水，在模殼灌入硅膠，裝上面罩，就是半成品模組。

Stage 4
Connection cables are then added to complete the finished LED display.

第四階段
將模組組裝成 LED 箱體，裝好電源，連上電源線、網線、排線，就是成品箱體。

GOOD!

Shopping Guide 購物指南

Product 1
Name: Indoor full-color display P6-3-in-1
Features: 1. High illumination
2. Remarkable dynamic effects
3. Reliable performance
Mass produced since: 2008
Price: RMB 27,000 per sqm

P6-3-in-1 室內全彩顯示屏亮度高,動態效果令
人驚歎,具有出色的可靠性。

Product 2
Name: Outdoor full-color display P16
Features: 1. Excellent uniformity
2. Big wide angle of 110 degree
3. Best competitive price
Mass produced since: 2008
Price: RMB 9,000 per sqm

產品 P16 系列室外全彩顯示屏擁有同等產品
種最高性能。其靈活性令其適用於多種場合。
超大視角,可視範圍廣,新技術有效地解決
了馬賽克現象,顯示效果一絕。

Best Seller!
Product 3
Name: Indoor Single Color Display C5
Features: 1. Maximum flatness
2. Good consistency
3. Better image quality
Mass produced since: 2007
Price: RMB 3,000 per sqm

獨特封裝技術,平整度好,具有良好的發光
一致性,使像素顯示效果好,可視角度大,
不偏色。

Product 4
Name: Outdoor single-color display P14
Features: 1. Extra high brightness LED
2. Super high refresh rate
3. Stable image
Mass produced since: 2006
Price: RMB 5,000 per sqm

採用超高亮發光二極管,在戶外太陽直射下現
實依然清晰。可自動調節色彩對比度、亮度,
超高刷新率使畫面穩定出色。

Product 5
Name: LED street light
Features: 1. Long service life
2. No discomforting glare
3. Lead free, low pollution
Mass produced since: 2008
Price: RMB 1,000

LED 路燈在配光性能、散熱性能、電氣性能、使用
壽命、功耗、啟動速度、頻閃、出光頻率、色溫、不
良眩光、環境效應等方面均具有優勢。

Exterior facade of the canteen 員工餐廳外觀

Canteen kitchen 員工餐廳廚房

Inside the canteen 員工餐廳室內環境

Lunch 午餐

Name: Canteen set lunch provided for workers
Features: Two dishes, rice and soup
Lunch time: 12:00–1:30 pm

Taste ranking: ★★★★

名稱：香芋排骨、蛋包肉、綠豆沙
特點：營養搭配合理，根據季節變換菜式
午飯時間：中午至下午 1:30

美味指數：★★★★

Dinner 晚餐

Name: Canteen set dinner provided for workers
Features: Three dishes, rice and soup
Dinner time: 5:00–6:30 pm

Taste ranking: ★★★★

名稱：魚香茄子、菜花雞柳、蒜蓉炒通菜、綠豆沙
特點：每天供應十款不同菜式的搭配，夏天時額外有綠
　　　豆沙供應
晚飯時間：下午 5:00–6:30

美味指數：★★★★

Accommodation 工人的住宿

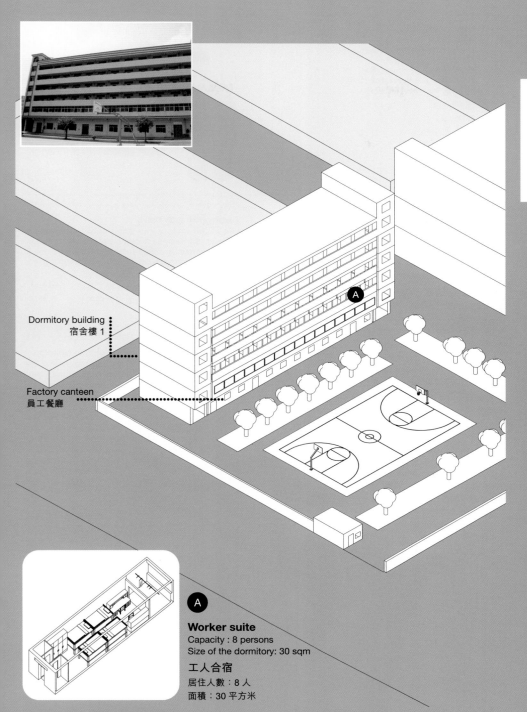

Dormitory building
宿舍樓 1

Factory canteen
員工餐廳

A

Worker suite
Capacity : 8 persons
Size of the dormitory: 30 sqm

工人合宿
居住人數：8 人
面積：30 平方米

Shenzhen 深圳

Newcolor Optoelectronics Co. Ltd. 新彩光電有限公司

Nickname: Qiu Ju
Age: 26
Hometown: Sichuan Province
Marital status: Single
Post: Assembly line worker
No. of years in the factory: 0.5
Monthly income: RMB 2,200

暱稱：秋菊
年齡：26
家鄉：四川省
婚姻狀況：單身
職位：生產線工人
在此工廠的年資：0.5 年
月薪：2,200 人民幣

Workers' uniform in the factory 職員制服

For a better salary
I was longing for a life outside our small village. My family couldn't support ourselves with the income from farming. That's why I came to Shenzhen to become a factory worker.

我不想待在農村，因為掙不到錢，而我的家庭需要更多的錢以維持生活。

Tough and happy times
Life in the factory can bring about ambivalent feelings. Sometimes it can be tough and boring; in other times, it brings me happiness because I get the chance to make friends with people from different parts of the country.

在工廠裏的日子有苦澀也有快樂。雖然工作略為枯燥，但是認識了很多來自五湖四海的朋友，在閒時我們會一起聊天。

Satisfactory living conditions
I am mostly content with my salary and the accommodation/food provided by the company.

我大致上滿意我的工資和公司安排的食宿。

More activities needed
I hope that this town can also become a place where we can pursue different activities in our leisure time..

我希望工廠區也能像城市一樣能有多姿多彩的生活，減少我們生活的枯燥。

Feelings of isolation
We are happy that we can earn our living, but we don't have as many activity choices as people who live in central Shenzhen do. Sometimes I have feelings of isolation and boredom. There is nothing to do during the weekends out here, so I often have to travel to the downtown area instead.

在工廠區感覺與市區隔絕了。市區的豐富多彩在這裏我們無法享受到。只有每到週末，花上幾個小時的車程到市區，我們才能感受到城市裏的熱鬧。

Around the Clock 他／她的一天

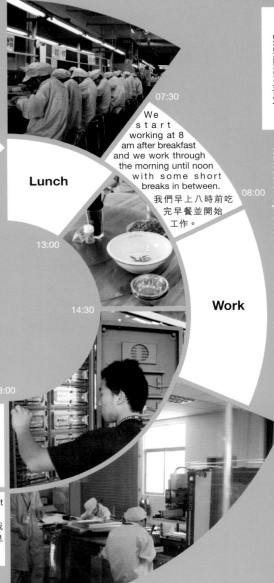

Start

12:00

Lunch time is one of the most important moments of the day because we can get some refreshment, and we can spend some time to walk to the shops or chat with friends.

午餐時刻是我們一日中最重要的時間之一。我們不但為下午的工作補充體力，還可到周圍的商店逛逛或與友人聊天。

Sleep

22:00

20:00

18:00

Dinner

10:00

Normally we have a break from around 10:00 to 10:20. We like to take this time to have a rest and chat with each other.

10:00 至 10:20 是休息時間。我們喜歡利用這個時間歇息並和朋友聊天。

09:30

Lunch

13:00

07:30

We start working at 8 am after breakfast and we work through the morning until noon with some short breaks in between.

我們早上八時前吃完早餐並開始工作。

08:00

14:30

Work

Shenzhen 深圳 Shekou Industrial Zone 蛇口工業區

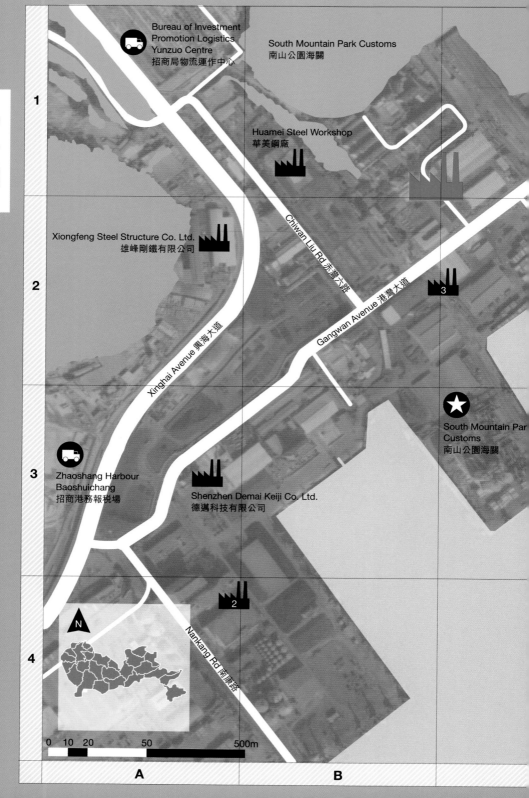

Bureau of Investment Promotion Logistics Yunzuo Centre
招商局物流運作中心

South Mountain Park Customs
南山公園海關

Huamei Steel Workshop
華美鋼廠

Xiongfeng Steel Structure Co. Ltd.
雄峰剛鐵有限公司

Chiwan Liu Rd 赤灣大路

Gangwan Avenue 港灣大道

Xinghai Avenue 興海大道

3

South Mountain Par Customs
南山公園海關

Zhaoshang Harbour Baoshuichang
招商港務報稅場

Shenzhen Demai Keiji Co. Ltd.
德邁科技有限公司

2

Nankang Rd 南康路

N

1   2

1

2

3

4

0   10 20   50   500m

A   B

QSI International School
of Shekou Middle School
蛇口科愛賽國際學校

Guanhai Rd 觀海路

Shekou Haitao Hotel
蛇口海濤酒店

Haishan World
海山世界

Shekou Ferry Terminal
蛇口客運碼頭

erchant Shekou Industrial Zone
商局蛇口工業局

D

Hong Tai Toy Manufacturer Co. Ltd.
鴻泰玩具工廠有限公司

Hong Tai Toy Manufacturer is one of many factories located in the PRD which produces toys mainly exported to North America and Europe. Managed through a Hong Kong head office, the factory produces over 1,500 toys on a daily basis.

鴻泰玩具工廠有限公司是珠三角小許剩下來的玩具工廠。所有玩具都是批發出口到美洲、歐洲的不同國家。工廠一天可生產 1,500 件玩具。

Lam Soon Flour Mills
南順麵粉工廠

Lam Soon Flour Mills is located in the heart of the Shekou Industrial Zone. The Hong Kong-based parent company, Lam Soon Corporate, owns many factories producing flour and cooking oil in the PRD.

南順麵粉工廠位於蛇口工廠區的中心。 設於香港的總公司現在於珠三角的多個城市地區擁有工廠，主要出產麵粉和食油。

CIMC Containers Manufacture Co. Ltd.
南方中集集裝箱製造有限公司

As the world's largest manufacturer of shipping containers, CIMC is committed to providing comprehensive equipment and services for modern transportation. CIMC focuses on providing value-added services to its customers in the form of container depot services in order to further expand its business.

集團致力為現代化交通運輸提供裝備和服務，針對這一定位，中集集團已經於 2003 年開始以深圳蛇口為試點，為客戶提供全套的集裝箱 M&R 服務，包括集裝箱堆存、維修、翻新、保養等，力求為客戶提供集裝箱從產品到保養的「一站式」服務，為客戶監控和保證產品的質量。

A1 A2 Xinghai Avenue 興海路

B1 B2 Loading and unloading area 上落貨物區

C1 Factory building 1 一號廠

D Billboards 新聞公告欄

C2 Factory building 2 二號廠

The factory owner puts a lot of effort into greening the site to improve the workers' living environment.

工廠很用心地去美化廠內的環境。

Factory billboards are a very important way of providing workers with regularly updated information about the company. Events such as New Year's celebrations, or company anniversary ceremonies are posted on the billboards.

新聞公告欄位於員工宿舍的前方。公告牌貼上一些公司的新聞和最新的活動。

Open space 小巷

E In between the factory buildings 廠與廠之間的空間

Factory name: Hong Tai Toy Manufacturer Co. Ltd.
Factory address: Xinghai Avenue, Nanshan District
Plot size: 3.5 hectares
No. of workers: 350
Construction era: 1990s

工廠名稱：鴻泰玩具工廠有限公司
工廠地址：南山區蛇口工廠區興海大道
用地面積：3.5 公頃
工人數量：350 人
建設年代：1990 年代

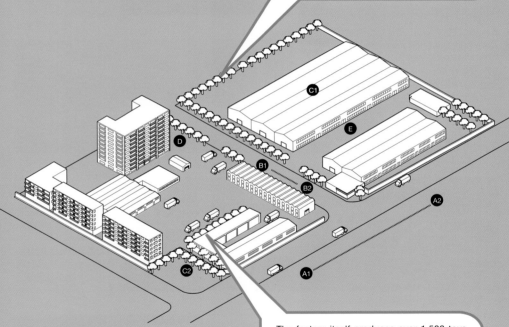

The factory is located in the Shekou Industrial Zone. Shekou is also known as the first industrial zone in China, established under the instructions of Mao Zedong in order to stimulate the development of the manufacturing industry.

工廠位於蛇口工廠區內。蛇口工廠區是毛澤東領導成立的全國第一個工廠區。

The factory itself produces over 1,500 toys a day and more than 80% of the products are exported internationally. The factory's location is logistically convenient, being next to Shekou's port. This reduces transportation costs and improves product mobility.

這工廠每天製造大約 1,500 件玩具，80% 的玩具都是輸出到外國，工廠位於港口附近，可省了運費。

Production Line 生產流程

Materials:
Plastic
(i.e. styrofoam, mix acetone)
Plastic sheets
Fabrics

原材料：
塑膠粒、塑膠片、布料

tchh chh kkk...

Stage 1
Preparing the basic materials in pieces to facilitate assembly (such as sewing doll clothing, producing masse smaller plastic pieces, etc.).

準備所有基本的材料方便裝配的程序，例如製作公仔的衣服與配件。

Stage 2
Assembling electronic and other small components.

第二階段是把電子配件與基本材料裝配在一起。完成程序後就可以運送到最後裝配程序了。

tap click click kkk

Stage 3
Final assembly of component parts, completing end products such as dolls or choo-choo trains.

第三個階段是把搭配件，如公仔的衣服、火車的配件等，安裝到裝配材料上。

Stage 4
The final stage is to verify the end product and to test the product for safety. Quality check is a very important step in toy production.

最後的程序就是要檢查製成品的品質是否合格和符合國際的標準。

BIP BIP!

Shenzhen 深圳

Hong Tai Toy Manufacturer Co. Ltd. 鴻泰玩具工廠有限公司

Best Seller!
Name: Ranger doll
Features: 1. Japanese collectibles
          2. Varieties of sizes and colors
          3. Different accessories to match
Mass produced since: 2007
Price: RMB 40

變形金剛是工廠銷路最好的產品。每一天有 800
多件變形金剛玩具製成。

Product 2
Name: Stress balls
Features: 1. Offered in many colors
        2. Cheap price; good value
Mass produced since: 2005
Price: RMB 5

壓力球是工廠最便宜的產品。雖然製
作過程很簡單，可是產品銷路一般。

Product 3
Name: Dress-Up dolls
Features: 1. Most recent fashion icon dolls
          2. Many accessories to match
Mass produced since: 2007
Price: RMB 50

娃娃玩具是最受小女孩歡迎的玩具。每天出產
的產品有大概 500 個娃娃玩具，是工廠銷量第
二名的產品。

Product 4
Name: Choo-Choo train
Features: 1. High quality materials
        2. Outstanding variety of
          colours
        3. Collectibles
Mass produced since: 2005
Price: RMB 100

小火車是工廠最別致的玩具產品之
一。因為產量不多，很多人會買來
作收藏品。

Shenzhen 深圳

Hong Tai Toy Manufacturer Co. Ltd. 鴻泰玩具員工廠有限公司

Kitchen 厨房

Exterior facade of the canteen 員工餐廳外觀

Snack station near canteen 小賣部

Set lunch for workers 員工午餐

Name: Workers' set lunch special
Features: Each worker may choose the dish of the day, including unlimited rice, soup of the day and fruits
Lunch time: 11:30 am–1:30 pm
Taste ranking: ★★★

名稱：員工級午餐
特點：每天供應款式不同的菜式，跟飯、是日湯和水果
午飯時間：上午 11:30- 下午 1:30
美味指數：★★★

Set lunch for managers 經理午餐

Name: Set lunch special for supervisors & managers
Features: In addition to the regular worker's option, supervisors and managers enjoy the choice on Western-style lunch sets
Lunch time: 11:30 am–1:30 pm
Taste ranking: ★★★★★

名稱：經理級午餐
特點：經理級職員可選擇中式午餐（跟員工午餐相同）或西式午餐，跟飯、是日湯和水果
午飯時間：上午 11:30- 下午 1:30
美味指數：★★★★★

Accommodation 工人的住宿

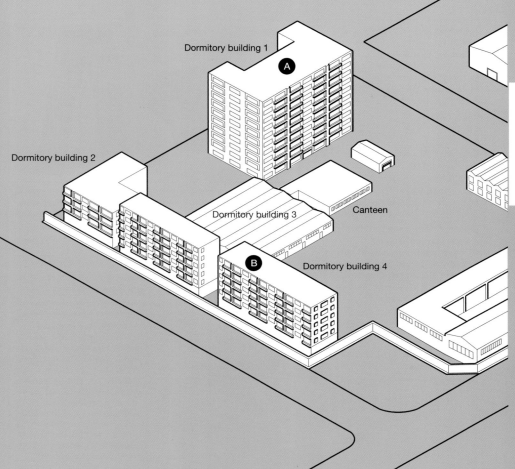

Dormitory building 1

 A

Dormitory building 2

Dormitory building 3

Canteen

B

Dormitory building 4

A
Double room (women)
Capacity: 2 persons
Size of the accommodation: 25 sqm

雙人房宿舍（女員工）
居住人數：2 人
面積：25 平方米

B
Standard worker room
Capacity : 4 persons
Size of the accommodation: 35 sqm

標準員工宿舍
居住人數：4 人
面積：35 平方米

Employee of the Day 今日之星

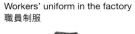

Name: Xiao Jing
Age: 30
Hometown: Shanxi Province
Marital status: Married with a daughter
Post: Quality control tester
No. of years in the factory: 12 years
Monthly income: RMB 2,200

暱稱：小晶
年齡：30
家鄉：山西
婚姻狀況：已婚，育有一女
職位：品質控制員
在此工廠的年資：12 年
月薪：RMB 2,200

Workers' uniform in the factory
職員制服

I used to work in the assembly line. Overtime work was a normal routine when I started the job. My life changed ever since I met my current husband. He is a very smart man. He is the current manager of the assembly line department.

我從前是個配裝工人，每天配裝同一樣的東西，很多時超時工作。可是當我遇見我現在的丈夫，他就改變了我一生。我丈夫現在是配裝部的經理。

A low starting salary
I have been working at this factory for almost twelve years. When I started working here, I was paid a very low salary of only 400 RMB per month.

超低起薪點
我在工廠裏已工作了 12 個年頭。我當時是一個小小的工廠員工，工資非常低。 當時的工資是大概 400 元人民幣吧。

Assembly line romance
My husband and I met in the factory twelve years ago and it was love at first sight. We dated for almost two years before getting married. I can't believe we have already reached our tenth anniversary. I can remember when we were dating it was difficult to find the time to see each other as we both worked such long hours.

我丈夫是我當年的上司哦！我當然愛他！可是當年根本沒時間去約會，因為我天天工作 12 小時。我想可能是因為我老公覺得我們見面的時間不夠，所以就娶了我吧！

Saving money
I feel very proud to be with my husband. He is a really intelligent and well-respected man. I hope to be able to save enough money to send our daughter to university.

我覺得我的人生升級了，因為我嫁了我老公。我老公是個讀書人，懂得很多。我希望我女兒也像她爸那樣，或送她到外國讀大學。

Working as a quality control tester is a very interesting job. I don't need to work overtime, which is great for my family. I can leave on time to go home and cook for my daughter. We don't live far from the factory. Of course, we own an apartment!

現在的我工作很舒服。我不需要加班，所以有很多時間陪伴家人。我現在可以在下班後去買菜做飯給女兒吃。我現在當然不住在宿舍呢！我們有自己的房子。

Around the Clock 他／她的一天

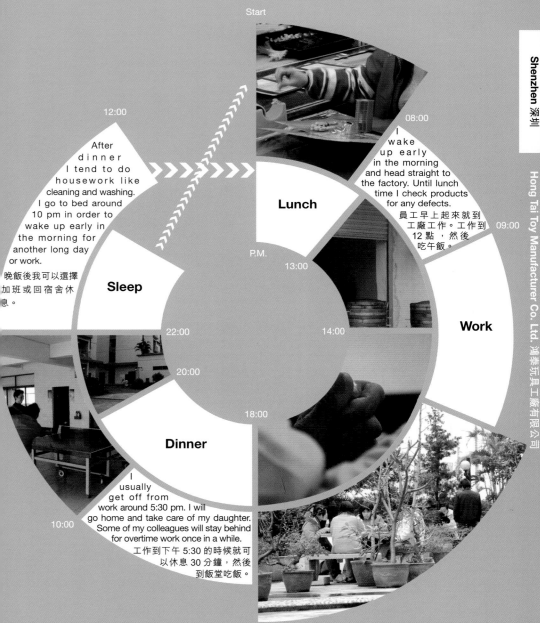

Start

08:00
I wake up early in the morning and head straight to the factory. Until lunch time I check products for any defects.
員工早上起來就到工廠工作。工作到 12 點，然後吃午飯。

09:00

Work

09:30

Lunch

P.M.

13:00

14:00

18:00

Dinner
I usually get off from work around 5:30 pm. I will go home and take care of my daughter. Some of my colleagues will stay behind for overtime work once in a while.
工作到下午 5:30 的時候就可以休息 30 分鐘，然後到飯堂吃飯。

10:00

20:00

22:00

Sleep

12:00
After dinner I tend to do housework like cleaning and washing. I go to bed around 10 pm in order to wake up early in the morning for another long day or work.
晚飯後我可以選擇加班或回宿舍休息。

DONGGUAN
東莞

Dongguan city is situated at 23'02" north latitude and 113'45" east longitude. It is located in the northeast part of the PRD with the Pearl River to the west, and also borders the cities of Guangzhou, Shenzhen and Huizhou.

In terms of administration, Dongguan is a prefecture-level city in Guangdong Province, governing 28 towns and central districts. It is one of only three prefecture-level cities in China without county level. This special administrative system provides every town in Dongguan an equal opportunity to develop.

After China adopted its "Open Door" policy, Dongguan began its fast economic development. Today Dongguan is a famous industrial hub, being home to all types of factories making many of the world's best-known brands. For a long time the city has offered great opportunities for both workers and investors, local and foreign.

Despite the competitive advantages the city has offered to industry, the recent global financial crisis has caused a number of smaller manufacturers to go out of business. Is this a temporary blip or is this a sign of things to come? Is the government's encouragement of the tertiary sector indicative of the city's postindustrial future?

廣東省東莞市位於北緯 23 度 02 分，東經 113 度 45 分，地處珠江三角洲東北部，西臨珠江口，與廣州市、深圳市、惠州市接壤。

從行政區域上而言，東莞市是隸屬於廣東省的一個地級城市，除了 4 個中心城區之外，管轄 28 個鎮，是全國三個不設縣級編制的地級市之一，特殊的城鎮體系帶給每一個鎮迅速發展的同等機會。

中國改革開放之後，東莞告別了農業時代，進入了一個工業高速發展的時代。如今，毫無疑問，東莞以其工業和服務業聞名世界，各種類型規模的工廠和酒店遍布市區和 28 個鎮。同時，發達的製造業和投資機會吸引着來自中國各省的工人和世界各地的投資商，這個城市用最廉價的勞動力創造着全世界最巨大的財富。然而，金融危機之後的東莞面對着中小企業關閉、廠房空置、舊工業區衰落的窘境，以及「退二進三」的國家政策。這座世界工廠將如何調整？工業還會在東莞興盛多少年？它會否將面對後工業時代的到來？

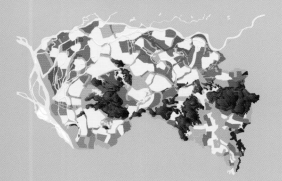

Land Use 土地利用

27% of the total area is water, 25% is forest, 13% is farmland, and 35% is urban.

東莞面積的 27％為水域，25％為森林，13％為耕地，35％為城市。

Subdistricts 城鎮體系

Dongguan is divided into 28 towns and 4 city proper districts.

東莞市管轄 4 個中心城區，28 個鎮，不設縣級編制。

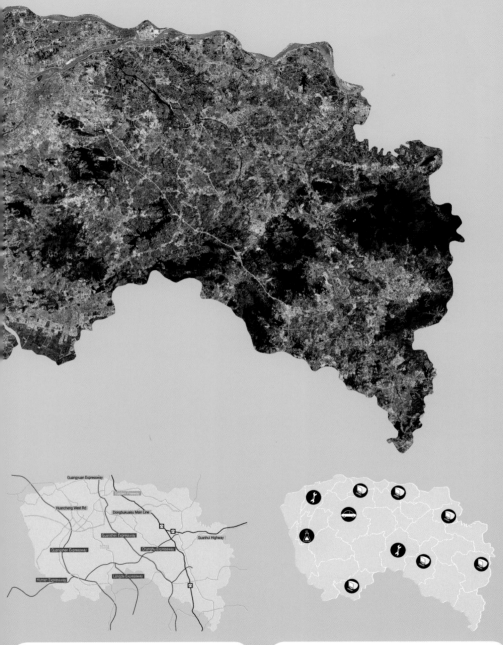

Road System 道路系統

Dongguan's main road system has a total length of 2970km. The city also offers connections between the standard and high-speed rail networks.

東莞全市擁有多條公路幹線，公路里程達 2970 公里，亦是多條鐵路和高速電路的交匯點。

Industries 工業類型

Dongguan produces a wide range of products, with its focus being the electronic and IT industries.

東莞的工業以資訊電子類產品為主，此外還涵蓋了製鞋、製衣、家具、機械等。

History 歷史

Dongguan has been designated into four historical conservation zones.
東莞劃定了四個文物保護區。

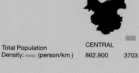

Major battles in the Opium War were fought at Humen Town, Dongguan.
「虎門銷煙」發生在東莞的虎門鎮。

ZHONGTANG 133.100 2218	GAOBU 125.200 4172	SHIJIE 222.300 6176	SHILONG 145.400 12864
QISHI 93.500 1670	QIAOTOU 119.900 2141	XIEGANG 92.900 902	MAYONG 110.000 1487
SHIPAI 125.400 2238	HONGMEI 47.700 1446	DAOJIAO 141.600 2247	CHASHAN 168.900 2964
WANGNIUDUN 67.900 1132	LIAOBU 250.000 2857	DONGKENG 100.400 3651	ZHANGMUTOU 181,700 1529
HENGLI 178.600 3571	CHANGPING 430.600 3981	HOUJIE 501,400 3979	DALINGSHAN 262.800 2398
QINGXI 366.100 2560	SHATIAN 430.600 922	HUMEN 731.700 4181	CHANGAN 733.200 8833
CENTRAL 862.900 3703	DALANG 250.100 2119	HUANGJIANG 213.600 2180	TANGXIA 372.300 2908
			FENGGANG 345.900 4192

Total Population Density: (person/km)

Qing Dynasty

1839

Qing Dynasty

1845

Republic of China

1925

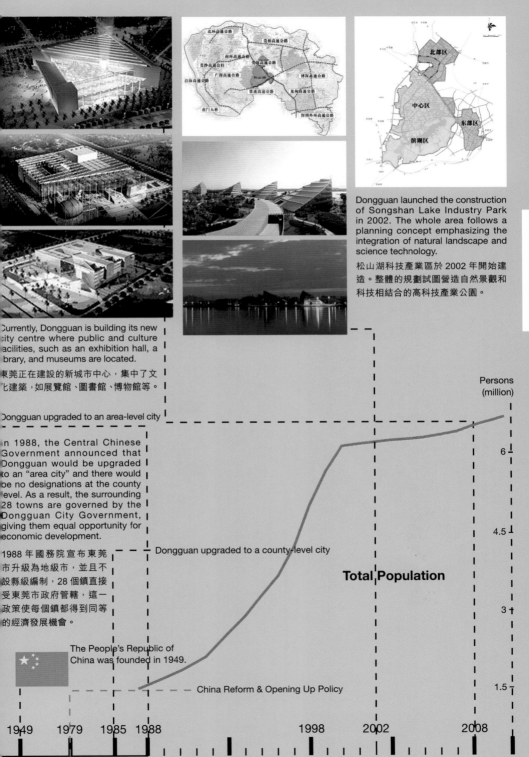

Dongguan launched the construction of Songshan Lake Industry Park in 2002. The whole area follows a planning concept emphasizing the integration of natural landscape and science technology.

松山湖科技產業區於 2002 年開始建造。整體的規劃試圖營造自然景觀和科技相結合的高科技產業公園。

Currently, Dongguan is building its new city centre where public and culture facilities, such as an exhibition hall, a library, and museums are located.

東莞正在建設的新城市中心，集中了文化建築，如展覽館、圖書館、博物館等。

Dongguan upgraded to an area-level city

In 1988, the Central Chinese Government announced that Dongguan would be upgraded to an "area city" and there would be no designations at the county level. As a result, the surrounding 28 towns are governed by the Dongguan City Government, giving them equal opportunity for economic development.

1988 年國務院宣布東莞市升級為地級市，並且不設縣級編制，28 個鎮直接受東莞市政府管轄，這一政策使每個鎮都得到同等的經濟發展機會。

The People's Republic of China was founded in 1949.

China Reform & Opening Up Policy

Dongguan upgraded to a county-level city

Persons (million)

Total Population

6

4.5

3

1.5

1949   1979   1985 1988   1998   2002   2008

Dongguan 東莞 Nancheng District 南城區

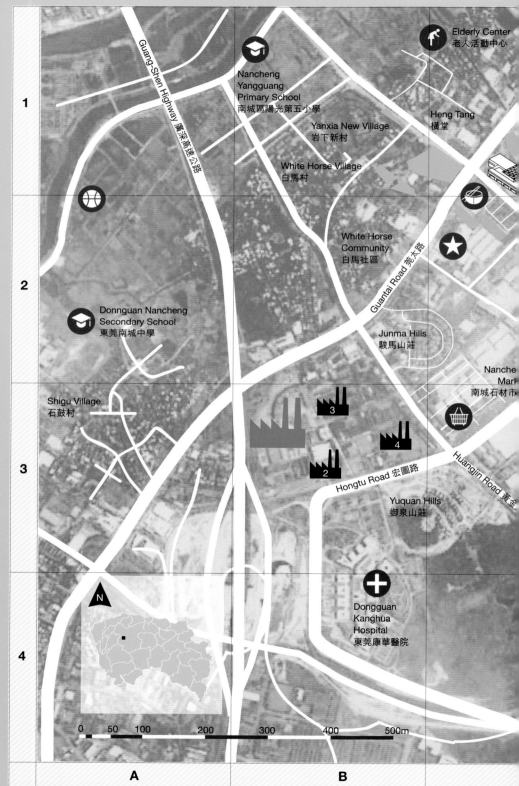

Guang-Shen Highway 廣深高速公路

Nancheng Yangguang Primary School
南城區陽光第五小學

Elderly Center
老人活動中心

Yanxia New Village
岩下新村

Heng Tang
橫堂

White Horse Village
白馬村

White Horse Community
白馬社區

Guantai Road 莞太大路

Nanche Mark
南城石材市

Junma Hills
駿馬山莊

Donnguan Nancheng Secondary School
東莞南城中學

Shigu Village
石鼓村

Hongtu Road 宏圖路

Huangjin Road 黃金

Yuquan Hills
御泉山莊

Dongguan Kanghua Hospital
東莞康華醫院

N

0   50   100   200   300   400   500m

1

2

3

4

A

B

Zhongli Hostel
東莞眾利賓館

...uan House
...ommunity
...屋邊社區

Manyee Hotel
萬怡酒店

Jiye Rencai
Building
基業人材大廈

Honger Road 宏二路

Da Jin Pu
大進埔

D

Dongguan Ideal Automobiles Co. Ltd.
東莞理想汽車公司

Ideal Automobiles was established in 2001 and it is located at the most accessible area near Guantai Road. The company has production lines, wholesales, and repair and maintenance services. It is one of the leading brands in China.

理想汽車公司於 2001 年在東莞莞太路設廠，對外交通完善，公司設有汽車製造、銷售及維修服務，是中國一代自主品牌汽車龍頭之一。

Wah Jian Group — Wah Bao Shoes Co. Ltd.
華堅集團—華寶鞋業有限公司

The company relocated its base in October 1996 from Nanchang of Jiangxi Province to Dongguan Nancheng district. Its products are exported to the European and the American markets.

華堅集團華寶鞋業有限公司於 1996 年 10 月由江西南昌遷至東莞市南城區，已逐步成為多元化業務，產品全部出口歐美。

Taiyo Cable (Dongguan) Co.Ltd.
太陽電線（東莞）有限公司

Taiyo Cable (Dongguan) Co. Ltd. was established in 1996, and is entirely invested by the Japanese Taiyo Cable joint-stock company.

太陽電線（東莞）有限公司成立於 1996 年，是由日本太陽電線株式會社 100% 出資的日本獨資企業。

Dong Xing Packing Paper Product Ltd.
東興紙品廠

The company was established in 1990, and its products are mainly exported to Taiwan.

東興紙品廠於 1990 年在東莞設廠，產品主要輸出台灣。

Dongguan Ideal Automobiles Co. Ltd. 東莞理想汽車公司

Ⓐ1 Ⓐ2 Guantai Road 莞太路

Ⓑ1 Ⓑ2 Golden One Road 黃金一路

Ⓒ Auto-parts building 汽車零部件廠

Ⓓ Spray painting & modeling building 噴漆和模版廠

Ⓔ Storage warehouse 零件倉庫

Ⓕ Showroom & sales area 展銷廳

Ⓖ Automobiles store area 汽車儲備場

Factory name: Dongguan Ideal Automobiles Co. Ltd.
Factory address: Guantai Road, Dongguan
Plot size: 7.0 hectares
No. of workers: 100
Construction era: 2000s

工廠名稱：東莞理想汽車公司
工廠地址：東莞市莞太路
用地面積：7 公頃
工人數量：100 人
建設年代：2000 年代

The factory has a storage capacity of 800 cars. This area also provides test drive areas. Ideal Automobiles sells approximately 100 cars per month, and is one of the most popular brands in China.

這裏有超過 800 部汽車存放在儲車場，又提供場地和駕車師父親身教授駕駛技術，學車人士無需另覓地方學車，既方便又安全。至於銷量方面，每月平均能賣出超過 100 輛汽車，可算是在國內受歡迎的品牌之一。

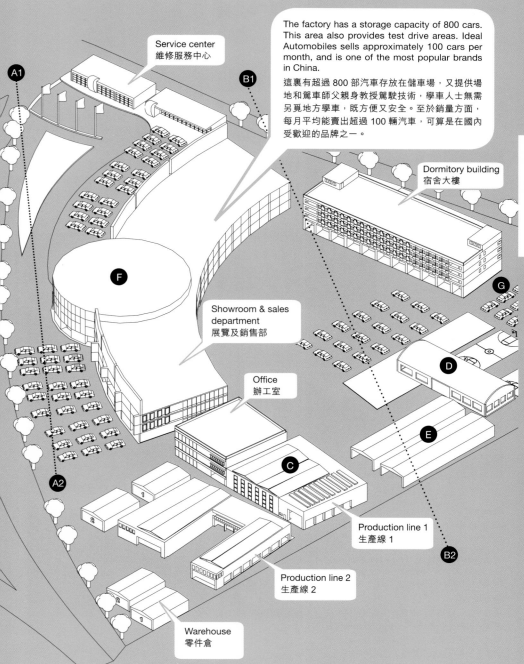

Service center
維修服務中心

Dormitory building
宿舍大樓

Showroom & sales department
展覽及銷售部

Office
辦工室

Production line 1
生產線 1

Production line 2
生產線 2

Warehouse
零件倉

A1
A2
B1
B2
F
G
D
E
C

Production Line 生產流程

Materials:
Aluminum alloy
Automobile parts
Engine

原材料：
鋁合金、零件、引擎

Stage 1
Transfer the car frame to the middle of the production line and carefully place the engine into the frame.

第一階段
先將預製的汽車車架放在運輸帶上，然後將引擎放上汽車上。

Stage 2
Installation of doors, glass panes and other accessories.

第二階段
安裝車門，汽車玻璃及其他零件。

嘭嘭嘭！

Stage 3
Installation of the bumper, intelligent transportation system, ABS safety system and air bags etc.

第三階段
再裝上防撞桿、電腦智能系統、安全氣袋等設備。

Quick!

Stage 4
After all the doors and accessories have been installed, technicians will check the lighting and computer system to make sure it is functional. The manufacturing process is now complete and the car is driven outside for testing.

第四階段
所有零件及設備裝上車身後，最後程序是檢查有沒有完全安裝成功，之後也會檢查電腦系統及照明設備，如一切妥善無誤，這部車就完成，可以推出試車場進行試車。

Beep Beep!

Shopping Guide 購物指南

Product 2 ★★★★

Name: F8 Leading brand

Features: 1. Two doors
2. Automatic open top

Mass produced since: 2010

Price: RMB 206,800

理想 F8 硬頂敞篷休閒轎跑車凝聚了理想多年成功造車經驗，融合了國際汽車製造領域最尖端的汽車科技，全面展現了理想汽車強大的技術研發實力，填補了國內硬頂敞篷轎跑車市場的空白，可謂里程碑式的經典之作。

Product 3 ★★★

Name: F8 Luxury brand

Features: 1. Two doors
2. Automatic transmission

Mass produced since: 2010

Price: RMB 169,800

F8 系列的豪華型，搭載理想自主研發的 BIVT2.0L 發動機，輸出 110kW，全自動變速箱可選。安全性配置有四安全氣囊，手感應、遙控、中控、行車自動上鎖車門鎖等。在都市居民忙裏偷閒、抓緊分秒享受生活的今天，F8 為年輕「潮」人一族帶來一陣「都市休閒主義」新風。

Best Seller! ★★★★★

Product 1

Name: F0 Modern brand

Features: 1. Four doors
2. Automatic transmission

Mass produced since: 2010

Price: RMB 46,900

F0 以「風格 JUST COOL 時尚」為設計理念的小車，吸收了歐洲最流行的設計元素，匯聚國際經典潮流，而且外觀漂亮、內飾時尚、動力強勁、養用經濟，是一款難得時尚小車。

Product 4 ★★★★

Name: F3 GL-i

Features: 1. Four doors
2. keyless smart security system

Mass produced since: 2006

Price: RMB 86,800

F3 定位面向家庭用戶，設計風格依然沒有擺脫日系車的設計思路，外形飽滿為內部留下足夠的空間基礎。圓滑的外形也為 G3 增加了不少親和力，也符合節能環保的潮流。

Product 5 ★★★☆

Name: F6 Luxury brand

Features: 1. Four doors
2. Five automatic transmission

Mass produced since: 2009

Price: RMB 159,800

F6 以「超豪外觀、超大空間、超強動力、超值享受、超省油耗、超高品質」等六項超值備受消費者青睞，F6 向消費者傳達的都是一種價值信號，即強調消費者的價值。不得不說 F6 的這張牌打的很「親民」，而 F6 十萬輛的下線也證明了市場給予非常正面的回應。

Wining and Dining 工人的飲食

Dongguan 東莞

Dongguan Ideal Automobiles Co. Ltd. 東莞理想汽車公司

Interior of the canteen 員工餐廳室內環境

Canteen kitchen 員工餐廳廚房

Exterior facade of the canteen 員工餐廳外觀

二素一肉
配搭清淡
非常健康
最合心意

Lunch 午餐

Name: canteen set lunch provided for workers
Features: with three kinds of cuisine, rice and fruits
Lunch time: 12:30 pm

Taste ranking: ★★★

名稱：玉米火腿、椰菜紅蘿蔔、青瓜、煎蛋、白飯
特點：每天供應三至四款不同菜式的配搭，多以蔬
　　　菜為主，食材非常健康
午飯時間：下午 12:30

美味指數：★★★

Dinner 晚餐

Name: canteen set lunch provided for workers
Features: With four kinds of cuisine, rice, soup and
fruits. Snacks & drinks provided when working
overtime.
Dinner time: 6:30 pm

Taste ranking: ★★★★

名稱：水煮魚、茄汁焗豆、菜心牛肉、清蒸豆腐、玉米湯、
　　　白飯、水果
特點：每天供應四種菜式一湯的配搭，晚上加班還可點小食及
　　　飲料
午飯時間：下午 6:30

美味指數：★★★★

Accommodation 工人的住宿

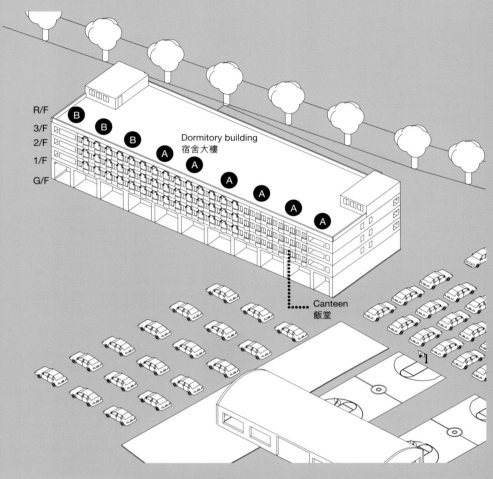

R/F
3/F
2/F
1/F
G/F

B **B** **B**

Dormitory building
宿舍大樓

A **A** **A** **A** **A** **A**

Canteen
飯堂

A

Family suite
Capacity : 3–4 persons
Size of the accommodation: 19 sqm

家庭戶型宿舍
居住人數：3–4 人
面積：19 平方米

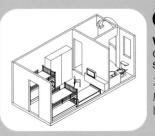

B

Worker suite
Capacity : 4–6 persons
Size of the accommodation: 19 sqm

工人合宿
居住人數：4–6 人
面積：19 平方米

Employee of the Day 今日之星

Dongguan 東莞

Dongguan Ideal Automobiles Co. Ltd. 東莞理想汽車公司

Nickname: Ah Ye
Age: 23
Hometown: Anhui Province
Marital status: Single
Education: Technical institute graduate
Post: Automobile technician
No. of years in the factory: 1
Monthly income: RMB 2,500
Other working experience : Nil

暱稱： 亞葉
年齡： 23
家鄉： 安徽省
婚姻狀況：未婚
學歷：2009 安徽技術學院畢業
職位： 汽車零件技術員
在此工廠的年資：1 年
月薪：RMB 2,500
其他工作經驗：沒有

Workers' uniform in the factory 職員制服

My first job
This is my first job after graduating from technical school. The job is challenging and I really enjoy working in here.
第一份工作
這是我從技術學院畢業後的第一份工作。我本身很有興趣從事汽車製造的行業。希望有一天能升為管理層。

What I think about the factory
The factory gives me a lot of opportunities to learn; the boss is nice and cares for everyone. Workers live in the dormitory; we can build up a close relationship with each other. I love the car industry and I really love this place.
對工廠的感覺
這裏提供很多學習機會，老闆也關心我們，常有聯誼活動。我也認識了很多好友，真的喜歡在這裏工作。

My leisure activities
Karaoke, basketball, mahjong, and table tennis
消閒活動
在閒日子時我比較喜歡和朋友打麻雀消磨時間，也會打藍球、乒乓球、KTV 等⋯⋯

Becoming a registered resident in Dongguan
Under the *hukou* system, I cannot enjoy any housing allowance and welfare in Dongguan, but after working here for 7 years, I may register as a nonagricultural resident in Dongguan. I will work hard, and I want to get married here.
為城市戶籍奮鬥
雖然我不能擁有城市戶籍，享有城市市民的各種房屋及醫療等福利，但隨着制度上的改變及放寬，只要在這裏工作滿七年，我希望能取得城市戶籍，在這裏落地生根。

Interesting anecdote
I once installed the tyres incorrectly, which led to my colleagues also making mistakes in the subsequent procedures.
入行有趣經歷
曾試過一次安裝汽車輪胎時錯誤地倒轉內外的安裝方向，令負責安裝彈簧的同事也裝錯了，哈哈！

Around the Clock 他／她的一天

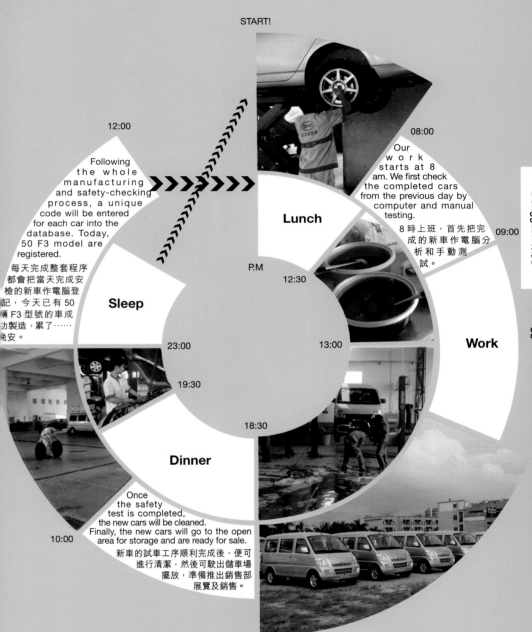

START!

12:00

08:00

Following the whole manufacturing and safety-checking process, a unique code will be entered for each car into the database. Today, 50 F3 model are registered.

每天完成整套程序都會把當天完成安檢的新車作電腦登記，今天已有 50 輛 F3 型號的車成功製造，累了⋯⋯晚安。

Our work starts at 8 am. We first check the completed cars from the previous day by computer and manual testing.

8 時上班，首先把完成的新車作電腦分析和手動測試。

09:00

Lunch

P.M

12:30

Sleep

23:00

13:00

Work

19:30

18:30

Dinner

10:00

Once the safety test is completed, the new cars will be cleaned. Finally, the new cars will go to the open area for storage and are ready for sale.

新車的試車工序順利完成後，便可進行清潔，然後可駛出儲車場擺放，準備推出銷售部展覽及銷售。

09:30

Dongguan 東莞

Dongguan Ideal Automobiles Co. Ltd. 東莞理想汽車公司

119

Dongguan 東莞 Huangjiang Town 黃江鎮

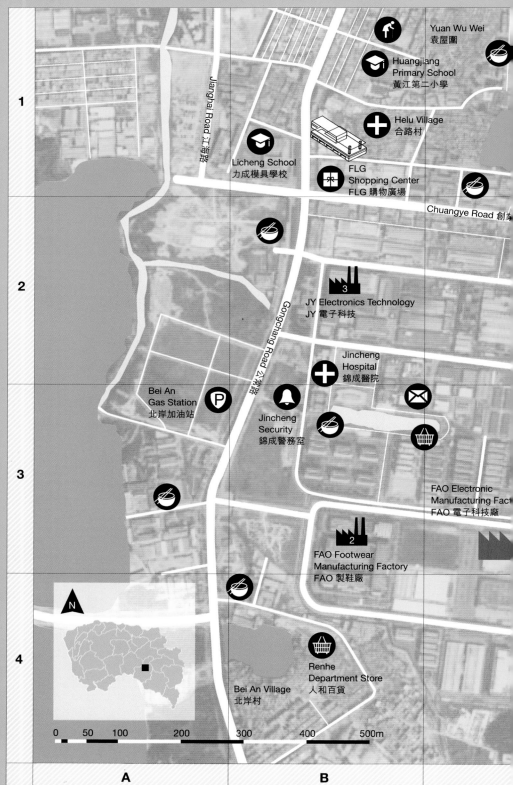

Yuan Wu Wei
袁屋圍

Huangjiang
Primary School
黃江第二小學

Helu Village
合路村

Licheng School
力成模具學校

FLG
Shopping Center
FLG 購物廣場

Jianghai Road 江海路

Chuangye Road 創業

JY Electronics Technology
JY 電子科技

Jincheng
Hospital
錦成醫院

Gongchang Road 公常路

Bei An
Gas Station
北岸加油站

Jincheng
Security
錦成警務室

FAO Electronic
Manufacturing Fact
FAO 電子科技廠

FAO Footwear
Manufacturing Factory
FAO 製鞋廠

N

Renhe
Department Store
人和百貨

Bei An Village
北岸村

0   50   100   200   300   400   500m

Huangjiang
Kindergarten
黃江中心幼兒園

Qiu Wu Wei
沆屋圍

Yuannei Road 園內路

Donghuan Road 東環路

D

FAO Electronic Manufacturing Factory
FAO 電子科技廠

The factory is owned by a large-scale enterprise from Taiwan. The company started out making printed circuit boards (PCBs) and then expanded into PCB assembly. Currently the company focuses on PCB production and electronics manufacturing services (EMS) business. Products include applications for consumer electronics, communications devices, mobile phones and automotive components.

成立於 1999 年，工廠位於黃江鎮一處大型工業園內，是一家大規模的台灣投資的企業。

工廠最初的業務是印刷電路板（PCB），之後拓展至印刷電路板組裝。如今，工廠以從事電子專業產品代工製造為核心業務，涵蓋消費類電子、通信設備、手提電話以及其他的自動化產品。

FAO Footwear Manufacturing Factory
FAO 製鞋廠

Founded in 1993, this footwear factory is owned by the same parent company as that of the electronics firm, FAO, and specializes in both original equipment manufacture (OEM) and original design manufacture (ODM) of footwear for international brand names.

製鞋廠成立於 1993 年，與電子廠同屬一家集團，為國際知名品牌代工製造或設計 (OEM/ODM) 運動鞋和休閒鞋的專業製鞋廠商。

JY Electronics Technology
JY 電子科技

Founded in 1993, also belonging to the same parent company, the factory is an important business unit responsible for surface mount technology (SMT) assembly, tooling, plastic and systems assembly, offering a total solution for electronic products.

園區內的一家電子科技廠，成立於1993年，屬於同一集團。工廠提供電子產品的全面解決方案，建立了從 SMT 貼裝、開模、注塑、塗裝，以及系統組裝的完整製作系統。

121

FAO Electronic Manufacturing Factory　FAO 電子科技廠

Bird's eye view of the whole industrial zone 工業區鳥瞰

Inside the industrial zone 工業園內

A Factory building 1 一號廠

B1 **B2** Main factory building 廠房大樓

C Loading bay 卸貨區

D View of factory 2
從廠房大樓望隔壁製鞋廠

E Factory building entrance 廠房大樓入口

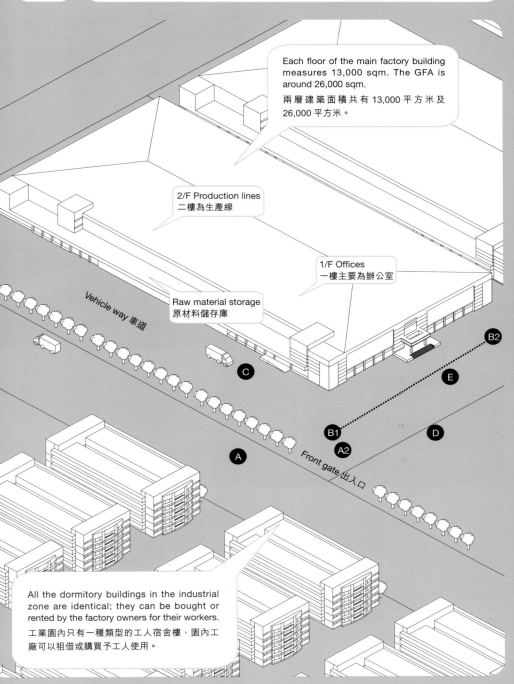

Factory name: FAO Electronic Manufacturing Factory
Factory address: Gongchang Road, Huangjiang
Plot size: 2.7 hectares
No. of workers: 1600
Construction era: 1990s

工廠名稱：FAO 電子科技廠
工廠地址：東莞市黃江鎮公常路
用地面積：2.7 公頃
工人數量：1,600 人
建設年代：1990 年代

Each floor of the main factory building measures 13,000 sqm. The GFA is around 26,000 sqm.

兩層建築面積共有 13,000 平方米及 26,000 平方米。

2/F Production lines
二樓為生產線

1/F Offices
一樓主要為辦公室

Raw material storage
原材料儲存庫

Vehicle way 車道

Front gate 出入口

All the dormitory buildings in the industrial zone are identical; they can be bought or rented by the factory owners for their workers.

工業園內只有一種類型的工人宿舍樓，園內工廠可以租借或購買予工人使用。

Production Line 生產流程

Materials:
Base boards (multiple sizes)
Chemical nickel and aurum
原材料：
基板（多種尺寸）
化金線

Stage 1
The PCB boards are first c
into shape. Then they g
through a series of steps, suc
as pressing, exposing, an
etching. Finally, the board
undergo a checked process.

第一階段
PCB 內層製作要先裁剪基
板，然後在基板上壓模，壓
模後經曝光、顯影、蝕刻
檢查成品。

咔嚓！

Stage 2
The completed board from
the previous stage is then
pressed with copper and other
plastic materials to create a
multi-layer board. The pressed
board is then drilled.

第二階段
將之前完成的內層，通過熱
壓方式，與銅箔、膠片一起
壓合成多層板，再經過鑽
孔、電鍍等步驟後成品。

cooling...

Stage 3
Repeating previous step
to produce the desire
exterior circuit networks.

第三階段
在內板上再次經過鍍膜、
曝光、顯影及蝕刻，作出
所需求的外層線路圖。

Stage 4
Printing text onto the
boards. Components are
then soldered onto the
boards. Finally the boards
go through a series of
rigorous tests.

第四階段
在板子上印上文字，與零件
組裝打線，衝模成型並裁
剪。最後，當然就是一連串
嚴格的檢驗。出貨啦！

DONE!!

Shopping Guide 購物指南

Writing Pad
Apart from the interior electronic circuit, the factory also designed the exterior case and packaging.

手寫板
特色：除了生產手寫板的內部電路主板之外，還包括外殼和包裝設計。

Best Seller!
Toy Model Machine
Features:
1. Popular toy in Western countries for children to make models
2. Interaction with personal computers
3. Two colors for boys and girls

玩具模型機
特色：暢銷歐美的玩具模型機，可以連接上電腦。有兩種不同顏色，適合男孩和女孩。

Air-conditioning Controller
Apart from the interior electronic circuit, the factory also designed the exterior case and packaging.

空調系統控制器
特色：除了生產該空調設備控制器的內部電路主板之外，還包括外殼和包裝設計。

LED Lighting Bulb
Features:
1. Energy efficient LED bulb
2. Various types for consumers

LED 燈泡
種類：成品
特色：1. 節能型燈泡。
2. 設有多種款式可供挑選。

Power Supply Device
Features: Providing a terminal device for power supply systems.

動力系統終端
特色：為動力系統提供終端設備。

Wining and Dining 工人的飲食

Exterior facade of the canteen 員工餐廳外觀

Canteen kitchen 員工餐廳廚房

Inside the canteen 員工餐廳室內環境

Lunch 午餐

Name: canteen set lunch provided for workers
Features: workers can pick four out of eight kinds of
    dishes, rice and fruits
Lunch time: 11:30 am

Taste ranking: ★★★

名稱：肉丸、炒蛋、青椒肉丁、腐竹
特點：每天供應八款不同菜式，工人可以選擇其中四
      種菜式，並有水果。
午飯時間：上午 11:30

美味指數：★★★

Dinner 晚餐

Name: outside restaurant
Features: more choices and more hometown flavors
Dinner time: 5:30 pm

Taste ranking: ★★★★★

名稱：家鄉紅燒肉、炒豌豆、青椒炒肉片、雞湯
特點：廠外餐廳有更多的家鄉口味和選擇
午飯時間：下午 5:30

美味指數：★★★★★

Accommodation 工人的住宿

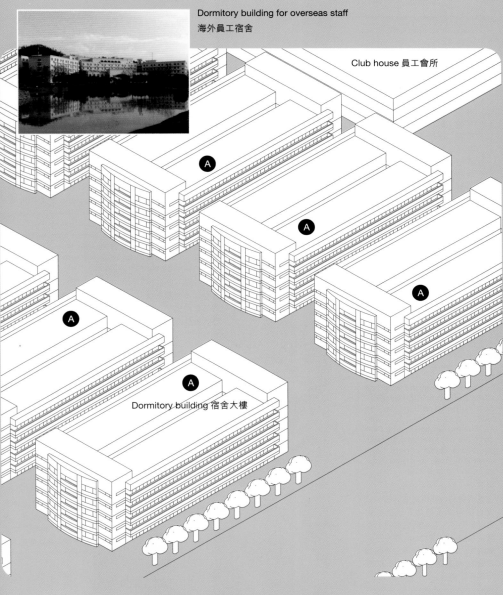

Dormitory building for overseas staff
海外員工宿舍

Club house 員工會所

A

A

A

A

A

Dormitory building 宿舍大樓

A

Worker suite
Capacity: 6 persons
Size of the accommodation: 26 sqm

工人合宿
居住人數：6 人
面積：26 平方米

Employee of the Day 今日之星

Nickname: Xiao Mei
Age: 22
Hometown: Sichuan Province
Marital status: Single
Post: Assembling worker
No. of years in the factory: 4
Monthly income: RMB 1,100

暱稱：小梅
年齡：22
家鄉：四川省
婚姻狀況：單身
職位：裝配工
在此工廠的年資：4 年
月薪：RMB 1,100

Workers' uniform in the factory 職員制服

How it started
I saw a recruitment advertisement at the entrance of the industry zone. There are many people looking for jobs at that gate every day.

如何開始
我就是由工業區門口的中介介紹下，找到這工作。園區門口有招工廣告，每天很多人在找工作。

Recent changes
Since the financial crisis, the orders have reduced a lot. So we don't need to work over time often. Many people left the factory. Most workers here are from Henan and Sichuan Provinces.

近況改變
自從去年金融危機以來，廠裏少了訂單，我們部門沒有很多加班了，很多人也離去了。廠裏河南人最多，然後就是四川人。

Nowadays
The environment and security here are good. The food is not bad. It is usually very late when our work is completed. Sometimes I will go to the internet cafe to chat on QQ with my friends. On weekends, I will go to the department store with my peers. Every month I will send 200 RMB to my parents, so I don't spend a lot.

現在
這裏環境和治安還是很好的，伙食也還可以。平常下班後，也已經很晚了，有空就去網吧上上網，和朋友聊聊 QQ。週末可能和同事去逛逛百貨公司。每個月我會給家裏寄 200 塊，所以平時都很節儉。

What I think about the factory
Before I started working in this factory, I thought the exterior looked grand and that it was a large factory; therefore, I wanted to work here. However once I started, I realized it was not up to my expectations.

對工廠感想
沒有進廠之前，覺得外表挺華麗，畢竟是大廠，很想進來看看，不過進來之後，覺得也就是這樣罷了。

Future plan
I am thinking to go somewhere else to have a look, maybe Shanghai or Ningbo. After all, I am still young.

未來計劃
再做幾年吧，然後可能換個地方去看看，可能去上海或寧波。反正我還年輕嘛。

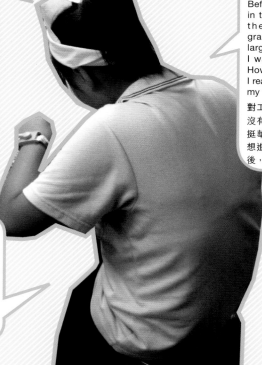

Around the Clock 他／她的一天

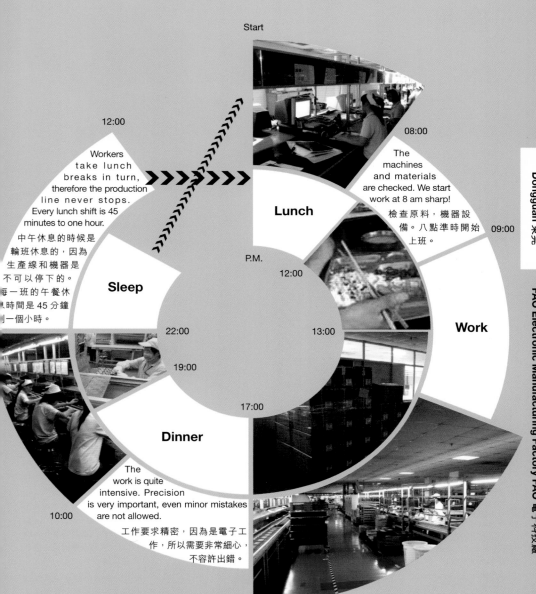

Start

08:00

12:00

Workers take lunch breaks in turn, therefore the production line never stops. Every lunch shift is 45 minutes to one hour.

中午休息的時候是輪班休息的，因為生產線和機器是不可以停下的。每一班的午餐休息時間是 45 分鐘到一個小時。

The machines and materials are checked. We start work at 8 am sharp!

檢查原料，機器設備。八點準時開始上班。

Lunch

Sleep

P.M.
12:00

22:00

13:00

19:00

Work

17:00

Dinner

The work is quite intensive. Precision is very important, even minor mistakes are not allowed.

工作要求精密，因為是電子工作，所以需要非常細心，不容許出錯。

10:00

09:30

GUANGZHOU
廣州

Guangzhou 廣州

Previously known in English
and other European languages
as Canton, Guangzhou is the
principal city of the Guangdong
Province of southern China. The
city is located north of the Pearl
River and about 120 km northwest
of Hong Kong.

At the 2000 census, the city had
an official population of 6 million, but a
consolidated urban population of roughly 12
million, making it the most populous city in the
province and the third most populous metropolitan
area in China.

Guangzhou is the main manufacturing hub of the Pearl
River Delta, and a key transportation hub and trading
port, with access to the South China Sea.

廣州從前被英國人和歐洲人稱為「廣東」。
她是中國廣東省的省會，位於珠江北面，約
於香港西北面 124 公里。

根據 2000 年官方人口統計，廣州有 600
萬人口，但據聞實際人口約有 1,200
萬，這使廣州成為廣東省最多人口
聚居之城，亦是全中國第三最多
人居住的都市。

由於位處南中國海，廣州是
珠三角的製造業、貿易和交
通樞紐。

Land Use 土地利用

Most of the development appears in the middle of the city along the Pearl River. The north of the city is contained by mountains and the south by wetlands.

廣州由於地理條件而呈現出北山南海中城的總體用地形態，主要的建設沿珠江河，建在市中心。

Administration 分區

Guangzhou is a sub-provincial city. It has direct jurisdiction over ten districts and two county-level cities.

目前廣州市管轄 10 個市轄區（市區）、代管 2 個縣級市（郊區），當中合共 130 個街道辦事處。

Subdistricts 城鎮體系

Guangzhou contains 34 subdistricts.

廣州市有 34 個鎮。

Road System 道路系統

The road system of Guangzhou is well developed, especially the highways. Guangzhou is the fourth city in China to have an underground metro system.

廣州道路交通建設，尤其是高架橋與內外環路、高速公路非常發達。廣州市是中國第四個擁有地鐵的城市。

Rail System 鐵路系統

Guangzhou has four main railway lines branching from two main stations. Baiyun airport lies within 7 km of the CBD.

廣州有四條主要的鐵路線和兩個站點。並與距離市中心約 7 公里的白雲機場連接。

Industries 工業類型

Guangzhou is one of the oldest industrial cities of China. The three pillar industries are automobile, petrochemical, and electronics manufacturing .

廣州是中國的老工業區。目前，汽車、石油化工、電子產品製造是廣州的三大支柱工業。

First map of Guangzhou
第一張廣州的地圖

Xiguan was located on the western side of ancient Guangzhou. It was the commercial center during the Ming and Qing dynasties. A typical Xiguan house was three stories high and housed wealthy businessmen and government officials.

西關位於廣州舊城區西面，在明清時期是業中心。西關的樓房常 3 層樓高，佔地 1 至 150 平方米。許富人和政府官員都住西關的大屋。

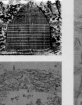

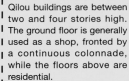

Qilou buildings are between two and four stories high. The ground floor is generally used as a shop, fronted by a continuous colonnade, while the floors above are residential.

騎樓在 1920 年開建設，每棟有兩四層樓高。在首的前面是連續的廊，門廊後面是店，樓上是住宅。

市州廣

Guangzhou

Southern Song Dynasty

1152

Qing Dynasty

1845

Republic of China

1925

COLL. IISG

鋼

以 鋼 为 纲．全面跃进
YI GANG WEI GANG QUAN MIAN YUE JIN

In May 1958, after the second session of the Party Congress, Guangdong pioneered the "Great Leap Forward." It focused on the production of steel and required such huge quantities of iron ore and fuel that it led to an unprecedented shortage. This prompted people to cut down trees for firewood, triggering natural disasters and a grain shortage which led to mass famine.

1958 年 5 月，中共八大二次會議後，廣東同全國各地掀起了「大躍進」高潮。煉鋼需要鐵礦、焦炭、燃料等材料。由於鐵礦不足，於是全民不下田耕作，改而上山採礦，使糧食產量大減。由於燃料不足，只好上山伐林，把一座又一座青山砍得光光，引發日後的天災。

The 16th Asian Games was held in Guangzhou in 2010. The city invested RMB 260 billion into the construction of stadiums and associated infrastructure.

第十六屆亞運會在 2010 年在廣州舉行，廣州投入了 260 億元人民幣建設基礎設施和比賽場館。

Persons 11
(million)

Total Population

China Reform & Open Door Policy

The People's Republic of China was founded in 1949.

10

9

8

1978 1988   1998   2008

Guangzhou 廣州 Liwan District 荔灣區

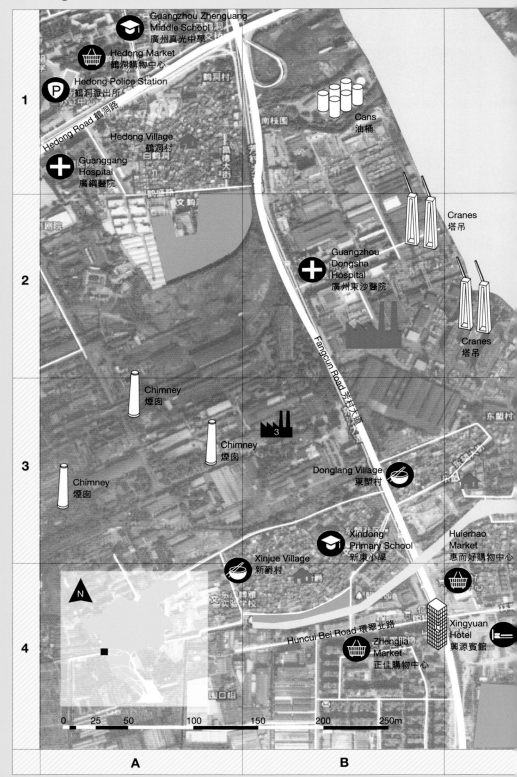

Guangzhou Zhenguang Middle School 廣州真光中學

Hedong Market 鶴洞購物中心

Hedong Police Station 鶴洞派出所

Hedong Road 鶴洞路

Hedong Village 鶴洞村

Guanggang Hospital 廣鋼醫院

Cans 油桶

Cranes 塔吊

Guangzhou Dongsha Hospital 廣州東沙醫院

Cranes 塔吊

Chimney 煙囪

Chimney 煙囪

Chimney 煙囪

Fangcun Road 芳村大道

Donglang Village 東塱村

Huierhao Market 惠而好購物中心

Xindong Primary School 新東小學

Xinjue Village 新爵村

Xingyuan Hotel 興源賓館

Huncui Bei Road 環翠北路

Zhengjia Market 正佳購物中心

N

0   25   50   100   150   200   250m

A   B

Shipyard 造船廠

The shipyard factory was founded in the 1950s. It has a long history in China. It produces and develops tankers. Because of the noise pollution it generates and the shortage of land, the factory has to move out of the city.

造船廠始建於 1950 年代，有着非常悠久的歷史。主要以造船為核心企業，研發靈便型液貨船。由於噪音與土地限制等問題，船廠將搬出市區，尋求更好的發展。

Paper factory 造紙廠

The paper factory has existed for more than 50 years and occupies more than 200 hectares along the Pearl River. The main product of this well-known factory is paper for newsprint papers.

50 多年歷史的造紙廠同樣位於珠江邊，佔地 200 多公頃。主要產品為報紙的紙張，風靡廣州。

Steel factory 鋼鐵廠

Established in the 1950s, this is the third steel factory in China. Because of the rising land value and air pollution caused by the factory, it will be relocated.

始創於 1950 年代，是中國第三大鋼鐵製造基地，隨着土地的升值及環境污染問題的日益嚴重，鋼廠同樣面臨着搬遷的問題。

Shipyard 造船廠

A1 **A2** Bird's eye view 鳥瞰圖

B Main production area 主要生產區

At the shipyard, the huge cranes, the old factory plants and the constant noise lend a unique industrial character to the site.

當置身於船廠的時候，巨大的機器結構，老舊的廠房，忙碌的人群還有無邊的噪聲，都顯示出該處的工業用途。

C1 Original building 舊樓

C2 New building 新樓

D Assembly area 分段區

E Offices 辦公區

F Manufacturing building 作業區

Factory name: Shipyard Factory
Factory address: Fangcun, Guangzhou
Plot size: 65 hectares
No. of workers: >5,000
Construction era: 1950s

工廠名稱：造船廠
工廠地址：廣州，芳村
用地面積：65 公頃
工人數量：> 5,000 人
建設年代：1950 年代

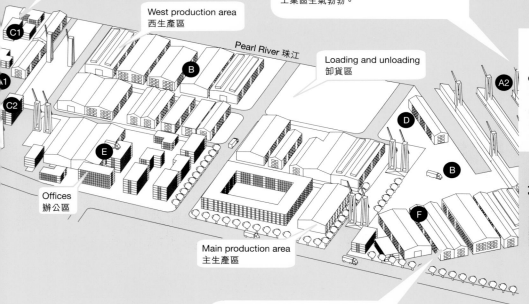

These buildings were initially used as offices until the exponential growth of the industry required their change of use into manufacturing buildings.

這些生產建築是廠區的老建築之一，由辦公室改造而來。猶如船廠的發展，空置多年後被重新利用。

The cranes can be considered as landmarks of the industrial area. They come in a variety of colors and heights, varying from 30 to 80 meters, and animate the skylines.

起重機是工廠的地標，他們色彩繽紛，高度從 30–80 米不等。他們在空中移動，令整個工業區生氣勃勃。

West production area
西生產區

Pearl River 珠江

Loading and unloading
卸貨區

Guangzhou 廣州

Shipyard 造船廠

Offices
辦公區

Main production area
主生產區

The old factory plants are built in an enigmatic 1950s Soviet style. The buildings are built with red bricks and contain a large interior space.

這些前蘇聯樣式的老廠房建於 60 年前。這些建築的特點是紅磚牆，簡潔及寬敞的空間，殘留着古老的記憶。

Production Line 生產流程

Materials:
Steel, iron, tubes, sections, mainly from Chongqing

原材料：
鋼鐵、鋼管、分段，主要來自重慶。

Stage 1
First, the different ship segments are welded together. The most labor-intensive job is the painting of the sections, which needs to be done outside.

第一步：
首先將分段船體焊接，員工們在不同的部份工作，最費時的工作是油漆，需要室外作業。

Sha Sha!
沙沙！

Stage 2
Operating cranes dominate the river bank, where they place the segments onto the dock. Only experienced workers can do this high-risk job.

第二步：
河邊的塔吊負責將準備好的的分段運輸到船塢上面。這工具需要專業人士駕馭，因為非常危險。

Careful!
小心！

Stage 3
Workers check details on the dock and weld the joints to consolidate the different pieces. Sometimes, the working conditions are so dangerous that workers are required to work in a team.

第三步：
工人們在船務上檢查細節，並焊接必要的結合點。有時工作環境較危險，需要安全工具。

Stage 4
Finally, engineers adjust the engine and test the performance of the ship in the Pearl River, together with the shipowners and workers.

第四步：
最後一步是工程師調試引擎，與船東和工人一起在珠江試航。

TESTING
試航

Shopping Guide 購物指南

Product 2
Name: Propeller
Features: 1. 360° full turn
        2. High efficiency

螺旋槳，360°高效全回轉，
適用於多種船型。

Best seller!
Product 1
Name: Tai An Kou
Features: 1. Carrying capacity: 17,550 tons
        2. Semi submerged ship
        3. Commercial and military use
Mass produced since: 2000
Length: 156 m

泰安口：擁有 17,550 噸搬運容量。適合商業和軍
用。在 2000 年開始大規模生產。全長 156m。

Product 3
Name: Mooring guide holes
Features: 1. Casting product
        2. Various sizes

導纜孔，適用於多種船型。

Product 4
Name: Hai Xun 31
Features: 1. Continuous deck
        2. Helipad
        3. Well designed exterior
Mass produced since: 2003
Length: 112 m

海巡 31：連續甲板，直昇機降落設備。 在 2003
年開始大規模生產。全長 112m。

Wining and Dining 工人的飲食

Shipowners' canteen 船東餐廳

Workers' canteen 員工餐廳

Canteen in urban village 城中的食堂

Lunch 午餐

Name: Canteen set lunch provided for workers
Features: Four kinds of dishes, including rice and fruits
Lunch time: 11:30 am

Taste ranking: ★★★★

名稱：清蒸鯇魚、西紅柿炒蛋、芥菜、白飯
特點：每天供應四款不同菜式，夏天時額外有涼茶供應
午飯時間：上午 11:30

美味指數：★★★★

Dinner 晚餐

Name: A set meal provided for workers by a
restaurant in the urban village
Features: Three kinds of dishes, including rice and
soup
Dinner time: 5:30 pm

Taste ranking: ★★★★★

名稱：清蒸鯇魚、西紅柿炒蛋、芥菜、白飯
特點：每天供應三款不同菜式，夏天時額外有涼茶
供應
午飯時間：下午 5:30

美味指數：★★★★★

Accommodation 工人的住宿

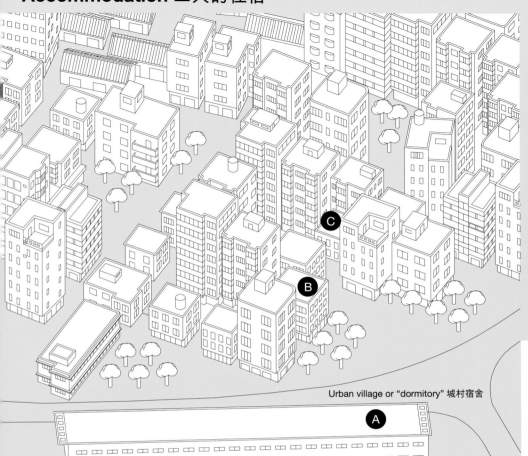

Urban village or "dormitory" 城村宿舍

A

Worker suite
Capacity: 4–6 persons
Size of the accommodation: 15 sqm

家庭戶型宿舍
居住人數：4–6 人
面積：15 平方米

B

Officer suite
Capacity: 2 persons
Size of the accommodation: 12 sqm

工人宿舍
容納人數：2 人
面積：12 平方米

C

Urban village for group of workers or family
Capacity: 1–4 persons
Size of the accommodation: 8–60 sqm

工人宿舍
容納人數：1–4 人
面積：8–60 平方米

Employee of the Day 今日之星

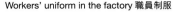

Nickname: Xiao Wu
Age: 30
Home Town: Hunan Province
Status: Married with two sons
Post: Painter
No. of years in the factory: 2
Monthly Income: RMB 1500

暱稱：小伍
年齡：30
家鄉：湖南省
婚姻狀況：已婚，育有兩子
職位：油漆工
在此工廠的年資：2 年
月薪：RMB 1500

Workers' uniform in the factory 職員制服

The color of each uniform refers to a different job. The most common one is blue, which belongs to the manufacturing workers. Workers also need to wear safety helmets for protection. A rule in the factory states that if you forget to wear a helmet, you will be fined.

不同的制服顏色代表不同的工作。最普通的是工人們穿的藍色。同時，他們需要佩戴安全帽。一旦忘記佩戴，會被罰款。

Away from my hometown

I am from Hunan Province. I have not been back to my hometown since I moved to Guangzhou two years ago.

我來自湖南，在廣州呆了兩年都沒有回過家鄉。

About my family

My wife and our children live in Guangzhou now. Since our sons are only one and four years old, my wife stays home in order to take care of them.

我的妻子和孩子都住在廣州。因為我們的孩子只有 4 歲和 1 歲，我妻子沒有時間上班。

Making ends meet

I am living in the urban village adjacent to the factory. The rent is about 500 RMB per month, which is relatively cheap but still leaves me little money to take care of my family.

我住在工廠附近的城中村，租金只要每月 500 塊，但是我還沒有足夠的錢養家。

After work

I like the urban village here because it is quite convenient and the living expenses are cheaper. After work I go home quickly to take care of my sons. I like taking my family to go shopping in the supermarket, which is my favorite pastime.

我喜歡住在城中村，方便又便宜。平時我沒有什麼娛樂，放工後就回家帶孩子。我只喜歡和家人一起去超市買東西。

We came here as a group

We were recruited in our hometown as a group of 100 people to work here. After five years, we may change to work for another factory.

我們是以團隊的形式來到這家工廠的，並且都是老鄉。這個工作將會持續五至六年，然後我們可能會去其他工廠。

Around the Clock 他／她的一天

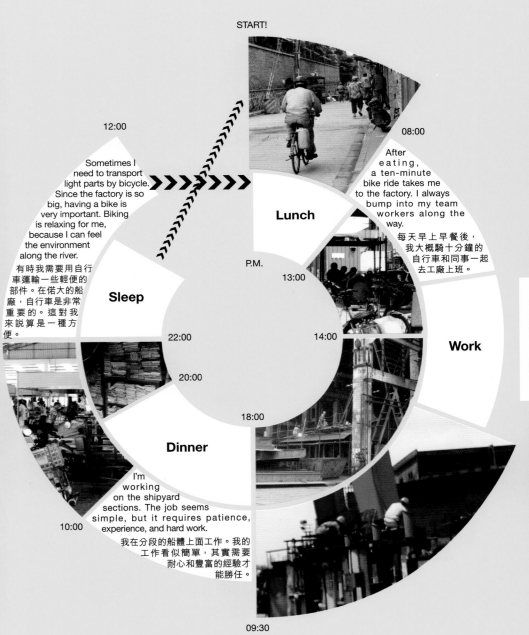

START!

08:00
After eating, a ten-minute bike ride takes me to the factory. I always bump into my team workers along the way.

每天早上早餐後，我大概騎十分鐘的自行車和同事一起去工廠上班。

12:00

Sometimes I need to transport light parts by bicycle. Since the factory is so big, having a bike is very important. Biking is relaxing for me, because I can feel the environment along the river.

有時我需要用自行車運輸一些輕便的部件。在偌大的船廠，自行車是非常重要的。這對我來說算是一種方便。

Lunch

P.M.

13:00

Sleep

14:00

22:00

Work

20:00

18:00

Dinner

10:00

I'm working on the shipyard sections. The job seems simple, but it requires patience, experience, and hard work.

我在分段的船體上面工作。我的工作看似簡單，其實需要耐心和豐富的經驗才能勝任。

09:30

Guangzhou 廣州

Shipyard 造船廠

143

Guangzhou 廣州 Donghuanjie Town 東環街鎮

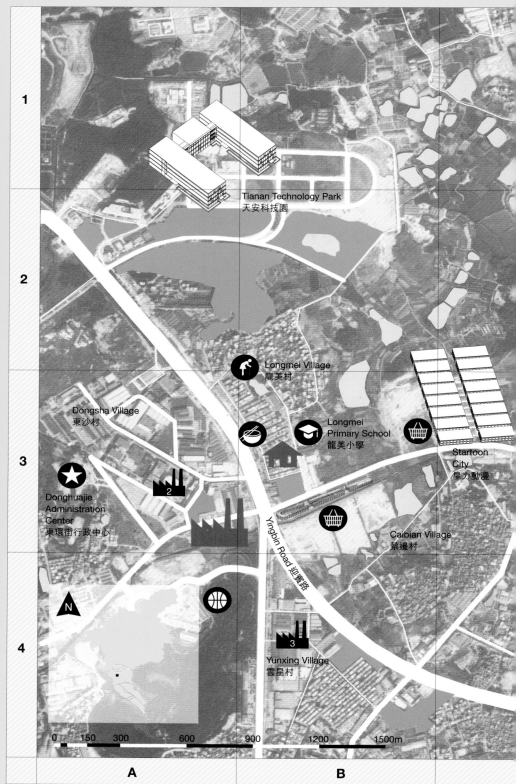

1

2

Tianan Technology Park
天安科技園

Longmei Village
龍美村

Dongsha Village
東沙村

Longmei
Primary School
龍美小學

Startoon
City
星力動漫

3

Donghuajie
Administration
Center
東環街行政中心

2

Caibian Village
蔡邊村

Yingbin Road 迎賓路

N

3

4

Yunxing Village
雲星村

0   150   300   600   900   1200   1500m

A   B

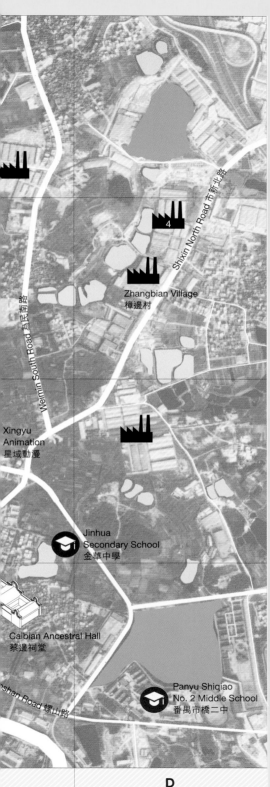

Shixin North Road 市新北路

Weimin South Road 為民南路

Zhangbian Village
樟邊村

Xingyu
Animation
星域動漫

Jinhua
Secondary School
金華中學

Caibian Ancestral Hall
蔡邊祠堂

'shan Road 螺山路

Panyu Shiqiao
No. 2 Middle School
番禺市橋二中

D

Video game assembly factory
電子遊戲機廠

Donghuan town produces video game machines and casino machines. As it is illegal to make casino machines in China, the production process has been distributed across the town. The factory produces gift machines, basketball machines, shooting machines, simulation machines, dance machines, and racing machines.

該廠主要生產禮品機、籃球機、射擊機、模擬機、跳舞機、賽車機等。

Video game CPU factory
電子遊戲機中央處理器工廠

The factory, built in 2008, produces the CPUs of video game machines. It employs 300 workers.

該廠主要生產遊戲機的中央處理器，共有 300 名工人。
該工廠建於 2008 年。

Video game accessory factory
電子遊戲機零部件工廠

This factory produces all kinds of video game machine accessories, such as coin boxes, control handles, and joysticks.

電子遊戲機零部件工廠生產各種各樣的零部件，包括投幣箱、控桿、按鈕等等。

Casino machine cabinet factory
賭博機外殼箱工廠

The casino machine cabinet factory is under heavy security by dogs and security guards.

賭博機外殼廠保安嚴密，有保安人員和狗看守。

145

Video game machine factory 電子遊戲機廠

Ⓐ1 Ⓐ2 Yingbin Road 迎賓路

Ⓑ1 Ⓑ2 Electronics street 電子街

This company develops and sells video game machines. It was set up in Nanjing in 1995. For business development purposes, the company moved to Panyu, Guangzhou in 1997, because of its close proximity to Hong Kong, Taiwan and Southeast Asia.

這是一家集系統集成、遊戲開發和銷售於一體的遊戲機生產企業。公司於 1995 年 8 月於南京成立，後因業務發展，於 1997 年遷到鄰近香港、台灣和東南亞的廣州番禺。

Ⓒ CPU building 中央處理器工廠

Ⓓ Loading bay 卸貨區

Ⓔ Warehouse A 倉庫甲

Ⓕ Warehouse B 倉庫乙

Factory name: Video game machine factory
Factory address: Dongsha Village, Panyu, Guangzhou
Plot size: 12 hectares
No. of workers: 1,000
Construction era: 1990s

工廠名稱：電子遊戲機工廠
工廠地址：廣州市番禺區東環街東沙村
用地面積：12 公頃
工人數量：1,000 人
建設年代：1990 年代

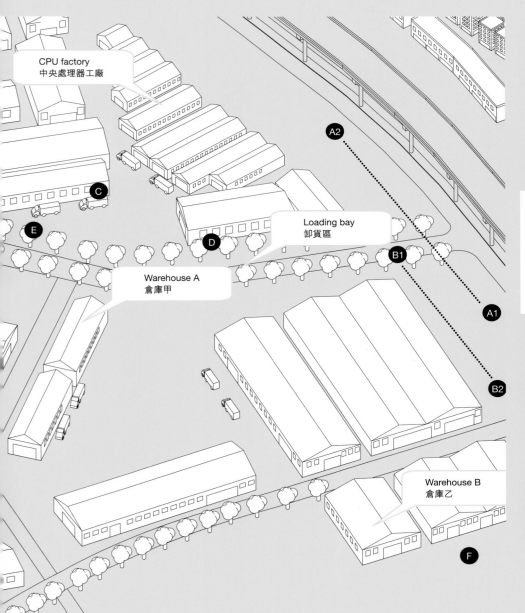

CPU factory
中央處理器工廠

Loading bay
卸貨區

Warehouse A
倉庫甲

Warehouse B
倉庫乙

Production Line 生產流程

Materials:
CPU
Machine component
Wood and plastic cabinet
原材料：
中央處理器、零部件、塑料
和木質機箱

> THIS IS JUST A PIECE OF CAKE...
> 這工作也太簡單了

Stage 1
Workers process th
cabinet using differen
machines. They assembl
and install the panels o
the production belt.

第一階段
工人用不同的機器為遊戲
機的機箱加工，在流水
線上將一塊塊板組裝在一
起。

> KACHA!
> 咔嚓！

Stage 2
Workers use a special
machine to examine the
CPU's functioning.

第二階段
工人通過一台特殊的機器檢
查中央處理器是否運作正
常。這需要耐心和細心。

> TIK TIK...
> 嘀嘀

Stage 3
Workers assemble and
install the CPU into the
cabinet, and weld it firmly
in place. Afterwards, they
examine it one more time.

第三階段
工人將中央處理器安裝到
機箱裏面，焊接穩固後，
再檢查一遍。

Stage 4
The final step in the
installation includes adding
finishing touches such as
buttons and small LED
lights.

第四階段
最後，工人將零部件按鈕及
燈安裝到機箱，整個遊戲機
的安裝過程就完成了。

> CHHH!
> 呇

Shopping Guide 購物指南

Product 2
Name: Race car arcade machine
Features: 1. Realistic experience
           2. Built-in movement
           3. Latest technology
Mass produced since: 2005
Price: RMB 2,200

沿用了八代的筐體設計，遊戲畫面表現進一步增強，操作感也相應革新，玩家在新作中能體驗完全不一樣的飆車手感。

Product 3
Name: Shooting machine
Features:
1. Realistic experience
2. Two-player option
3. Second player can join or quit any time
Mass produced since: 2006
Price: RMB 1,800

Shooting 42 寸高清液晶，震撼的槍戰場景，讓玩家能身臨其境地感受與敵人搏鬥的驚險與刺激。

Product 4
Name: Basketball machine
Features: 1. Keeps the players fit
           2. Easy to learn and play
           3. High amusement value
Mass produced since: 2006
Price: RMB 2,000

Basketball 系列採用超級得分王專用電腦板，時尚動感金屬質感外形設計，組合式機架方便組裝。

Best Seller!
Product 1
Name: Coin-pushing machine
Features 1. Easy to learn and play
          2. Legally approved casino
             machine
          3. Built-in video game
Mass produced since: 2006
Price: RMB 2,500

合法化的賭博機，程序和做工相對複雜，所以價錢較高，越來越受到市場的歡迎。

Product 5
Name: Dancing machine
Features: 1. Keeps the players fit
           2. Easy to learn and play
           3. High amusement value
Mass produced since: 2006
Price: RMB 2,500

Dancing 系列擁有雙屏顯示，玩家可更有自信地展示多變舞姿；3D 立體圖畫，高清顯示屏，視覺更清晰，帶來更大享受；歌曲全新，勁ú流行。

Product 6
Name: Simulation machine
Features: 1. High quality and low price
           2. Easy to learn and play
           3. High amusement value
Mass produced since: 2004
Price: RMB 1,000

Simulation 系列高清顯示屏，視覺更清晰，帶來更大享受，時尚動感金屬質感外形設計，組合式機架方便組裝。

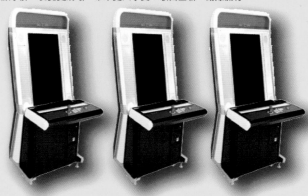

Wining and Dining 工人的飲食

Exterior facade of the restaurant 餐廳外觀

Restaurant kitchen 餐廳廚房

Inside the restaurant 餐廳內環境

Lunch 午餐

Name: Fried rice, sandwiches, bread, soy milk
Features: With four kinds of dishes, rice and drinks
Lunch time: 12:00 pm

Taste ranking: ★★★★★

名稱：肉和菜、麵包、三文治、豆奶
特點：每天供應四款不同菜式，有例湯和豆奶選擇
午飯時間：中午 12:00

美味指數：★★★★★

Dinner 晚餐

Name: Guilin rice noodle with beef
Features: Simple and cheap
Dinner time: 7:30 pm

Taste ranking: ★★

名稱：牛肉桂林米粉
特點：簡單省時，由於午餐比較豐富和下班時間較晚，
　　　晚餐相對簡單
午飯時間：下午 7:30

美味指數：★★

Accommodation 工人的住宿

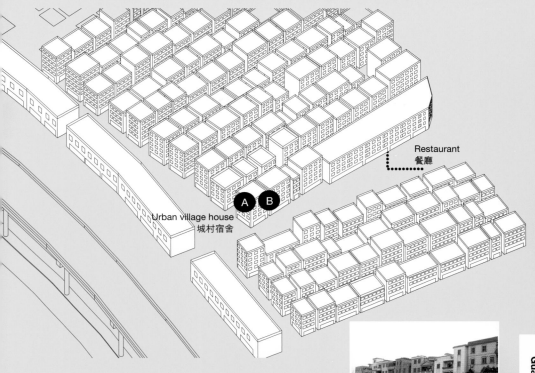

Restaurant
餐廳

 Urban village house
城村宿舍

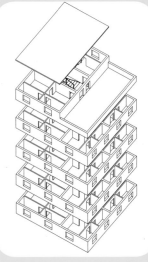

Ⓐ Family suite
Capacity: 2–4 persons
Size of the accommodation:
24 sqm

家庭戶型宿舍
居住人數：2–4 人
面積：24 平方米

Ⓑ Worker suite
Capacity: 2–4 persons
Size of the accommodation:
21 sqm

工人合宿
居住人數：2–4 人
面積：21 平方米

Typical house in urban village
Capacity: 40–80 persons
Size of the accommodation: 550 sqm

典型城村住宅
容納人數：40–80 人
面積：550 平方米

Guangzhou 廣州

Video game machine factory 電子遊戲機廠

151

Employee of the Day 今日之星

Nickname: Xiao Ming
Age: 20
Hometown: Zhaoqing, Guangdong Province
Marital status: Single
Post: Assembly worker
No. of years in the factory: 2
Monthly income: RMB 2,000
Other working experience : None

暱稱：小明
年齡：20
家鄉：廣東省肇慶市
婚姻狀況：單身
職位：裝配工人
在此工廠的年資：2 年
月薪：RMB 2,000
其他工作經驗：沒有

Workers' uniform in the factory 職員制服

About my job
My job is pretty easy and there is not a lot of work to do. I work for eight hours a day. If there is no order, I can have a rest and chat with colleagues.

在這裏工作不算太忙，一天 8 個小時，沒有訂單的時候，還可以休息一下，和同事聊聊天。

Saving money
The salary here is reasonable; they pay me 1,500–2,300 RMB per month. The harder you work, the more you get paid. I manage to save about 800–1,200 RMB per month.

這裏的工資待遇算是不錯了。1,500–2,300 元一個月，多勞多得。我通常每個月能存 800 到 1,200 元。

Getting married
I am single now. I am getting married to a local girl next year. Then I will work here permanently.

我還沒有結婚，計劃明年和本地的女朋友結婚，還是在這裏工作生活，不打算回老家了。

About my leisure time
After work, I like to play basketball with my friends in the village. Sometimes I like to play video games.

平時下班後，我喜歡在村裏的籃球場和朋友打籃球，或者去遊戲機室玩遊戲機。

A crowded home
I live in the urban village nearby. It takes about five minutes to go to the factory by foot. The urban village is very crowded; buildings are very close to one another. If I have enough money, I would like to move out.

我住在附近的城村，上班大概需要五分鐘的步行時間。不過城村很擁擠，住宅都靠得很近。如果我有足夠的錢，我想搬離這裏。

Around the Clock 他／她的一天

START

12:00

I have two hours' break at noon. The factory offers several free lunch options, such as fried rice, bread, sandwiches, and soy milk.

中午我通常有兩個小時的休息時間，工廠免費提供二餐，包括多種選擇，如炒飯、麵包、文治、豆奶等。

Sleep

Lunch

P.M.

13:00

22:00

14:00

20:00

Work

18:00

Dinner

In the morning, we have less work to do. Typically, we just do the work that was not finished the day before.

早上的工作通常比較輕鬆——就是完成昨天沒有完成的工作。

10:00

09:30

08:00

I usually go to Hubei Restaurant to have breakfast. Noodles are delicious and cost only RMB 5.

我喜歡去湖北餐廳吃早餐，我喜歡吃麵，那裏的麵便宜好吃，只需要五塊錢。

09:00

Video game machine factory 電子遊戲機廠

FOSHAN
佛山

The town of Foshan is many centuries old and is famous for its porcelain industries. It is the third largest city in Guangdong and has become relatively affluent compared to other Chinese cities; it is now the home of many large private enterprises. Foshan is also famous for its numerous martial arts "Wing Chun" schools which attract many people into the town to train and spar. Foshan has recently seen transformations triggered by China's booming economy.

In January 2009 the National People's Congress approved a development plan for the Pearl River Delta Region. On March 19, 2009, the Guangzhou Municipal Government and Foshan Municipal Government both agreed to establish a framework to merge the two cities together.

There are many examples of Chinese temples and Chinese architecture in Foshan. One example is the old Zu temple, which housed the city's guardians. It has stood in Foshan for hundreds of years despite enduring many wars and the Cultural Revolution. Much of its original architecture is still intact. The temple is now used to stage traditional Cantonese operas at night.

Foshan 佛山

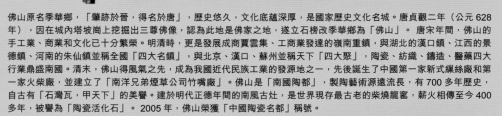

佛山原名季華鄉，「肇跡於晉，得名於唐」，歷史悠久，文化底蘊深厚，是國家歷史文化名城。唐貞觀二年（公元 628 年），因在城內塔坡崗上挖掘出三尊佛像，認為此地是佛家之地，遂立石榜改季華鄉為「佛山」。 唐宋年間，佛山的手工業、商業和文化已十分繁榮。明清時，更是發展成商賈雲集、工商業發達的嶺南重鎮，與湖北的漢口鎮、江西的景德鎮、河南的朱仙鎮並稱全國「四大名鎮」，與北京、漢口、蘇州並稱天下「四大聚」，陶瓷、紡織、鑄造、醫藥四大行業鼎盛南國。清末，佛山得風氣之先，成為我國近代民族工業的發源地之一，先後誕生了中國第一家新式繅絲廠和第一家火柴廠，並建立了「南洋兄弟煙草公司竹嘴廠」。佛山是「南國陶都」，製陶藝術源遠流長，有 700 多年歷史，自古有「石灣瓦，甲天下」的美譽。建於明代正德年間的南風古灶，是世界現存最古老的柴燒龍窯，薪火相傳至今 400 多年，被譽為「陶瓷活化石」。 2005 年，佛山榮獲「中國陶瓷名都」稱號。

佛山是聞名的武術之鄉，是中國南派武術的主要發源地。明初，佛山武術已相當普及。清末民初，佛山武術流派紛呈，湧現出一批有國際影響的武術家和武術組織，並通過各種途徑走向世界，現在世界上廣泛流行的蔡李佛拳、洪拳、詠春拳等不少拳種和流派的根都在佛山，著名武術大師黃飛鴻，武打明星李小龍等祖籍及師承亦在佛山。佛山是「獅藝之鄉」，是南獅的發源地。龍獅起舞既是融武術、舞蹈、音樂等為一體的體育競技活動，更是佛山武術重要項目之一，每年的「獅王爭霸賽」吸引了國內外廣大武術愛好者參與。禪城區是「中國龍獅運動之鄉」，南海區西樵鎮是全國唯一「中國龍獅名鎮」。

154

Road System 道路系統

Foshan is serviced by national and provincial highways. The Guangfo Highway connects Foshan with adjacent cities. The Foshan 1st Ring Road encircles the city itself.

佛山市與多條國家和省級公路連接，其中廣佛高速公路把佛山市和鄰近市鎮連接一起，另有佛山一環公路，環繞城區。

Railway System 鐵路系統

Foshan is a main interchange for railway lines linking Guangzhou, Hong Kong and the western Guangdong Province. The Guangfo Metro will provide connections to adjacent cities.

佛山是連接廣州、香港和廣東省西部鐵路主要的交通匯點。廣佛地鐵線將連接兩地。

Industries 工業類型

Foshan is the third largest manufacturing base in the PRD. Its economic strength lies in private firms and township enterprises in Shunde and Nanhai.

佛山是珠三角第三大生產基地，經濟實力集中於順德和南海的私人和鄉鎮企業。

Land Use 土地利用

Other than the major manufacturing zone at the city center, "Agricultural Model Districts" exist.

除了主要的市中心生產區域，佛山市設有農業示範區。

Administration 分區

The city of Foshan has five county-level districts: Chancheng, Nanhai, Sanshui, Gaoming and Shunde. There are 64 township-level divisions, including 37 towns and 27 subdistricts.

佛山全市有 5 個縣級區，包括：禪城、南海、三水、高明和順德。佛山分成 64 個城鎮區域。

History 歷史

Ancient map of Foshan
Chancheng was part of Sanshui in Qing Dynasty
佛山古地圖：今天的禪城在清朝時是三水的一部分

Known as one of the four most prominent
ceramics towns in ancient China
中國古代四大陶瓷城鎮

Quarrying in Jihuaxiang 季華鄉採石場

Ceramics
陶瓷
Furnitures
家具
Nonmetal ore
非金屬礦
Stainless steel products
不銹鋼產品
Plastic products
塑料製品
Electronics and communications
電子及通信
Household electrical appliance and tools
家庭電器和工具

Development of manufacturing
industries started
佛山開始發展製造業

Foshan Town was
established
佛山鎮成立

Foshan Town
佛山鎮

It was part of
Sanshui
禪城當時是三水
的一部分

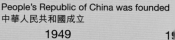

Eastern Jin Dynasty
東晉

Ming Dynasty
明朝

Qing Dynasty
清朝

People's Republic of China was founded
中華人民共和國成立

398

1506

1845

1949

19

TV was a popular electrical appliance only seen in the "ten-thousand-yuan" households during the 1980s.

1980 年代初 「萬元戶」的時髦家用電器—電視機。

Urban renewal projects initiated around Foshan. The Dongping area is the planned new city center.

佛山展開城市更新項目，東平地區將規劃成新市中心。

Upgraded to Foshan City
升格為佛山市

City Area 城市範圍

Water 河道
153 sq km

Urban 都市
690 sq km

Pollution policy: heavy industries to be moved out of Foshan
針對污染的政策，重工業遷出佛山。

Persons
(Million) 6

Guangzhou and Foshan signed the City Merge Cooperation Framework
廣佛同城合作框架協議

Merger with the Nanhai district
南海區被合併成佛山市一部分

5

Total Municipal Population
總市民人口

4

3

Foshan city with 5 districts
佛山市的五個區

Guangfo City
廣佛同城

2

1983   1988   1993   1998   2003   2010

Foshan 佛山 Shiwan Town 石灣鎮

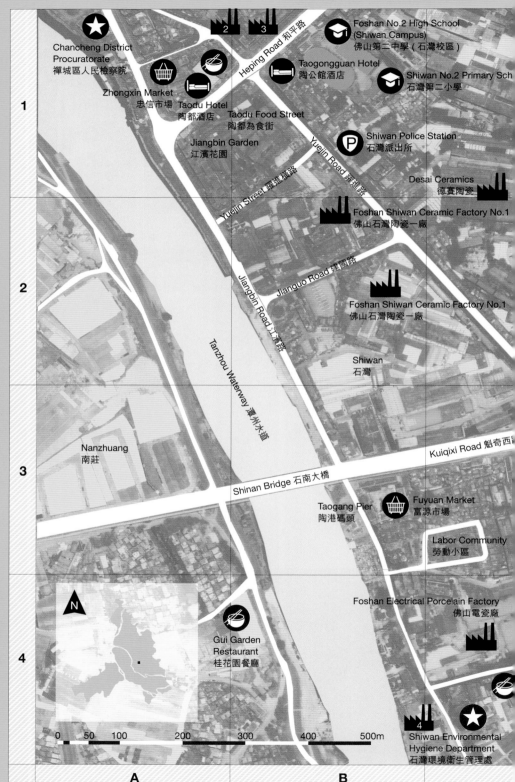

Chancheng District Procuratorate
禪城區人民檢察院

Zhongxin Market
忠信市場

Taodu Hotel
陶都酒店

Taodu Food Street
陶都為食街

Jiangbin Garden
江濱花園

Heping Road 和平路

Foshan No.2 High School (Shiwan Campus)
佛山第二中學 (石灣校區)

Taogongguan Hotel
陶公館酒店

Shiwan No.2 Primary Sch
石灣第二小學

Shiwan Police Station
石灣派出所

Desai Ceramics
德賽陶瓷

Yuelin Street 躍進街路

Yuelin Road 躍進路

Foshan Shiwan Ceramic Factory No.1
佛山石灣陶瓷一廠

Jianguo Road 建國路

Foshan Shiwan Ceramic Factory No.1
佛山石灣陶瓷一廠

Shiwan
石灣

Jiangbin Road 江濱路

Tanzhou Waterway 潭州水道

Nanzhuang
南莊

Kuiqixi Road 魁奇西路

Shinan Bridge 石南大橋

Taogang Pier
陶港碼頭

Fuyuan Market
富源市場

Labor Community
勞動小區

Foshan Electrical Porcelain Factory
佛山電瓷廠

N

Gui Garden Restaurant
桂花園餐廳

Shiwan Environmental Hygiene Department
石灣環境衛生管理處

0   50   100   200   300   400   500m

A   B

Shiwan Artistic Ceramic Factory 石灣美術陶瓷廠

Foshan 佛山

Shiwan Culture Plaza
石灣文化廣場

Shiwan Central
Wholesale Market
石灣中心批發市場

Maoxiang Road
茂祥路

Zhenzhong Road 鎮中路

NW Swan Restaurant
東北白天鵝餐廳

Heping Community
和平社區

Gui Garden Restaurant
桂花園餐廳

Shiwan Industrial Ceramic Factory
石灣工業陶瓷廠

iwan Collection Center
灣收藏天地

Tianduobao Store
天多寶百貨商店

Gongnong Road 工農路

Ziwei Road 紫薇路

Community canteen
大眾飯店

Shiwan Vocational School
石灣成校

Shiwan Seagull
Ceramic Shop
石灣海鷗陶瓷

D

Shiwan Artistic Ceramic Factory 石灣美術陶瓷廠

New Shiwan Artistic Ceramic Co. Ltd.
新石灣美術陶瓷廠有限公司
Foshan Red Lion Ceramic Co. Ltd.
佛山紅獅陶瓷有限公司

Shiwan Artistic Ceramic Factory was founded in 1956. It has more than fifty years of history, specializing in architectural and decorative ceramics.

石灣美術陶瓷廠始建於 1956 年，已有逾 50 年歷史，專業生產建築裝飾陶瓷。

Nanfeng Kiln 南風古灶

Nanfeng Kiln was built in 1506 (Ming Dynasty). Together with several ceramic factories, these form a valuable cultural site for the study of Chinese ceramics production technology.

南風古灶始建於 1506 年明朝正德年間，是對研究中國陶瓷生產技術的發展具有重要價值的全國重點文物保護單位。

Dongpeng Ceramics Co. Ltd 東鵬陶瓷股份有限公司

Dongpeng Ceramics Co. Ltd. was established in 2001. Formerly known as Foshan Dongping Ceramic Factory, it specializes in ceramic wall, floor tiles and sanitary equipment. It owns several prominent brands.

廣東東鵬陶瓷股份有限公司成立於 2001 年，前身為佛山市石灣東平陶瓷廠，專業生產牆地磚及潔具的陶瓷企業之一，擁有東鵬和金意陶品牌。

Foshan Diamond Ceramic Co. Ltd.
佛山鑽石瓷磚有限公司

Foshan Diamond Ceramic Co. Ltd. has thirty years of history. It is one of the largest ceramic factories.

佛山鑽石瓷磚有限公司有 30 多年歷史，是其中一個最大的陶瓷工廠。

Shiwan Artistic Ceramic Factory 石灣美術陶瓷廠

A1 **A2** Nanfeng Kiln 南風古灶

B1 **B2** Dongfeng Road/ Kuiqixi Road 東風路／魁奇西路

C Factory building 1 一號廠   **D** Factory building 2 and showroom 二號廠及展廳

E Loading bay 卸貨區

F Front gate 前門   **G** Factory outdoor exhibition and reception area 工廠戶外陳列空間

Shiwan Artistic Ceramic Factory 石灣美術陶瓷廠

Foshan 佛山

Factory name: Shiwan Artistic Ceramic Factory
(New Shiwan Artistic Ceramic Co. Ltd. & Foshan Red
Lion Ceramic Co. Ltd.)
Factory address: 17 Dongfeng Road, Shiwan, Foshan
Plot size: 3 hectares
No. of workers: 400
Construction era: 1980s

工廠名稱：石灣美術陶瓷廠
（新石灣美術陶瓷廠有限公司及佛山紅獅陶
瓷有限公司）
工廠地址：佛山市石灣鎮東風路 17 號
用地面積：3 公頃
工人數量：400
建設年代：1980 年代

Shiwan Artistic Ceramic Factory has fifty years of
history and was rebranded into two different companies
in 2006. They specialize in Shiwan traditional figures
and "Red Lion" building decorations. The factory has
been designated as an industrial tourist attraction.

石灣美術陶瓷廠有 50 多年的歷史，並於 2006 年更注冊
為兩間有限公司，分別專製石灣公仔和紅獅裝飾建築材
料。現時，陶瓷廠被譽為工業旅遊景點。

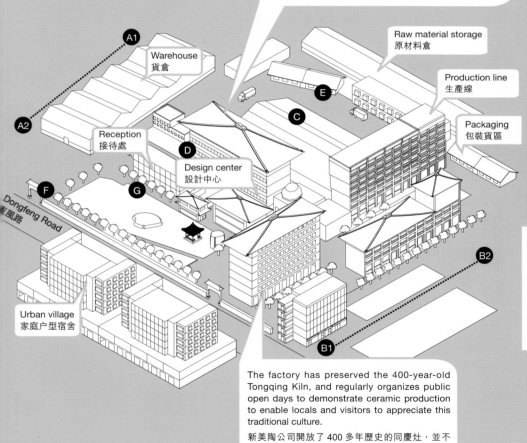

A1

Warehouse
貨倉

A2

Raw material storage
原材料倉

E

C

Production line
生產線

Reception
接待處

D

Packaging
包裝貨區

Design center
設計中心

F

G

Dongfeng Road
東風路

B2

Urban village
家庭户型宿舍

B1

The factory has preserved the 400-year-old
Tongqing Kiln, and regularly organizes public
open days to demonstrate ceramic production
to enable locals and visitors to appreciate this
traditional culture.

新美陶公司開放了 400 多年歷史的同慶灶，並不
時燒製陶藝品供人欣賞，展示石灣陶藝發展。

Production Line 生產流程

Materials:
Gypsum; clay slurry
porcelain glaze, ceramic
grain

原材料：
石膏、泥漿、釉彩和陶瓷原泥

Clay slurry 泥漿

Ceramic grain 陶瓷原泥

專注設計！

Stage 1
Design the artworks
設計原件

Stage 2
Mold-making: Gypsum is
plastered on the original
artworks.
製模：把石膏塗在原件上，
待其凝固後製成石膏模。石
膏模可重複使用。

Gypsum mould 製成石膏模

Stage 3
Shaping: clay slurry is poured
into the molds. The mold
can then be taken apart into
two halves to remove the
solidified clay item after 20
to 40 minutes.

注漿成型：把泥漿注入石膏
模內。由於石膏具吸水性，
靠近石膏的部分泥漿會在 20
至 40 分鐘內凝固並成型。

Pouring clay slurry 注入泥漿

Solidified pieces 凝固組件

Striving for
perfection
上品

Stage 4
Assembling: the artworks
are assembled by putting
several separate parts
together according to the
design of the original piece.

修補：工藝品分幾部分成型，
修補的工作就是按原作風貌
把組件安裝修整成一件完整
的工藝品。

Assembling 安裝和修整組件

Glazing 上釉

Stage 5
Glazing: After desiccation,
different colors are glazed
on the surface of the artworks.
上釉：修補完畢並經乾燥後。

Stage 6
Firing: It takes approximately
12 hours to finalize the artistic
pieces in a shuttle kiln burning
at 1250 degrees Celsius.

煆燒：將工藝品置入窯內，
用 1250 攝氏度的高溫經 12
小時煆燒，出窯後即為成品。

Kiln 工藝品燒陶窯

出窯！

Shopping Guide 購物指南

Good Fortune (Fu), Prosperity (Lu), and Longevity (Shou)
Type: Sculpture
Dimensions: 440x230; 460x250; 400x230 (mm)
Feature: Designed by nationally-known sculptors

三星喜臨門
種類：陶像
特色：三星喜臨門為陶瓷
藝術收藏品，高檔品，
由中國工藝美術大師創作。

Vase of Peace
Type: Vase
Features: 1. Traditional decorative
          patterns symbolizing
          peace and prosperity
       2. Colorful pattern

竹報平安
種類：花瓶
特色：民間吉祥圖案有畫竹和兒童
放爆竹，寓意報平安。

Lu Yu Tea Sculpture
Type: Sculpture
Dimensions: 150x130 (mm)
Features: 1. Traditional character
       2. Icon of Chinese tea culture

陸羽品茶
種類：陶像
特色：陸羽品茶筆觸精細，場景
生動，人物神態捕捉準確，刻畫
細緻入微，唯妙唯肖。

Shiwan Artistic Ceramic Factory 石灣美術陶瓷廠

Best Seller!
Kungfu master Wong Fei-hung
Type: Sculpture
Dimension: 350x260 (mm)
Features: 1. Kungfu posture
       2. A Foshan classic
       3. Handcraft

黃飛鴻
種類：陶像
特色：黃飛鴻是佛山傳奇，結合石灣精美手藝，
屬紀念品首選

Foshan 佛山

Chinese style roof tiles
Type: Roof tiles
Dimension: 170×103×60 (mm); 190x215x10 (mm)
Features: 1. Traditional garden style
       2. Artistic floral pattern
       3. Waterproof

紅獅滿面筒及瓦品
種類：屋頂瓦品
特色：琉璃滿面筒擁有耀眼的色彩和簡約的花紋，
品讀出悠久的歷史和傳統園林文化。

Dragon Ridge
Type: Roof decoration
Dimension: 2300x140x550 (mm)
Features: 1. Traditional color
       2. Adheres to national standards

紅獅脊上龍
種類：屋頂裝飾
特色：紅獅園林琉璃瓦品種繁多，脊上龍按國家標準生產，並有多
種釉色供使用者選擇，是賓館別墅、園林亭台樓閣等理想裝飾產品。

Exterior facade of the canteen 員工餐廳外觀

Inside the canteen 員工餐廳室內環境

Kitchen 員工餐廳廚房

Lunch 午餐

Name: Canteen set lunch provided for workers
Features: Steamed fish, assorted vegetables, fried eggs,
　　　　　red sausage, barbecue pork, soup, bean curd,
　　　　　with rice
Lunch time: 11:30 am

Taste ranking: ★★★★

名稱：食堂為工人提供午餐
特點：清蒸魚，煎蛋，炒菜，紅腸，燒肉，老火湯，蒸豆
　　　腐，白飯
午飯時間：上午 11:30

美味指數：★★★★

Dinner 晚餐

Name: Home-cooked dinner, not provided by factory
Features: Steamed fish, assorted vegetables, meat,
　　　　　soup, with rice
Dinner time: 7:00 pm

Taste ranking: ★★★★

名稱：員工自備晚餐，不是由工廠提供
特點：清蒸魚，炒菜，肉，湯，白飯
晚飯時間：下午 7:00

美味指數：★★★★

Accommodation 工人的住宿

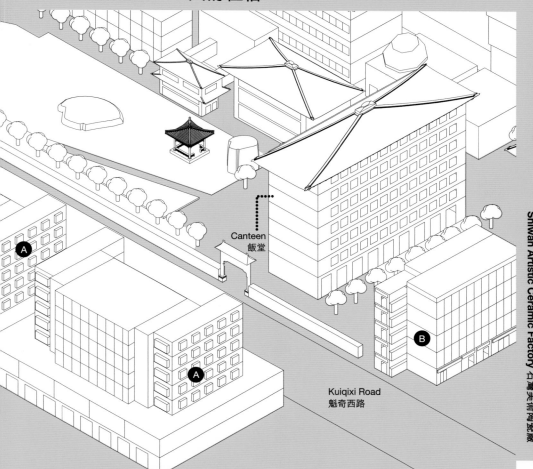

Canteen
飯堂

Kuiqixi Road
魁奇西路

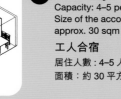

A **Urban village**
Capacity: 3–4 persons
Size of the accommodation:
approx. 45 sqm

家庭戶型宿舍
居住人數：3–4 人
面積：約 45 平方米

B **Dormitory**
Capacity: 4–5 persons
Size of the accommodation:
approx. 30 sqm

工人合宿
居住人數：4–5 人
面積：約 30 平方米

Employee of the Day 今日之星

Nickname: Cui Jie
Age: 32
Hometown: Shiwan, Foshan, Guangdong
Marital Status: Married with a 16-year-old son
Post: Mold-making worker
No. of years in the factory: 16
Monthly income: RMB 1,200

暱稱：翠姐
年齡：32
家鄉：廣東省佛山市石灣鎮
婚姻狀況：已婚，育有一名 16 歲兒子
職位：製模工
在此工廠的年資：16 年
月薪：RMB 1,200

Workers' uniform in the factory 職員制服

My family history in ceramics

I was born in Shiwan and have spent all my life here. My father raised me by working in a ceramic factory too. I joined this factory when I was young. I met my husband in the factory as he is also a worker here. My son is not interested in ceramics.

自我出生以來我一家也居住在石灣。我爸爸從前也是在陶瓷廠工作的。我十幾歲的時候就開始在這工廠打工，也是在工廠裏認識我的丈夫的，他也是這裏的工人。我們的兒子對陶瓷無興趣。

Boring work

The days here are boring and mundane. We work day and night and repeat the same procedures every day. There are no opportunities for entertainment nor resting; I spend all my time either working or on my family.

在工廠裏的日子是挺悶的，每天也重複着一樣的工序，我把所有時間都放在家和工作上。勿論什麼娛樂了，在這裏幾乎沒有休息可言。

From time to time, some celebrities would come over to look at the artworks. I have seen two movie stars from Hong Kong (Liza Wong and Law Ka Ying).

有時候，會有名人來工廠看陶藝品。我就曾經遇過兩位香港的演員—汪明荃和羅家英。

Limited prospects

Although ceramic making is a traditional art, it doesn't require much skill or knowledge; all you need is labor and practice. You don't have prospects working as a mold-making worker. I wouldn't want my son to work in a ceramic factory like myself. I wish that he could enter university and become some kind of professional in the future.

雖然做陶製品也算是一門傳統手藝，可是這工作根本不需要什麼技術，只有勞力，熟能生巧，做陶瓷工人也沒有前途。我不想我的兒子跟爸媽一樣當工人，我還是希望他能多讀點書，考上大學，學個專業。

I have made many kinds of sculptures. At the beginning, I was only allowed to pour clay slurry as it is the easiest procedure of all. Later I became more experienced and skillful, and was assigned to do the assembling. Practice makes perfect in this field.

做了 20 年，我什麼陶藝品都做過了。起初，我只被安排做最簡單的倒漿工作。慢慢，我的經驗多了，手藝純熟了，就被安排做修補的工作。這一行就是熟能生巧。多練習，誰都能做出陶製品。

Around the Clock 他／她的一天

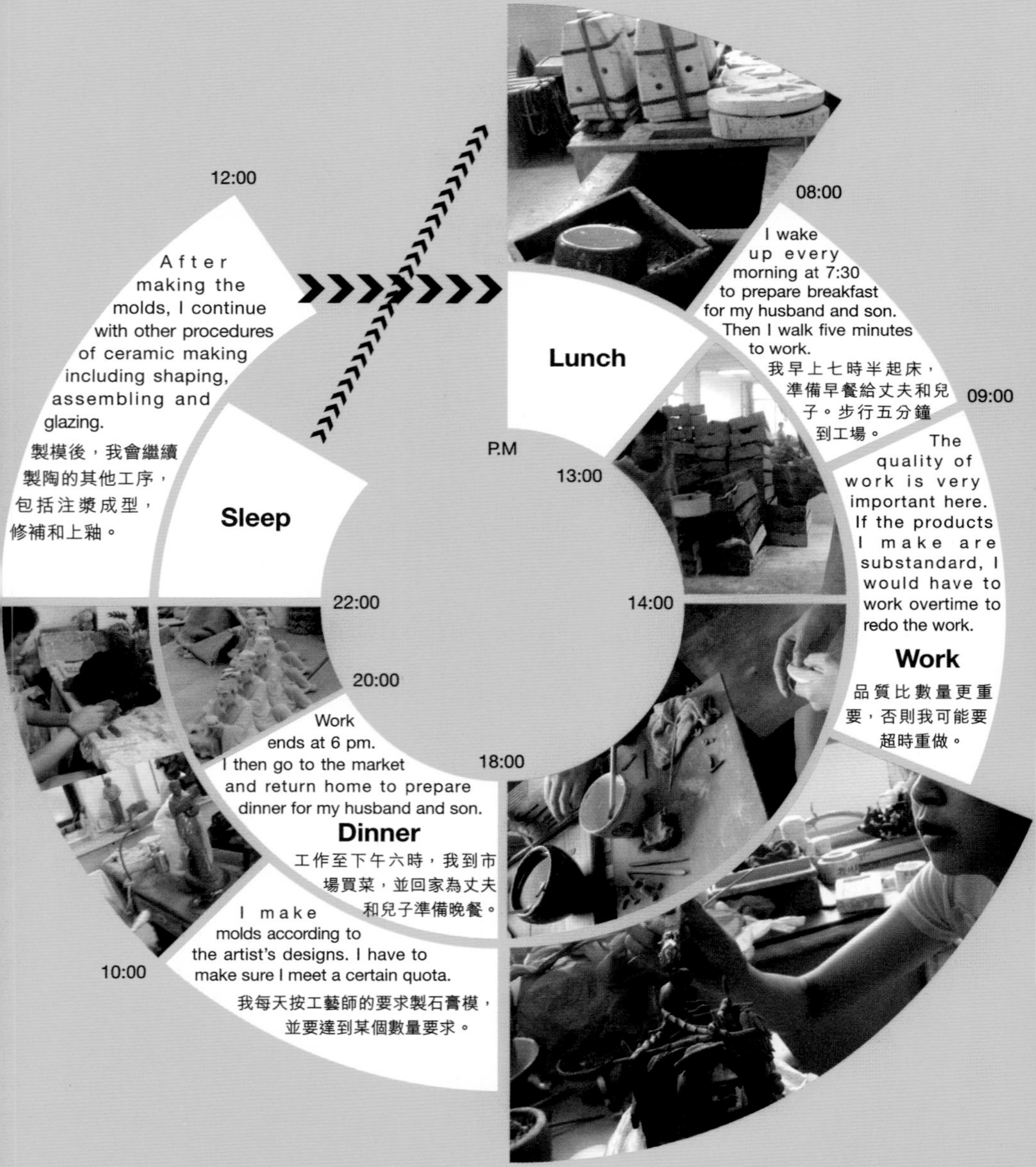

START!

12:00

08:00

After making the molds, I continue with other procedures of ceramic making including shaping, assembling and glazing.

製模後，我會繼續製陶的其他工序，包括注漿成型，修補和上釉。

I wake up every morning at 7:30 to prepare breakfast for my husband and son. Then I walk five minutes to work.

我早上七時半起床，準備早餐給丈夫和兒子。步行五分鐘到工場。

09:00

The quality of work is very important here. If the products I make are substandard, I would have to work overtime to redo the work.

品質比數量更重要，否則我可能要超時重做。

Lunch

P.M

13:00

14:00

Work

Sleep

22:00

20:00

18:00

Work ends at 6 pm. I then go to the market and return home to prepare dinner for my husband and son.

工作至下午六時，我到市場買菜，並回家為丈夫和兒子準備晚餐。

Dinner

I make molds according to the artist's designs. I have to make sure I meet a certain quota.

我每天按工藝師的要求製石膏模，並要達到某個數量要求。

10:00

09:30

Shiwan Artistic Ceramic Factory 石灣美術陶瓷廠

Foshan 佛山

Foshan 佛山 Shiwan Town 石灣鎮

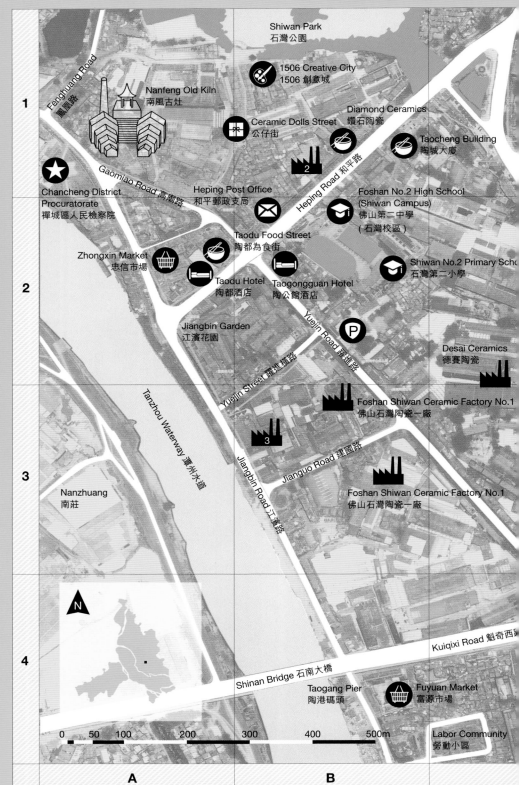

Shiwan Park
石灣公園

1506 Creative City
1506 創意城

Nanfeng Old Kiln
南風古灶

Diamond Ceramics
鑽石陶瓷

Ceramic Dolls Street
公仔街

Taocheng Building
陶城大廈

Fenghuang Road 鳳凰路

Chancheng District
Procuratorate
禪城區人民檢察院

Gaomiao Road 高廟路

Heping Post Office
和平郵政支局

Heping Road 和平路

Foshan No.2 High School
(Shiwan Campus)
佛山第二中學
(石灣校區)

Taodu Food Street
陶都為食街

Zhongxin Market
忠信市場

Taodu Hotel
陶都酒店

Taogongguan Hotel
陶公館酒店

Shiwan No.2 Primary Scho
石灣第二小學

Jiangbin Garden
江濱花園

Yuelin Road 躍進橋路

Tanzhou Waterway 潭州水道

Yuelin Street 躍進橋路

Desai Ceramics
德賽陶瓷

Foshan Shiwan Ceramic Factory No.1
佛山石灣陶瓷一廠

Jianguo Road 建國路

Nanzhuang
南莊

Jiangbin Road 江濱路

Foshan Shiwan Ceramic Factory No.1
佛山石灣陶瓷一廠

Huanqiu Ceramics Factory 環球陶瓷廠

Foshan 佛山

N

Kuiqixi Road 魁奇西路

Shinan Bridge 石南大橋

Taogang Pier
陶港碼頭

Fuyuan Market
富源市場

0   50 100   200   300   400   500m

Labor Community
勞動小區

A   B

Huanqiu Ceramics Factory 環球陶瓷廠

The factory was originally a state-owned enterprise specializing in the manufacturing of ceramic floor and wall tiles for the country. Currently it is a medium-sized privately owned enterprise, providing ceramic products for public facilities, such as schools, hospitals and government offices, as well as for large private development projects.

原為國有企業，專為國家生產陶瓷牆地磚，現已轉型為中型民營企業，主要為公共設施，例如學校、醫院等提供陶瓷磚建材，亦為私人大型發展項目提供建材。

Jianguo Ceramics Factory (Abandoned)
建國陶瓷廠 (已廢棄)

The factory was formerly a well-known state-owned ceramics factory in Foshan, established in the early 50s, specializing in ceramic daily necessities. The factory was closed and abandoned in 2003.

一家為老佛山人所熟悉的國營陶瓷廠，成立於 1950 年代初，主要生產日用陶瓷，工廠於 2003 年關閉。

Guangdong Shiwan Winery (Taiji Winery)
廣東石灣酒廠 (太吉酒廠)

Established in the Qing Dynasty (1830), the winery is famous for its history and its "Shiwan Brand" rice wine in China. It is probably the only winery in Guangdong that is still manufacturing in its original location for over a hundred years.

始創於清朝道光年間 (1830 年)，是一家以其歷史及其「石灣牌」米酒聞名於國內的酒廠，亦可能是廣東唯一證實還在原址生產的百年老字號。

Huanqiu Ceramics Factory 環球陶瓷廠

A1 **A2** View from the dormitory building 從宿舍大樓看工廠

B Company headquarters 公司總部大樓

C Entrance of production line 1 第一生產線入口

D Production line 1 and vehicular way
第一生產線及行車通道

E Former dormitory 前工人宿舍

F Raw material storage 原物料儲存庫

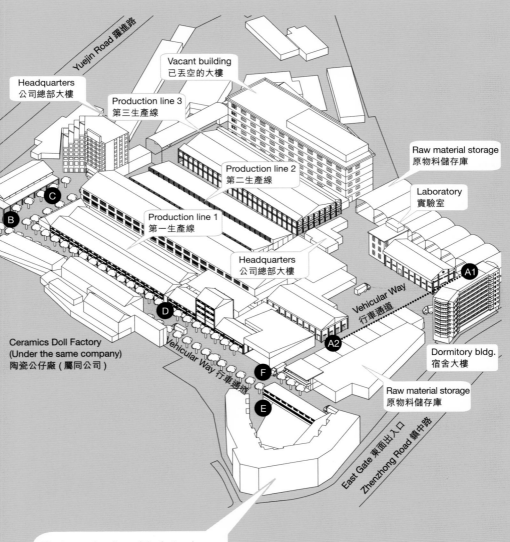

Factory name: Huanqiu Ceramics Factory
Address: 148 Yue jin Road, Shiwan Town,
Chancheng district, Foshan
Plot size: approx. 8 hectares
No. of workers: approx. 600
Construction era: 1950s

工廠名稱：環球陶瓷廠
工廠地址：佛山市禪城區石灣鎮躍進路 148 號
用地面積：約 8 公頃
工人數量：約 600 人
建設年代：1950 年代

Yuejin Road 躍進路

Headquarters
公司總部大樓

Vacant building
已丟空的大樓

Production line 3
第三生產線

Production line 2
第二生產線

Production line 1
第一生產線

Headquarters
公司總部大樓

Raw material storage
原物料儲存庫

Laboratory
實驗室

Vehicular Way
行車通道

A1

Dormitory bldg.
宿舍大樓

Ceramics Doll Factory
(Under the same company)
陶瓷公仔廠 (屬同公司)

Vehicular Way 行車通道

A2

Raw material storage
原物料儲存庫

East Gate 東面出入口

Zhenzhong Road 鎮中路

The former dormitory of the factory is now
sold to retired workers and their family
members testifying to the factory's long
history.
前身為工廠宿舍，現在均售予退休職工及其
家屬居住，足證工廠悠久的歷史。

Production Line 生產流程

Materials:
Ceramic grains
Porcelain ball
(for the ball grinding process)
etc.

原材料：
陶瓷原粒、瓷球 (球磨過程所用
工具) 等。

Ceramic grains 陶瓷原粒　　　　Porcelain ball 瓷球

Ball grinding mill 球磨機

轟隆轟隆 !!!

Stage 1
The first step is the grinding process. The ceramic grains are mixed with the porcelain balls in the ball grinding mill. It is then further processed to remove dust and sulphur, and for wet mixing.

第一階段
陶瓷原粒會首先進行破碎，與瓷球在球磨機進行球磨過程，再經過除塵、脫硫、濕混等加工步驟。

Stage 2
Processed clay will then be molded into required sizes and shapes and dried.

第二階段
經處理過的陶泥首先會被壓製成指定的大小和形狀，然後再進行乾燥工序。

Molding process 壓製成形　　　　Drying process 乾燥工序

It's over 40°C in here!
這裏的溫度超過 40 度！

Glazing machine 施釉機整組件　　　Kiln 燒陶窯

Stage 3
The ceramic tiles will then be transferred to the glazing machine if they require additional coloring. Afterwards, the tiles are transferred to the kiln for baking. Some of the tiles need to be cut beforehand.

第三階段
陶瓷磚經壓制成形和乾燥後，若該陶瓷磚需要顏色處理，便要施釉，再運往燒陶窯燒製。某些陶瓷磚需要先切割。

Stage 4
After the baking process, some ceramic tiles are then transferred to the polishing machine. Finally, the tiles are packed into boxes.

第四階段
陶瓷磚燒成後，某些陶瓷磚會運送往拋光機，最後所有陶瓷磚會在生產線末端進行包裝。

Hurry up!
快點快點！

Shopping Guide 購物指南

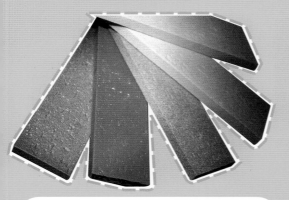

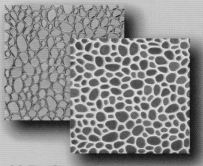

Best Seller!
Villa Tile

Type: Exterior wall tile
Features:
1. The most popular exterior tile designed by the factory
2. Widely used on exterior facades of residential projects
3. Expression of rustic and natural style

別墅磚

種類：外牆磚

特色：常為住宅項目所採用的外牆磚，亦是工廠最受歡迎
　　　的產品，此磚散發着濃郁的鄉土氣息和自然風格。

QQ Fine Stone Tile

Type: Interior wall and floor tile
Features:
1. Cobblestone pattern
2. Glazing on the recess areas and polishing on
the protruded areas
3. Usually used in balconies, bathrooms and
kitchens of the residence

QQ 美石磚

種類：室內用地牆磚

特色：具有獨特鵝卵石花紋，凹面作色釉處理：
　　　凸面則作拋光處理，適用於家居陽台、洗
　　　手間及廚房等。

International Standard Swimming Pool Tile

Type: Swimming pool tile
Features:
1. With glazed surface or wave pattern designs
2. Wear-proof, skid-proof, water pressure resistant and temperature
change resistant
3. Government-specified tiles for public swimming pool facilities

國際標準游泳池專用磚

種類：泳池磚

特色：分別有拋光設計及波紋設計兩大類，具有耐磨、防滑、抗水壓、
　　　抗溫差等主要性能，為國家體育局指定用泳池磚。

Bee-cloud Combination Tile

Type: Interior wall and floor tile
Features:
1. Antique looking tile with high temperature
matt glazing, slightly rough and
uneven surface
2. Stain resistant, wear-proof and skid-
proof, good for homes furnishing

蜂雲組合磚

種類：室內用地牆磚

特色：具有高溫啞光色釉和少許凹凸不平
　　　效果的仿古磚。抗污、耐磨及防滑
　　　等特點令此磚成為家居裝修的合適
　　　材料。

Lappato Tile

Type: Interior wall and floor tile
Features:
1. Antique looking tile with partly
polished surface, partly rough
surface and embossing
2. Suitable for interior decor of hotels,
especially for lobbies and corridors;
also suitable for furnishing homes

倫巴圖磚

種類：室內用地牆磚

特色：一種部分拋光，部分作凹凸不平
　　　堆積處理，並有印花選擇的仿古磚，尤
　　　其適合用於酒店大堂、走廊及電梯間，
　　　亦適用於家居裝修。

173

Wining and Dining 工人的飲食

Exterior facade of the canteen 員工餐廳外觀

Service counter 服務櫃檯

Inside the canteen 員工餐廳室內環境

Shiwan cuisine—Fish bean curd
石灣名菜—魚腐

Originated in Shiwan Town, fish bean curd is a famous cuisine in Southern China. It is made by mixing diced fish with cornflour and egg yolk, which is then deep fried to create similar texture with bean curd. It is now a common dish for lunch or dinner.

Taste ranking: ★★★★

魚腐是華南地區著名的菜色，源自佛山石灣鎮。魚腐由鯪魚肉打成膠狀後，加上生粉、蛋黃後酥炸而成，質感與豆腐相似，故名魚腐。現在已成為午飯或晚飯時的家常小菜。

美味指數：★★★★

Shiwan speciality—Rice wine
石灣特產—米酒

First developed in the Qing Dynasty, Shiwan Rice Wine has a history of 170 years. Today it is still brewed using traditional method of rice-cooking in a large vessel in the winery. It is a famous alcoholic drink in Southern China.

Taste ranking: ★★★★

石灣米酒已有 170 年歷史，由清朝起源至今。時至今天石灣米酒仍然採用以大鍋煮飯的傳統釀造方法。石灣米酒是華南地區知名的酒精飲料。

美味指數：★★★★

Accommodation 工人的住宿

Dormitory building
宿舍大樓

Ceramics company shop
陶瓷公司門市部

Motorcycle and
bicycle parking
摩托車及
自行車停放處

Entrance 入口

A

Worker suite
Capacity: 8–10 persons
Size of the accommodation:
40 sqm

工人宿舍
居住人數：8–10 人
面積：40 平方米

B

Private family suite
Capacity: 5–6 persons
Size of the accommodation:
45 sqm

私人家庭宿舍
居住人數：5–6 人
面積：45 平方米

Employee of the Day 今日之星

Nickname: Uncle Wah
Age: over 40
Hometown: Heshan, Guangdong Province
Marital status: Married with a son and a daughter
Post: Tile packing worker
No. of years in the factory: Approx. 10
Monthly income: approx. RMB 1,200
Other information: has been working in Foshan for over 20 years

暱稱：華叔
年齡：超過 40 歲
家鄉：廣東省鶴山市
婚姻狀況：已婚，育有一子一女
職位：陶瓷磚包裝工
在此工廠的年資：超過 10 年
月薪：約 1,200 人民幣
其他資料：他在佛山生活和工作超過 20 年

Workers' uniform in the factory 職員制服

A laborious job

It is a laborious job to pack the baked tiles from the kiln onto the trolleys, because the tiles are heavy and the environment is very hot. It is difficult for the factory to find new workers now. Most workers in this factory are in their middle age, and youngsters are not willing to work in ceramics factories anymore.

從燒陶窰的出口撿剛燒成的磚，是一門費力的工作，因為磚塊很重，工作環境又很熱。現在工廠都很難再找新的工人了，大部分在這裏工作的都是中年人，年青人都不太願意來陶瓷廠工作。

A good factory

This factory is good because the salary is paid on time and it seems that I have never experienced late payment.

這家工廠很好，因為糧期夠準，我幾乎沒有試過遲收工資。

Working schedule

I work four days a week and eight hours each working day. I normally have lunch around 2:30 pm.

我一星期工作 4 天，每天工作 8 小時，通常會在下午 2:30 吃午飯。

What to do on holidays?

I always go back to Heshan to spend time with my wife and children during the weekends. The travel duration via coach is only two and a half hours between Foshan and Heshan.

我經常回鶴山與妻兒們過週末，因為從佛山坐長途車回鶴山只需 2 個半小時。

The factory owner cares for us

Due to the extremely high temperatures in the workshop, the owners installed larger electric fans in the factory to improve the situation. In summer, Chinese herb teas are provided for us as a relief from the harsh conditions caused by staying inside the workshop.

因為車間的環境實在太熱，工廠在幾年前為我們裝了更大的電風扇，情況大大改善了，夏天時工廠更會煮涼茶給我們喝，清熱解暑，工廠對工人算是不錯。

Around the Clock 他／她的一天

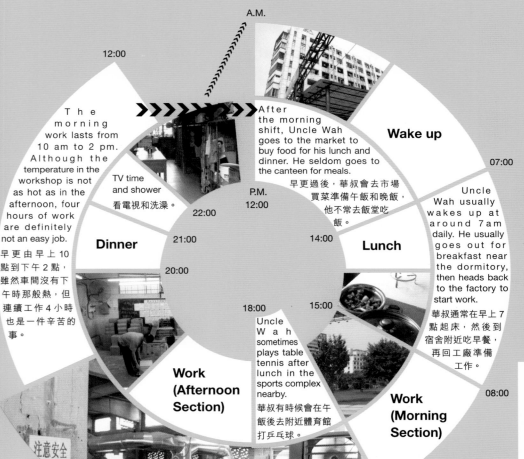

A.M.

12:00

The morning work lasts from 10 am to 2 pm. Although the temperature in the workshop is not as hot as in the afternoon, four hours of work are definitely not an easy job.

早更由早上 10 點到下午 2 點，雖然車間沒有下午時那般熱，但連續工作 4 小時也是一件辛苦的事。

TV time and shower
看電視和洗澡。

Dinner

22:00

21:00

20:00

18:00

Work (Afternoon Section)

注意安全

P.M.
12:00

After the morning shift, Uncle Wah goes to the market to buy food for his lunch and dinner. He seldom goes to the canteen for meals.

早更過後，華叔會去市場買菜準備午飯和晚飯，他不常去飯堂吃飯。

Wake up

07:00

Uncle Wah usually wakes up at around 7 am daily. He usually goes out for breakfast near the dormitory, then heads back to the factory to start work.

華叔通常在早上 7 點起床，然後到宿舍附近吃早餐，再回工廠準備工作。

08:00

14:00

Lunch

15:00

Uncle Wah sometimes plays table tennis after lunch in the sports complex nearby.

華叔有時候會在午飯後去附近體育館打乒乓球。

Work (Morning Section)

Huanqiu Ceramics Factory 環球陶瓷廠

Foshan 佛山

177

ZHONGSHAN
中山

Zhongshan is a prefecture-level city of the Guangdong Province. It has no county-level division, which is an uncommon administrative feature. The city government directly administers sixteen towns, four district offices (corresponding to the urban areas of Zhongshan) and a development zone.

Zhongshan is bordered by Guangzhou to the northeast, Foshan to the northwest, Jiangmen to the west and the Pearl River to the east. Shenzhen lies in the east across the river, while Zhuhai and Macao lie to the south.

The city was originally a county renamed in honor of Dr Sun Zhongshan, more widely known as Sun Yat-sen and is considered by many to be the "Father of modern China." Dr. Sun was born in Cuiheng Village (now part of Nanlang Town) located just outside of downtown Zhongshan.

Zhongshan is a city famous for the numerous leafy parks, wide boulevards and various monuments. A notable sight include: Sunwen Road West in Zhongshan Old Town — a pedestrian mall lined with dozens of restored buildings from the colonial period in treaty port style. Several of these buildings were built during the 1920s.

The seven-storey Fufeng Pagoda, built in 1606, is visible from all over the city. It is located on a hill in Zhongshan Park, which abuts on the western end of Sunwen Road West immediately to its north. A Sun Yat-sen memorial pavilion stands near the pagoda. Sunwen Memorial Park, located at the southern end of Xingzhong Road, is home to the largest bronze sculpture of Sun Yat-sen in the world.

The city covers an area of 1,800 square kilometers and has a population of around 3.1 million people, creating an average density of around 1,700 persons per square kilometer.

The city is the ancestral home of many overseas Chinese who, in particular, have emigrated to Australia, Europe, and the USA.

這個城市原是一個縣,是為紀念國父孫中山先生而命名的。孫中山先生出生於翠亨村(現為南朗鎮的一部分)。

中山是一個擁有許多公園、林蔭大道和各種紀念碑的城市。景點很多,包括位於中山舊城區的孫文西路,這裏的步行街的兩旁,都是建於二十世紀殖民時期的建築物,充滿當時的通商口岸的風格。

扶風寶塔建於 1606 年,在全市均看得見。它位於中山公園的一個小山丘上,鄰接孫文西路的西端和其北面。孫中山紀念館就在附近。孫文公園在興中道的南端,這裏置有世界最大的孫中山先生的銅雕塑。

中山全市面積有 1,800 平方公里,人口約 310 萬,每平方公里約有 1,700 人。這城市亦是許多海外華人的故鄉,他們的祖先很多移居到澳洲、歐洲和美國。

Land Use 土地利用

Large areas of Zhongshan are still used for agricultural purposes. Urban areas are consolidated.

中山大部分土地仍用於農業用途。城市地區比較集中。

Subdistricts 城鎮體系

The administrative area of Zhongshan is comprised of eighteen towns and four central districts of the city proper.

中山市的行政區域是由 18 個鎮和 4 個中心城區組成。

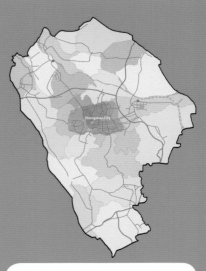

Road System 道路系統

Zhongshan is connected to the rest of the PRD and China by the Jingzhu and Fukai expressways.

中山市是以京珠和富凱高速公路連接到其他珠三角城市。

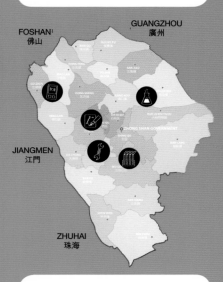

Industries 工業類型

Each town in Zhongshan specializes in a different industry, e.g., Guzhen specializes in lighting products.

每個鎮在中山專門從事不同的行業，如古鎮集中從事燈飾產品。

Zhongshan 中山

History 歷史

First map of Xiangshan 中山的第一版地圖

The "big four" department stores of Shanghai & Found
上海四大百貨公司

Zhongshan was originally called Xiangshan during ancient Chinese periods.
在中國古代時期，中山原稱為香山。

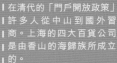

With the "open door policy" of the Qing Dynasty, many people from Xiangshan went abroad to study or do business. The "big four" department stores of Shanghai were founded by overseas Chinese returnees from Xiangshan.

在清代的「門戶開放政策」，許多人從中山到國外習商。上海的四大百貨公司是由香山的海歸族所成立的。

Zhongshan

The city was renamed i honor of Dr Sun Yat-sen i 1925, who is considere by many to be the "Fathe of modern China."

中山在 1925 年依孫中山博士之名改，其被視為現代中國的國父。

Portugal occupied Macao in 1553, and the occupation lasted 446 years.
葡萄牙於 1553 年佔領澳門，為期 446 年。

including Macao & most of Zhuhai
包括澳門與大部分珠海

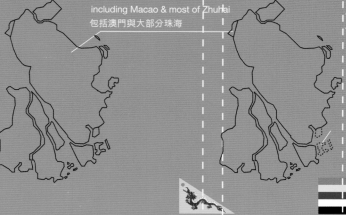

| Southern Song Dynasty | Qing Dynasty | Republic of China | |
| 1152 | 1845 | 1925 | 194 |

Sun Yat-sen died in 1925
孫中山於 1925 年去世

People came to Zhongshan to seek employment after the 1980s.
1980 年代後許多人來到中山求職

People returned to their hometown or went to other places rather than staying in the PRD after the financial crisis.
金融危機後許多人回到家鄉或到其他地方而不再留在珠江三角洲

中山市

Zhongshan upgraded to city level.
中山升等為城市

Persons (Million) 5-

The size of Zhongshan reduced by 43% between 1952 and 1965.
在 1952 至 1965 年間中山的規模縮小了 43%

Total Population
總人口

The People's Republic of China was founded in 1949.
中華人民共和國在 1949 年成立

China Reform & Open Door Policy
中國改革與門戶開放政策

4-

3-

2-

1978   1988   1998   2008

Zhongshan 中山 City Center 市中心

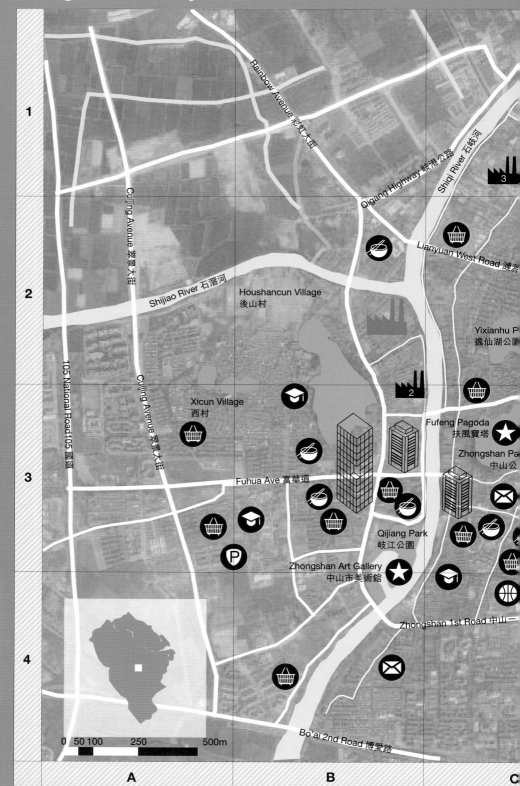

Rainbow Avenue 彩虹大街

Qigang Highway 岐港公路

Shiqi River 石岐河

Cuijing Avenue 翠景大街

Lianyuan West Road 濂源

Shijiao River 石滘河

Houshancun Village 後山村

Yixianhu P 逸仙湖公園

105 National Road 105 國道

Xicun Village 西村

Fufeng Pagoda 扶風寶塔

Zhongshan Pa 中山公

Cuijing Avenue 翠景大街

Fuhua Ave 富華道

Qijiang Park 岐江公園

Zhongshan Art Gallery 中山市美術館

Zhongshan 1st Road 中山一

Bo'ai 2nd Road 博愛路

0 50 100   250   500m

A   **B**   **C**

ngli village
丨村

Yuanfeng Village
元豐村

Zhongshan Museum
中山市博物館

D

Zhongshan Seasoning Co. Ltd.
中山市調味品有限公司

With a history of over 100 years, the company currently employs over 1000 workers in the production of soy sauce, chicken essence, oyster sauce, vinegar, bean curd, seasoning sauce, seasoning powder and MSG. Products are sold in over thirty countries including the UK, France, Japan, Russia and Australia.

歷史可以追溯到 100 年前，公司目前擁有員工超過 1,000 人。生產線生產醬油、雞精、蠔油醬、醋、豆腐、調味醬、調味粉、味精。產品銷往 30 多個國家，包括英國、法國、日本、俄羅斯和澳洲。

Taishan Siliao Co. Ltd.
泰山飼料有限公司

Siliao means animal feed. This factory is one of the few remaining in Zhongshan which continues to use the Shiqi River as a means of transport for its materials and products.

這家生產動物飼料的工廠是少數繼續留在中山石岐河生產的工廠，主要使用河道運送材料和產品。

Aestar (Zhongshan) Co. Ltd.
凱達（中山）有限公司

Aestar is China's largest aerosol production base, and employs more than 900 workers in their head office. More than 40% of the staff is involved in research and development, while the remainders is split into departments specializing in pesticides, air fresheners and household sanitary products departments.

中國最大的氣霧劑生產基地，總部合共有超過 900 名員工，超過百分之四十的工作人員參與研究和開發，其餘分為殺蟲劑、空氣清新劑、家用清潔產品部門。

Zhongshan Seasoning Co. Ltd. 中山市調味品有限公司

A1 A2 Shiqi River 石岐河

B Main building 主樓

The company's history extends to a time before Xiangshan was renamed in honor of Dr Sun Yat-sen to Zhongshan. The factory has evolved over time, displaying a snapshot of factory development in Southern China over the last 100 years. The company is poised to move to the new premises in the Zhongshan Torch—a high-tech industrial park.

公司成立時，香山還未改名為中山，工廠隨着時代演變，呈現出過去 100 年間中國南方的工業發展。工廠現準備遷往中山市火炬高新技術產業園區。

C Building 2 二號產樓

D Warehouse 倉庫

Adjoining park 鄰近公園

Adjacent residential buildings 鄰近的住宅

Former warehouse 前倉庫

E Loading bay 卸貨區

Factory name: Zhongshan Seasoning Co. Ltd.
Factory address: Xianghe Street, Zhongshan
Plot size: 2.5 hectares
No. of workers: 1000
Construction era: 1920s–1980s

工廠名稱：中山市調味品有限公司
工廠地址：中山市香河街
用地面積：2.5 公頃
工人數量號：1000 人
建設年代：1920 年 –1980 年

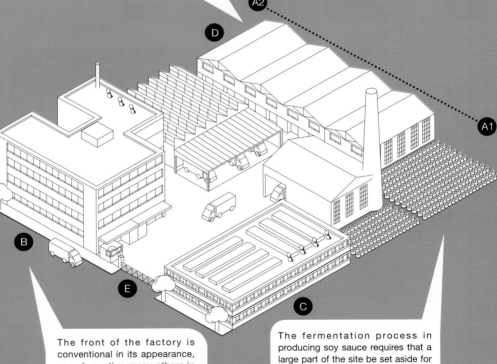

The site is adjacent to the Shiqi River, which the factory still uses for the transportation of goods. Due to the long history of the company, the site accommodates a range of different buildings from different eras.

該工廠位於石岐河，並向來一直使用河道輸送貨物。由於公司歷史悠久，該工廠由各種不同年齡的建築物組建而成。

The front of the factory is conventional in its appearance, complementing many others in the local area. The rear of the site is more traditional in terms of appearance, thus it gives a sense of China's industrial past.

工廠正面的外觀跟鄰近的許多其他工廠相似，呈一般工廠大廈的建築模式。背面則較傳統，展示出中國工業的背景。

The fermentation process in producing soy sauce requires that a large part of the site be set aside for large fermentation tanks.

工廠撥出較大空間裝置大型發酵糟，用來發酵醬油。

Production Line 生產流程

Materials:
Soybeans
Wheat
Salt and water
Aspergillus
Yeast

材料：
黃豆、小麥、鹽、水 及
曲霉

Hiiissssss!!

Stage 1

The soybeans are first soaked and then steamed, while the wheat is roasted and crushed. These ingredients are mixed together with the fermentation culture apergillus.

先讓黃豆浸泡，再蒸熟；小麥經烘烤後進行壓碎。然後這些成分與曲霉混合一起。

Stage 2

The ingredients are left to incubate for three days and then are mixed with salt, water and yeast. The resultant mash is then ready for the fermentation process.

混好的材料在 3 天後，再混合鹽水和酵母成糊狀物，準備發酵。

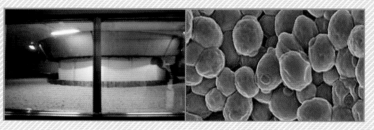

Stage 3

The mixture is then allowed to ferment for several months. During this time, several chemical reactions take place, including lactic acid, alcoholic, and organic acid fermentation. These provide the rich flavor and aroma of soy sauce.

發酵的步驟長達數月，期間產生的化學作用包括乳酸、酒精和有機酸發酵，造就了醬油濃郁的味道和香氣。

Blub ...
Blub ...

Stage 4

Once suitably aged, the mash is then pressed through multiple layers of fabric over a ten-hour period to remove all remnant solids. The raw soy sauce is then clarified, pasteurized and bottled, ready to be packed and shipped.

發酵完畢，用多層織物將剩餘固體分隔，進行 10 小時的處理。淨化的醬油以巴氏殺菌法消毒後，即可裝瓶，準備包裝和運送。

Flooosh!

Shopping Guide 購物指南

Product 2
Name: Chili Bean Curd
Features: 1. Unique flavor
2. Great for stir-frying
3. Premium all-purpose condiment
Sizes: 118g, 268g, 368g
Price: From RMB 16

特點： 1. 味道獨特
2. 炒菜最佳用料
3. 多用途調味品

Product 3
Name: White Bean Curd
Features: 1. Smooth texture
2. Unique flavor
3. All-purpose
Size: 225g
Price: RMB 14

特點： 1. 香滑口感
2. 味道獨特
3. 多用途調味品

Best Seller!
Product 1
Name: Soy Sauce
Features: 1. Premium soy sauce
2. Suits all cooking styles
3. Rich flavor
Sizes: 180g, 500g, 2kg
Price: From RMB 12

特點： 1. 一級醬油
2. 適合所有類型的烹飪
3. 味道香濃

Product 4
Name: Oyster Sauce
Features: 1. Appetizing aroma
2. Smooth texture
3. Finest oyster extract
Sizes: 330g, 510g, 730g, 2.27g
Price: From RMB 18

特點： 1. 芳香開胃
2. 香滑口感
3. 最佳鮮蠔精華

Product 5
Name: Vinegar
Features: 1. Flavor enhancing
2. Multi-purpose
3. Nutritious and healthy
Size: 420ml
Price: RMB 15

特點： 1. 增味作用
2. 多用途調味品
3. 營養、健康

Product 6
Name: Chicken Powder
Features: 1. Natural and fragrant
2. Soft color
3. Rich nutrition
Size: 140g, 227g, 1kg, 2kg
Price: From RMB 22

特點： 1. 天然芳香
2. 色彩柔和
3. 營養豐富

Zhongshan Seasoning Co., Ltd. 中山市調味品有限公司

Zhongshan 中山

187

Zhongshan Seasoning Co. Ltd. 中山市調味品有限公司

Zhongshan 中山

Local supermarket 當地的超市

Dinner lady 餐室員工／晚膳侍應

Inside the canteen 員工餐廳室內環境

Lunch 午餐

Name: Canteen set lunch provided for workers
Features: Rice, noodles, and soup with one main dish
Lunch time: 12:30 pm

Taste ranking: ★★★

名稱：食堂為工人提供午餐
特點：白飯、麵條、湯和一主菜
午餐時間：下午 12:30

美味指數：★★★

Dinner 晚餐

Name: Home-cooked
Features: Ingredients bought at local supermarket
Dinner time: 7:30 pm

Taste ranking: ★★★★★

名稱：家常菜
特點：當地的超市買
晚餐時間：下午 7:30

美味指數：★★★★★

Accommodation 工人的住宿

Local apartment building
Levels: 5
Apartment units: 80
Constructed: circa 1980

層數：5
單位數目：80
建造年份：1980s

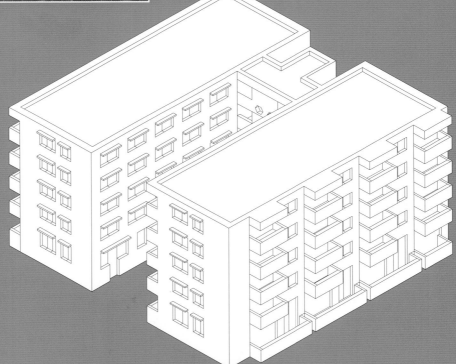

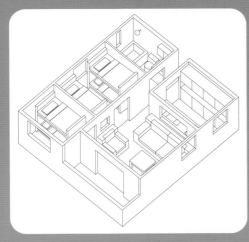

Typical apartment
Capacity : 6 persons
No. of bedrooms: 2
Size: Approx. 42 sqm

容量：6人
睡房：2
尺寸：約 42 sqm

Employee of the Day 今日之星

Name: Ho Kai-Ying (Karren)
Age: 23
Hometown: Hunan Province
Post: Accounts administrator
No. of years in the factory: 1.5
Monthly income: RMB 2,100

暱稱：何啟英
年齡：23
家鄉：湖南省
職位：帳戶管理員
在工廠的年資：1.5 年
月薪：RMB 2,100

Workers' uniform in the factory 職員制服

My current job

I found this job in the job market after I left my last job in Foshan to return home for New Year in 2009. I got the job because of my previous experience in office work, and because I am good at dealing with customers.

2009 年我回家過年，因此離開了上一份工作，其後在就業市場找到現時的工作，我擁有辦公室工作經驗，又擅於與客戶打交道，所以獲聘了。

I was nineteen when I first started working. My older sister was working at a household appliance factory and she got me a job there.

我 19 歲開始工作。當時我的姐姐在一家家用電器工廠打工，她替我在那裏找到一份工作。

Zhongshan

I like living in Zhongshan because it is not as large as some of the other cities, so you don't feel too overwhelmed. Things are calmer here and there are nice parks and landscaped streetscapes.

我喜歡住在中山，因為它不像某些城市大得令人目眩。這裏較平靜，有多個公園，街道上綠樹成蔭。

Spare time

Because I don't work on the production floor, I have more spare time. I enjoy going into town with friends, walking and reading. I have also taken courses to help my career and I am currently learning English.

我不是生產層工作，閒暇的時間也較多。我喜歡和朋友到城市裏逛逛、散步或看書。我正在修讀一些職業進修課程，同時也在學習英語。

Future plan

I hope to stay here in Zhongshan and continue to learn and develop my career further before settling down.

我希望留在中山，在這裏繼續學習、發展我的專業。

Around the Clock 他／她的一天

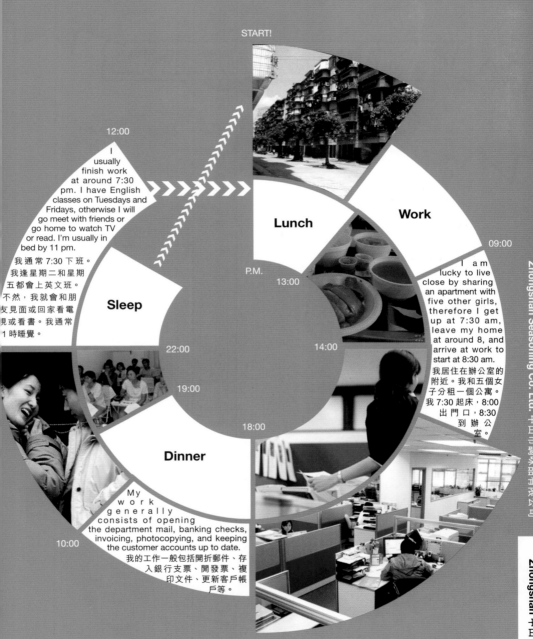

START!

Work

09:00

I am lucky to live close by sharing an apartment with five other girls, therefore I get up at 7:30 am, leave my home at around 8, and arrive at work to start at 8:30 am.

我居住在辦公室的附近。我和五個女子分租一個公寓。我 7:30 起床，8:00 出門口，8:30 到辦公室。

Lunch

P.M.

13:00

14:00

Dinner

18:00

19:00

My work generally consists of opening the department mail, banking checks, invoicing, photocopying, and keeping the customer accounts up to date.

我的工作一般包括開折郵件、存入銀行支票、開發票、複印文件、更新客戶帳戶等。

10:00

09:30

Sleep

22:00

12:00

I usually finish work at around 7:30 pm. I have English classes on Tuesdays and Fridays, otherwise I will go meet with friends or go home to watch TV or read. I'm usually in bed by 11 pm.

我通常 7:30 下班。我逢星期二和星期五都會上英文班。不然，我就會和朋友見面或回家看電視或看書。我通常 11 時睡覺。

Zhongshan Seasoning Co. Ltd. 中山市調味品有限公司

Zhongshan 中山

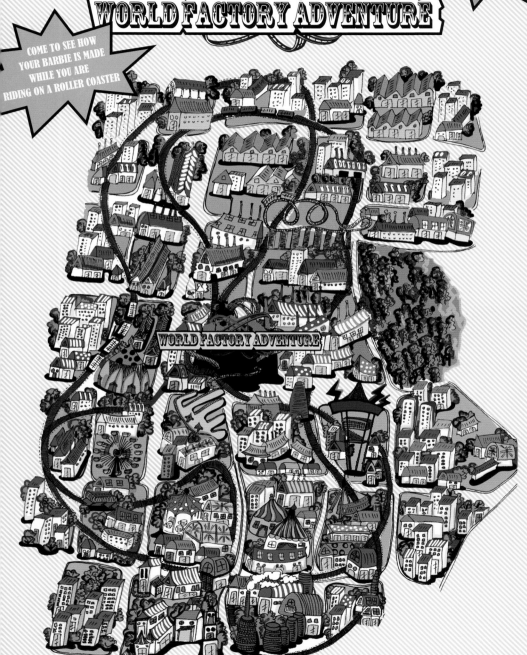

世界工廠探險

Village system for sale now !
村莊工業系統出售！

A,B,C,D,E

"Villaging industry"simulates the randomness of urban villages;
本系統模擬現存城村的亂中有序的自然模式；
an organic growth system to meet all your needs.
提供能滿足任何你所需的工業系統。

A Well-Designed Circulation
精心策劃

Visitor Flow 遊客動線

Customer Flow 顧客動線

Design Firm / Headquarters 設計公司/總部

Company Showroom 公司陳列室

Retail Stores 零售店

Design Firm Dorm 設計公司宿舍 Design School 設計學校

Exhibition Hall / Venue for Furniture Design Fair 展覽中心 / 傢俱設計展場區

Plaza 廣場

Gallery 藝廊

Exhibition Space 展覽空間
Furniture Assembly 傢俱組裝
Product Showcase 產品展示
Furniture Warehouse 傢俱倉儲

Design Sector 設計區

Expo Sector 展覽區

Manufacturing Flow 製造業動線

Manufacturing Sector 製造區

Assembly 組裝
Visitor 遊客
Visitor 遊客
Buyer (Wholesale) 批發商買家
Visiting 參觀
Customer (Retail) 零售顧客
Order 訂購

Transparent Factory 透明工廠
Furniture Assembly Line X Showcase 傢俱組裝 X 展覽陳列

Here, cooperation makes design successful.

在這裏，協作令設計更成功。

Manufacturing 製造
Design 設計
Expo 展覽

Foshan
Industrial Design Town
佛山工業設計村

Hong Kong
01 Kwun Tong Industrial Town: Printing Factory

Shenzhen
02 Fuyong Town: Optoelectronics Factory
03 Shekou Industrial Zone: Toy Factory

Dongguan
04 Nancheng District: Car Factory
05 Huangjiang Town: Electronics Factory

Guangzhou
06 Liwan District: Shipyard
07 Donghuanjie Town: Video Game Machine Factory

Foshan
08 Shiwan Town: Artistic Ceramic Factory
09 Shiwan Town: Ceramic Tiling Factory

Zongshan
10 City Center: Seasoning Factory

01

Bibliography

Burtynsky, Edward, Ted Fishman, Mark Kingwell, and Marc Mayer. 2005. *China*. Göttingen: Steidl.

Bray, David. 2005. *Social Space and Governance in Urban China: The Danwei System from Origins to Reform*. Palo Alto: Stanford University Press.

Campanella, Thomas. 2008. *The Concrete Dragon: China's Urban Revolution and What it Means for the World*. Princeton: Princeton Architectural Press.

Chan, Anita. 2001. *China's Workers Under Assault: The Exploitation of Labor in a Globalizing Economy*. Armonk, New York: M.E. Sharpe.

Chang, Leslie. 2008. *Factory Girls: From Village to City in a Changing China*. New York: Spiegel and Grau.

Chung, Chuihua Judy, Jeffrey Inaba, Rem Koolhaas, and Sze Tsung Leong. 2002. *Great Leap Forward/Harvard Design School Project on the City*. Cambridge: Taschen.

Enright, Michael, Edith Scott, and Ka-mun Chang. 2005. *Regional Powerhouse: The Greater Pearl River Delta and the Rise of China*. 1st ed. Wiley, June 24.

Friedmann, John. 2005. *China's Urban Transition*. Minneapolis: University of Minnesota Press.

Hessler, Peter. 2010. *Country Driving: A Journey through China from Farm to Factory*. New York: Harper.

Hsing, You-tien. 1998. *Making Capitalism in China: The Taiwan Connection*. New York: Oxford University Press.

Jun, Jiang, ed. *Urban China Magazine*.

Lee, Ching Kwan. 1998. *Gender and the South China Miracle: Two Worlds of Factory Women*. Berkeley: University of California Press.

———. 2007. *Against the Law: Labor Protests in China's Rustbelt and Sunbelt*. Berkeley: University of California Press.

Lin, George C. S. 1997. *Red Capitalism in South China Growth and Development of the Pearl River Delta*. Seattle: University of Washington Press.

Logan, John, ed. 2002. *The New Chinese City: Globalization and Market Reform*. Oxford: Blackwell.

Mars, Neville, and Adrian Hornsby. 2010. *The Chinese Dream: A Society under Construction*. Rotterdam: 010.

Ngai, Pun. 2005. *Made in China: Women Factory Workers in a Global Workplace*. Durham: Duke University Press.

Vogel, Ezra. 1989. *One Step Ahead of China: Guangdong under Reform*. Cambridge: Harvard University Press.

Wu, Fulong, ed. 2008. *China's Emerging Cities: The Making of New Urbanism*. New York: Routledge.

Yeh, Anthony Gar-on, Yok-shiu F. Lee, Tunney Lee, and Nien Dak Sze. 2002. *Building a Competitive Pearl River Delta Region*. Hong Kong: Hong Kong University Press.